Praise for *Finding Meaning in the S...*

". . . nourishing. . . . Like a master chef, Jam[es Hollis...]... food for the soul cannot be ordered to go."
—*The Plain Dealer* (Cleveland)

"[O]ffers insight into the process of finding true meaning later in life. . . . challenging . . . earnest."
—*The Houston Chronicle*

"How to find your way out of the woods (figuratively) . . . What's at stake is what Hollis calls the biggest project of midlife: reclaiming one's personal authority. This means leaving behind what's comfortable but confining."
—*More* magazine

"Everyone seems to be obsessing about the monetary cost of the graying of the American population, but there's very little talk about the soul. James Hollis, one of the foremost Jungian analytical psychologists in the world, has plenty to say about the soul. . . . [E]rudite and cultured but also accessible."
—*Portland Tribune*

"[A] deep Jungian exploration of individuation . . . humane and compassionate . . . [Hollis's] focus on the underlying meaning of life will resonate for many."
—*Publishers Weekly*

"[C]ontains the writing of a gentle and insightful soul who does not bog down in analytical dryness, but speaks to and teaches from the heart . . . genuine vision and genuine humanity is a rare and valuable gift, and readers will find both in this work."
—Clarissa Pinkola Estés, author of *Women Who Run with the Wolves*

"[An] important book, which, as it strips away illusions, posits the soul-work that's necessary for the difficult task of making our lives meaningful."
—Stephen Dunn, Pulitzer Prize–winning poet

"James Hollis's new book is a work of soul-making. It brings solace and wisdom to those of us who find ourselves in a dark wood in the second half of life."
—Edward Hirsch, author of *How to Read a Poem and Fall in Love with Poetry*

"Midlife is a time when people can lose their way and flounder. Jungian analyst James Hollis knows this terrain, describes it well and asks the important questions that can lead to clarity, maturity, and meaning."
—Jean Shinoda Bolen, M.D., author of *Goddesses in Everywoman* and *Gods in Everyman*

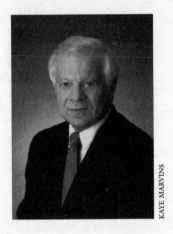

KAYE MARVINS

James Hollis, Ph.D., is a Jungian analyst in private practice and executive director of the C. G. Jung Educational Center of Houston, Texas. He received an A.B. from Manchester College and a Ph.D. from Drew University. He taught humanities for twenty-six years in various colleges and universities before becoming a Jungian analyst at the Jung Institute in Zurich, Switzerland, where he received a diploma in analytical psychology. He lectures frequently throughout the country and worldwide, lives in Houston, Texas, with his wife, and has four grown children.

Finding Meaning in the Second Half of Life

JAMES HOLLIS, PH.D.

GOTHAM
BOOKS

GOTHAM BOOKS
Published by Penguin Group (USA) Inc.
375 Hudson Street, New York, New York 10014, U.S.A.

Penguin Group (Canada), 90 Eglinton Avenue East, Suite 700, Toronto, Ontario, Canada M4P 2Y3
(a division of Pearson Penguin Canada Inc.); Penguin Books Ltd, 80 Strand, London WC2R 0RL,
England; Penguin Ireland, 25 St Stephen's Green, Dublin 2, Ireland (a division of Penguin Books Ltd);
Penguin Group (Australia), 250 Camberwell Road, Camberwell, Victoria 3124, Australia (a division of
Pearson Australia Group Pty Ltd); Penguin Books India Pvt Ltd, 11 Community Centre, Panchsheel
Park, New Delhi - 110 017, India; Penguin Group (NZ), Cnr Airborne and Rosedale Roads, Albany,
Auckland, New Zealand (a division of Pearson New Zealand Ltd); Penguin Books (South Africa) (Pty)
Ltd, 24 Sturdee Avenue, Rosebank, Johannesburg 2196, South Africa

Penguin Books Ltd, Registered Offices: 80 Strand, London WC2R 0RL, England

Published by Gotham Books, a division of Penguin Group (USA) Inc.
Previously published as a Gotham Books hardcover edition.

First trade paperback printing, May 2006

7   9   10   8

Copyright © 2005 by James Hollis, Ph.D.
All rights reserved

GRATEFUL ACKNOWLEDGMENT IS MADE FOR PERMISSION TO REPRINT THE FOLLOWING:

Quote from *Steppenwolf* by Herman Hesse. English language translation © 1929, 1963
by Henry Holt & Co. Reprinted by permission of Henry Holt & Co., LLC.

An excerpt from *The Essential Rumi* by Jeladaden Rumi, translated by Coleman Barks.
English translation © by Coleman Barks. Reprinted by permission of Coleman Barks.

Excerpt, from "After Making Love," from *Loosestrife* by Stephen Dunn.
Copyright © 1996 by Stephen Dunn. Used by permission of W. W. Norton & Company, Inc.

Gotham Books and the skyscraper logo are trademarks of Penguin Group (USA) Inc.

The Library of Congress has cataloged the hardcover edition of this title as follows:

Hollis, James, 1940–
    Finding meaning in the second half of life / James Hollis.
        p.   cm.
    Includes bibliographical references and index.
    ISBN 1-592-40120-1 (hardcover)   ISBN 1-592-40207-0 (paperback)
    1. Adulthood.   2. Maturation (Psychology)   3. Middle aged persons—Psychology.   I. Title.
HQ1061.H56 2005
155.6'6—dc22   2004060880

Printed in the United States of America
Set in Galliard and Medici Script

For Jill,

And for our children,
Taryn and Tim, Jonah and Seah,

And the people of
The Jung Center of Houston

Contents

"And then the knowledge comes to me that I have space within me for a second, timeless, larger life."

R. M. Rilke,
"I Love My Being's Dark Hours"

"O lost, and by the wind grieved, ghost, come back again."

Thomas Wolfe,
Look Homeward, Angel

Your Life Is Addressing These Questions to You:

What has brought you to this place in your
journey, this moment in your life?

What gods, what forces, what family, what
social environment, has framed your reality,
perhaps supported, perhaps constricted it?

Whose life have you been living?

Why, even when things are going well,
do things feel not quite right?

Why does so much seem a disappointment,
a betrayal, a bankruptcy of expectations?

Why do you believe that you have to hide so
much, from others, from yourself?

Why does life seem a script written elsewhere,
and you barely consulted, if at all?

Why have you come to this book,
or why has it come to you, now?

Why does the idea of your *soul* trouble you,
and feel familiar as a long-lost companion?

Why is the life you are living too small for the
soul's desire?

Why is now the time, if ever it is to happen,
for you to answer the summons of the soul,
the invitation to the second, larger life?

Introduction

The Dark Wood

SOMETIMES, TO OUR DISMAY, we find that we have been living someone else's life, that their values have and are directing our choices. While this life we are leading never quite feels right, it seems to be the only alternative. Even when we win the applause of others, we secretly feel fraudulent. Consider this true story: The man had spent his life in academia and brilliantly served the life of the mind. Now retired, he fell into a depression, for he had no structure to carry his psychological energies for him, no insistent agenda of values to serve, no sense of who he was apart from his role, his committees, his teaching task. One day, driving home after an hour of therapy, he began to weep, unaccountably weep, and no image or reason presented itself to his shaken consciousness. This man, who had lived quite successfully out of his head, confessed how humbling it was to be pulled so helplessly down into the body. That evening he dreamed that he was back in the university setting, that he was sitting for an exam for which he was unprepared, and that everyone else was far ahead of him on the test. The female instructor walked over to him and said, "I am not going to let you fail this course." He recalled that as a child his mother was forever directing his energies, setting her goals as his goals, and frequently intervened for him with the same tone this instructor used. Powerless as all children are, he knew Mother's will had to be his, and so he lived out her ambitions for him. But in this dream, "All of a sudden, it came to me that I didn't have to take this course. I thought, 'This test means nothing to me! I am beyond being tested in this way!' Relief overwhelmed me. I tore up the blue book and walked out of the room." And into the beginning of a different life—his life.

Or consider the thirty-eight-year-old woman who had risen to be a vice president of sales in her medical instruments company. She was flying from JFK to DEN, reading a book, and somewhere over Nebraska, a startling thought intruded on her consciousness: "I hate my life." She had identified her life with the achievement of her professional goals, but from that moment on, at thirty-five thousand feet, she knew that she had been walking on the uncertain crust of a depression all the while.

Or consider the first dream I had in Zurich, just as I was beginning analysis in midlife. I was a knight upon the ramparts of a medieval castle with a storm of arrows flying all about me. At the forest's edge I saw a witchlike figure who was directing the assault. I felt great anxiety, for I feared the castle would fall, and at the end of the dream its fate was very much in doubt. My analyst suggested that it was finally time to lower the drawbridge of my castle and go out and meet the witch, and find why she was so irritated with me. Naturally, I feared such an encounter, for who among us will willingly leave his reinforced castle and stand undefended before that which he fears? But I knew that my analyst's advice was sound, that I was at the beginning of a long journey through a dark wood, a wood in which I had already lived for many years, before it had come to consciousness.

What do these quite different people have in common? Each of them experienced an insurgency of the soul, an overthrow of the ego's understanding of self and world, and a rather demanding invitation to live more consciously in the second half of life. But first came the confounding of consciousness, and the sense that each of them had moved, or better, been pulled, from a familiar environment into some darker wood. Who does not resonate to this familiar image of voyaging through a dark wood? The poet Dante began his famous, fabulous descent into the underworld with the recognition that midway in life he found himself in a dark wood, having lost his way. Despite our best intentions, we, too, frequently find ourselves in a dark wood. No amount of good intentions, conscientious intelligence, forethought, planning, prayer, or guidance from others can spare us these periodic encounters with confusion, disorientation, boredom, depression, disappointment in ourselves and others, and dissolution of the plans and stratagems that seemed to work before. What can this apparently autonomous process, which overthrows the conscious conduct of our lives, mean to us, and how can we grow from such upsetting encounters with darkness? If the questions at the beginning of this book speak to you, scare you a bit, challenge you—then you, too, are already in this process, and have been for some time. This movement from the old moorings, perhaps confounding your quite understandable desire for comfort, security, predictability, is a deep motion of the psyche that has meaning, healing, and wholeness as its motive. In the midst of these psychological dislocations, we frequently consider ourselves victimized, and cannot imagine that there could be some enlarging purpose arising from our suffering. Often, much later, we are able to recognize that something *was* moving us purposefully, initiating a new phase of our journey, though it certainly didn't feel like it at the time. We may grudgingly admit that even the suffering enlarged us, and made us more richly human.

Acknowledging these deep currents, which initially course beneath our conscious awareness, is the beginning of what we may legitimately call wisdom. Aeschylus, the first great tragedian, observed that the gods ordained a solemn decree that from suffering alone comes wisdom. Such earned wisdom brings greater dignity and depth to our lives, and we are blessed by the spiritual enlargement that is its byproduct. For those in the midst of such suffering, talk of enlargement seems gratuitous, or insensitive, and yet, much later, they often come to realize that they have acquired a more differentiated consciousness, a more complex understanding of themselves, and, greatest of all, a more interesting life. Their lives grew spiritually, psychologically richer, and they earned this growth. Their own soul came rushing toward them, refusing any quarter, any denial, and demanding greater embodiment through them.

For many years I have had the privilege of working with people in the midst of their suffering. I am humbled by their willingness to share their most private places with me and to trust me as a companion on their journey. Together, we have been humbled by our joint encounters with the *Self,* Carl Jung's metaphor for that inherent, unique, knowing, directive, intelligence that lies so wholly beyond our ordinary ego consciousness. The metaphor of the Self arises from our intuitive knowledge that something within each of us not only monitors our organic biochemical processes, develops us from less complex to more complex creatures, but, much more, seeks that state of being that is the apparent purpose of our incarnation in the first place.

Soul is another word that, ironically, has been banished by most of modern psychology and psychiatry, even though the word *psyche*, which lies at the heart of *psychology, psychiatry, psychopathology, psychopharmacology,* and *psychotherapy,* is the Greek word for *soul*. Almost as egregious, the soul has been sentimentalized by much so-called New Age thinking, or imprisoned in fearful, defensive dogma by religious fundamentalists. Yet I will risk using the words *soul* and *psyche* interchangeably in this book, for in each of us, the Self* is in service to the soul; which is to say, the directive, purposeful energies that govern our lives are themselves in service to meaning, though a transcendent meaning that often has little to do with our narrow frame of conscious understanding. I recall reading about a woman who had been buried under rubble with her child after an earthquake in one of the former states of the USSR. Her child survived with her because the woman had slit her flesh and nursed her child with her own blood during the many days it took to find them. You might think that the first order of business is always self-preservation, but this mother's sacrifice of herself for her child shows that even this activity of the Self may come to serve the soul's demand for meaning. Remarkably, the "idea" of her child was more meaningful to this mother than the "idea" of herself. This story of subordination of the Self's interests to the task of

---

*The Self, the archetypal dynamic seeking wholeness, is capitalized to avoid confusing it with our ordinary, quite limited ego consciousness. In my dream, the ego consciousness is the knight, the witch the split-off part of my feeling life, but the Self is the architect of the whole dream, which summons consciousness and asks greater accountability of it.

meaning is repeated in various versions in all our lives. And when we live without meaning, we suffer the greatest illness of all. An ancient Egyptian text, *The World-Weary Man in Search of His Ba* (soul), illustrates the universality of this dilemma. Though thousands of years old, how modern is this title! Do you not see the tired commuter, the depleted homemaker, the businessman with the third martini—all longing, yearning, for something larger in their lives? Whenever we can bring consciousness to the meeting place with soul, we will be changed and, whether we wish or not, enlarged.

Millennia ago, the pre-Socratic philosopher Heraclitus concluded that the soul is a distant country whose breadth and boundaries can never wholly be explored. And yet all of us intuitively know what we mean by the word *soul. Soul* is the word we use to intimate that deepest intuitive relationship we have had with ourselves from our earliest moments of reflection to the present. *Soul* is our intuited sense of our own depth, our deepest-running, purposeful energy, our longing for meaning, and our participation in something much greater than ordinary consciousness can grasp. *Soul* is what makes us most profoundly human, and unceasingly drives us toward more conscious, evolved engagement in the four abiding orders of mystery in which our journey plays out: (1) the immense *cosmos* through which we are flung at warp velocity, (2) ambient *nature,* which is our home and our context, (3) each proximate *other* who brings the challenge of relationship, and (4) our own elusive, insurgent *Self,* forever asking, insisting, not to be forgotten.

We are the meaning-seeking, meaning-creating animals. Our fellow creatures live out their biological life cycles just as we do, but do not, apparently, have the capacity to reflect upon themselves, create abstractions, or build complex social structures as the carriers of their values. They may fight to live, but they are not anxious about their mortality. They carry the mystery of being as their instinctual heritage, as we do, but ours is the peculiar species that so often grows estranged from its own natural, instinctual ground. Our tendency toward idiosyncratic self-reflection, our discovery of metaphor, symbol, analogy, and abstraction, and that unnamable yearning that so typifies our nature, express our desire for meaning. This profound, irresistible urge toward meaning, and our anguish at the loss of meaning, give some inkling of our soul's parameters, and its insistent agenda. As Nobel Prize nominee Andre Malraux wrote in *The Walnut Trees of Altenburg:*

> *The greatest mystery is not that we have been flung at random between the profusion of the earth and the galaxy of the stars, but that in this prison we can fashion images of ourselves sufficiently powerful to deny our nothingness.* *

A life that constricts meaning wounds the soul. How often I have sat with couples who profess good intentions toward each other, but whose archaic agendas continue to impose themselves on each other. When I ask them, "How much do you want to live with a depressed, angry, reluctant partner?" each quickly responds that they desire the contrary. Yet their own actions, driven from hidden sources, create precisely that fractious, reluctant partner they dread. Relationships that are supposed to make both partners larger so often diminish both. The soul of each is constricted, and expresses itself through the familiar pathologies of daily discord.

Whether in a relationship or not, each of us has a profound need to feel the resonant support of the soul, to feel that we are participants in a divinely generated story. As Jung wrote in his memoir,

---

*Malraux, *The Walnut Trees of Altenburg*, p. 74.

"Meaninglessness inhibits fullness of life and is therefore equivalent to illness. Meaning makes a great many things endurable—perhaps everything."* As a Jungian analyst, I am privileged to witness the evolution of meaning out of great suffering and ignoble defeat in countless numbers of clients, as well as to track enlarging encounters with the dynamic unconscious. As the etymology of the word *psychotherapy* ("to observe or attend the soul") suggests, this work of spiritual enlargement is our common work, whether in a formal therapeutic setting or in the conduct of daily life.

Jung once observed that one can travel no further with another than one has traveled on one's own. This observation may seem commonplace to the reader, but most people don't know that very few psychotherapists have gone through analysis themselves. (Being driven into my own first hour of therapy—at age thirty-five, humbled by a classic midlife depression—felt very much like a defeat to me at the time, surely not the beginning of the second half of life.) Only those schools of thought and practice that are *psychodynamic,* that is, which seek a deepened conversation between the conscious and unconscious life, require the personal therapy of the practitioner. Today most therapists are *behaviorists,* seeking to modify non-productive behaviors and replace them with more effective strategies. The second largest group practices some form of *cognitive therapy,* which identifies various "bad ideas" we have acquired that reflexively make self-defeating choices for us and seeks to replace them with more effective ideas. Both of these approaches to the human condition are eminently logical and generally useful, and I have employed them many times myself.

Moreover, increasingly, the therapeutic scene is dominated by

*Jung, *Memories, Dreams, Reflections,* p. 340.

psychopharmacology. There are many individuals who suffer from chemical imbalances, whose problems are best treated by medical intervention. Once the biological playing field has been leveled, these individuals can then begin to deal with what Freud called the normal miseries of life. But I also believe that pharmacological treatment is vastly overprescribed because it is simpler, cost-effective, and relatively available to all. These are virtues, but more troubling is the possibility that, as a hidden agenda, pharmacology may conveniently allow one to avoid the larger questions of life, which, if ignored, are the secret source of suffering. This is not a virtue! Indeed, pharmacology, while helping diminish painful symptoms, may sometimes deflect or even derail our appointment with the soul.

Each of these three approaches, valuable as they may be in any given situation, can represent a failure of nerve to take on the larger questions of the soul. We may improve our chemistry or our behaviors, but in service to what ends? What brings us to our various dark woods is frequently interpreted as an external violation of the soul, an intrusion on a smoothly flowing life, whether from the acts of others, from the fates, or by our own choices. Yet just as often, inexplicably, it is the soul itself that has brought us to that difficult place in order to enlarge us, to ask more of us than we planned on giving. Only by attending the wounding of the soul, as well as learning to align our choices with its mysterious correctives, can we actively cooperate with this imperious summons to healing. Whatever we do to avoid the question of soul will prolong our reliance on the detritus of the old life, and the meaninglessness of its suffering. Only through making the meaning of that suffering and its agenda for spiritual enlargement conscious, can we ever emerge from the dark wood.

The second half of life presents a rich possibility for spiritual enlargement, for we are never going to have greater powers of choice, never have more lessons of history from which to learn, and never possess more emotional resilience, more insight into what works for us and what does not, or a deeper, sometimes more desperate, conviction of the importance of getting our life back. We are already survivors, and that counts for a lot. How, or even whether, we finally use these accumulated strengths to redeem our life from our history will count for even more.

Just what are those inner imperatives that rise to support us and challenge us in the journey of the second half of life? Perhaps Jung's most compelling contribution is the idea of *individuation,* that is, the lifelong project of becoming more nearly the whole person we were meant to be—what the gods intended, not the parents, or the tribe, or, especially, the easily intimidated or inflated ego. While revering the mystery of others, our individuation summons each of us to stand in the presence of our own mystery, and become more fully responsible for who we are in this journey we call our life. So often the idea of individuation has been confused with self-indulgence or mere individualism, but what individuation more often asks of us is the surrender of the ego's agenda of security and emotional reinforcement, in favor of humbling service to the soul's intent. This is quite the opposite of self-indulgence; it is the service of the ego to the higher order manifested to us through the Self.

The Self is the embodiment of the totality of the life of the organism. It is the architect of wholeness. What is monitoring your biological equilibrium as you read these lines? What moves your emotional and mental responses? What provides constancy when consciousness is distracted or asleep? A larger presence, which we all intuited when we were children and then lost contact with, moves and directs the total organism toward survival, growth, development, and meaning. Who we think we are is only a limited function of the ego, that thin wafer of consciousness floating on an iridescent ocean called the soul. Given the ego's tendency to try to solidify what is in flux, it is better to think of the Self as a verb than as a noun. The Self *selves;* it is always *selving,* even when, to the ego's consternation, it moves us toward our own mortal ends. This dynamic model of the psyche's totality was intuited by the nineteenth-century priest Gerard Manley Hopkins in his opulent lines:

Each mortal thing does one thing and the same:
Deals out that being indoors each one dwells;
Selves—goes itself; myself it speaks and spells,
Crying What I do is me: for that I came.*

The Self is the embodiment of nature's plan for us, or the will of the gods—whichever metaphor works better for you. Sometimes our journey takes place in the context of a vital, mythologically grounded culture, whereby one feels open to and supported by the mysteries. Then one experiences purpose in being, a sense of harmony with the world and with one's self—both the world and the individual journey are clothed in meaning. For so many more of us, our journey takes place amid the debris of history, the distractions of a noisy culture, and the experience of the loss of meaning. Either way, the intent of this metaphor—the summons of the soul to a larger life—is to invite your consciousness to a more mindful relationship to your journey. If we are in service to the Self, we can

---

*Hopkins, "As Kingfishers Catch Fire," *A Hopkins Reader*, p. 67.

seldom be in service to the herd as well. And how often do we have to learn that one cannot serve two masters without paying a crucifying cost?

Your Self is seeking itself, so to speak, through the realization of the possibilities inherent in you. At the same time, the ego is called to collaborate with the transcendent will of the Self, or it will be undermined by those eruptions that we call psychopathology in individuals and sociopathy in society. Service to the Self is quite the same as the achievement of enlightenment, or service to the will of God, as all great religions proclaimed, so often right before they fell into dogmatic forms and institutional claims that supplanted the sovereignty of the individual soul. As Jesus is reported to have said in the Gnostic Gospel of Thomas, "If you bring forth what is within you, what you bring forth will save you. If you do not bring forth what is within you, what you do not bring forth will destroy you." This is the essence of what Jung means by individuation. It is a service not to ego, but to *what wishes to live through us*. While the ego may fear this overthrow, our greatest freedom is found, paradoxically, in surrender to that which seeks fuller expression through us. Enlarged being is what we are called to bring into this world, contribute to our society and our families, and share with others. It is wholly false to think that individuation cuts a person off from others. It cuts a person off from the herd, from collectivity, but it deepens the range in which more authentic relationships can occur. It may be necessary for us from time to time to absent ourselves from the world in order to reflect, regroup, or revision our journey, but ultimately, we are to bring that larger person back to the world. Jung describes the dialectic of isolation and community in this way: "As the individual is not just a single, separate being, but by his very existence presupposes a collective relationship, it follows that the process of individuation must lead to more intense and broader collective relationships and not to isolation."*

We realize how tenuous our hold upon life is at such moments of existential choice. We all suffer from the lingering message of childhood: that the world is big and powerful, and that we are vulnerable and dependent. Stepping forth into larger shoes, more spacious psychologies, remains intimidating throughout our lives. We should never underestimate this disempowering paradigm, or the many ways in which it infiltrates new situations with familiar dynamics, producing unintended, regressive results. Moreover, virtually all of us lack a deep sense of permission to lead our own lives. We learned very early that the world exacted conditions that, if not met, could result in punishment or abandonment. That message, overlearned and internalized, remains a formidable block to the ego's capacity to elect its own path. Only when the ego has reached a certain measure of strength, or perhaps more commonly, is driven by desperation to make a different choice, can we overthrow this tyranny of history. Otherwise we all tend to slumber in history's unmade bed. Yet it is clear that we cannot choose not to choose, for not choosing is a choice from which consequences flow, and the inner split between soul and world widens. In most lives, permission to live one's life is not something one is given; it is to be seized, if not in early ego election then later in desperation, for the alternative is so much worse.

Separating from the herd the way the adolescent attempts to is typified by rebellion, a rebellion that quickly becomes another form of compliance. Separating from one's tribe as a mature person is

---

*Jung, *Psychological Types,* CW 6, para. 755.

fraught with risk, but derives from what one might call a religious imperative, namely to stand more honestly in relationship to that which is transcendent. Paradoxically, the withdrawal of compliance with the herd is the best way in which in time to return to the world and serve. As Jung notes:

> *Individuation cuts one off from personal conformity and hence from collectivity. That is the guilt which the individual leaves behind him for the world, that is the guilt he must endeavor to redeem. He must offer a ransom in place of himself, that is, he must bring forth values which are an equivalent substitute for his absence in the collective personal sphere.* *

In calling individuation a myth, we mean that such an image, charged with affect, rich with possibility, and related to transcendent purpose, is a psychologically grounding force field for the conduct of a conscious life. Most culturally charged alternatives of our time have noticeably failed because in the end they are not effective, do not satisfy the soul; only the myth of individuation deepens and ennobles our journey. Rather than ask, what does my tribe demand of me, what will win me collective approval, what will please my parents, we ask, what do the gods intend through me? It is a quite different question, and the answers will vary with the stage of life, and from one person to another. The necessary choices will never prove easy, but asking this question, and suffering it honestly, leads through the vicissitudes of life to larger places of meaning and purpose. One finds so much richness of experience, so much growth of consciousness, so much enlargement of one's vi-

---

*Jung, *The Symbolic Life, CW 18,* para. 1095.

sion that the work proves well worth it. The false gods of our culture, power, materialism, hedonism, and narcissism, those upon which we have projected our longing for transcendence, only narrow and diminish. Of each critical juncture of choice, one may usefully ask: "Does this path enlarge or diminish me?" Usually, we know the answer to that question. We know it intuitively, instinctively, in the gut. Choosing the path that enlarges is always going to mean choosing the path of individuation. The gods want us to grow up, to step up to that high calling that each soul carries as its destiny. Choosing the path that enlarges rather than diminishes will serve us well in navigating through our idol-ridden, clamorous, but sterile time and move us further toward meeting the person we are meant to be.

• • •

THIS BOOK IS NOT a typical "how to" book. My chief desire is to stir thought, trouble sleep, and provide some wider perspective. It will not tell you how to find God, meet the perfect mate, or win friends and influence people. That is your job, not mine. It is a book that respects your powers perhaps more than you do. It knows that you will still need to pass through all the trials of life, that you are surrounded by distractions, and that you are undermined by fear and by powerfully repetitious history. It believes that for you to make your own way you will have to become more responsible than any of us really wishes to be. It recognizes the immense importance of spirituality in this process of reclaiming your life, though it professes no specific belief for you to embrace. Again, that is your job. This book respects you, and asks that you do the same, and, together, we will come through this life with greater integrity and purpose.

This book is based on a personal journey, decades of working with others in their journey, and several books that have come before, some of which are included in the bibliography at the end. Each of those books, *The Middle Passage, Swamplands of the Soul, Under Saturn's Shadow, Creating a Life,* and *On This Journey We Call Our Life,* examine facets of this complex story, and I recommend them to readers who wish to focus on one aspect or another. *Finding Meaning in the Second Half of Life* is an effort to examine the shifting agenda of the second half of life from the perspective of depth psychology, in a language and style that's accessible to everyone. I seek to write as I might talk to you across a table, clearly and respectfully, yet always challenging you to find your own answers to the ongoing questions that your life asks of you.

I am especially grateful to Liz Williams for proposing this book, and for shepherding it through its various manifestations. And I am grateful for the editorial vision and support from Bill Shinker, Lauren Marino, and Hilary Terrell, who also believed in the need for this book, and made sure that it happened. From the beginning, we had one common desire: to address the universal journey of our separate, quite discrete lives with respect, with dignity, and with compassion for all people.

Despite the permutations that each of us brings to our unique journey, the story that follows is universal; it is the story of us all. Yet each of us is obliged to find our personal path through the dark wood. In the medieval Grail legend the knights, having seen the Grail, and intuiting that it symbolized their search for meaning, undertook the challenge and began their descent into the dark wood. But the text tells us that each one chose a separate place of entry "where there was no path, for it is a shameful thing to take the path that someone has trod before." Your journey is your journey, not someone else's. It is never too late to begin it anew.

Chapter One

Expensive Ghosts: How Did We Get to This Point?

"The chief cause of human error is to be found in prejudices picked up in childhood."
René Descartes, *Discourse on Method*

"We drag
expensive ghosts through
memory's unmade bed."
Paul Hoover, "Theory of Margins"

HAVE YOU NOT HAD THE FEELING, amid the evening rush hour drive, or while sitting on the beach, or at 3 A.M., the hour of the wolf, that you have no idea who you are, or what this busy business is about? If we have not had such moments of genuine confusion, perplexity, and doubt, chances are we are simply living on automatic pilot. I recently heard a lawyer recount how an insurance company he represented had been obliged to give a man a huge settlement. This worthy gentleman had bought a mobile home, set off on the interstate, then walked back in the mobile home to fix a cup of coffee. When the vehicle crashed and injured him, he claimed that he was not at fault because the dealer had not explained that "cruise control" was not the same as "automatic pilot." Improbably, the jury sided with him. Wouldn't it be nice to have someone award us for stupidity, for remaining unconscious, and for having no responsibility for being at the driver's wheel of our life? Our greatest sin may be choosing to remain unconscious, in spite of all the evidence that mounts through the years that other elements within us are actively making choices on our behalf, often with disastrous consequences.

So what has brought you to this point in your life? Have you chosen this life you lead, these consequences? What forces shaped you, perhaps diverted you, wounded and distorted you; what forces perhaps supported you, and are still at work within you, whether you acknowledge them or not? The one question none of us can answer is: *of what are we unconscious?* But that which is unconscious has great power in our lives, may currently be making choices for us, and most certainly has been implicitly constructing the patterns of our personal history. No one awakens in the morning, looks in the mirror, and says, "I think I will repeat my mistakes today," or "I expect that today I will do something really stupid, repetitive, regressive, and against my best interests." But, frequently, this replication of history is precisely what we do, because we are unaware of the silent presence of those programmed energies, the core ideas we have acquired, internalized, and surrendered to. As Shakespeare observed in *Twelfth Night,* no prisons are more confining than those we know not we are in.

Cynthia* prided herself on having freed herself from the constrictions of her family. She had fled the farming community into

---

*All names in this book are pseudonyms, all case examples composites, but all dreams are transcribed exactly as reported by the analysand, and I have permission to quote from them.

which she was born, attained a law degree, married an upwardly mobile man, and achieved her flourishing practice before her thirties ended. By forty she had reached all her goals, and felt miserable. How could she not be happy, having achieved what her cultural milieu, and her fine brain, valued so highly? Yet her depression grew; her body ached, and she found herself having to will herself to work each Monday. She reported her malaise to her internist and began taking a series of antidepressants. She found they took the edge off, but she also felt strangely depersonalized. When she came to therapy she brought this initial dream:

> *I am in my office, but it is also my parents' bedroom.*
> *I can't see them, but I know they are present.*

It is a short dream—one we all could have dreamed, for who ever leaves those ancestral specters wholly behind? The dream is a clue brought to us by the Self, solicits the attention of consciousness, and asks a question. "How is it possible that I can be in my world, and that of my parents at the same time?" Cynthia had to ask herself. In the weeks that followed she came to realize that in seeking to throw off their definitions of what and who she had to be, she had invested herself in their opposites. The more she chose the opposite of their instructions, the more those invisible presences dictated her choices. Having rejected their plans for her, and their dismal alternatives, Cynthia discovered to her dismay that she had not really been such a free agent in her own life as she supposed. She was reactively driven to reject her parents' constrictive world, and to elect what her middle-class culture endorsed, but still not to choose a life in accord with her soul's own desire. From the old messages of safety and constriction, she had fled into a compensatory professional world, yet found herself more constricted than she could ever have imagined. Why wouldn't she be depressed at such a predicament? Why would we not expect the body to revolt, and the psyche to withdraw energy from the place where the complex-driven ego wishes to invest it? Yet this troubling insurgency in the psyche is a friend, for it brings to Cynthia an accounting, and the possibility of greater consciousness. At this writing, she is conscientiously sorting through her choices, learning which ones are really hers and which ones derivative. It is a discernment process that must continue for the rest of her journey, as must ours. We all live with expensive ghosts in memory's unmade bed, for what we do not remember remembers us nonetheless.

It is unlikely that any of us would ever be called to reflect on the possibility of such autonomous forces in our lives if by some happy accident we made choices wholly consistent with our own nature. When we are young, our ready assumption is that, conscious beings that we are, we will make right choices and avoid the stupidities of those who have preceded us. Nonetheless, the ensuing conflict between our conscious choices and our nature's symptomatic commentary tells us that something is amiss. As a therapist, I am never happy to see people suffering, and yet the presence of suffering is already a manifestation of the psyche at work. The Self autonomously, sometimes dramatically, protests through symptoms—through addictions, through affective states such as anxiety or depression, or through conflicts in the external world—which, despite our frantic efforts, resist change through mere acts of ego intention. None of us is pleased to learn that our will is not enough, and that our good intentions often bring unintended consequences to ourselves or others. (As that ironic bumper sticker has it: "No good deed goes unpunished.")

As a therapist, my first clue to this large drama that plays out in the theater of our lives is found in the nature and dynamics of the symptom; thereafter, our joint task is to track the symptom or pattern to its origin. There is always a "logical" connection between a surface symptom or pattern and a historic wounding to the soul. Even though the external symptoms may seem irrational, even "crazy," they always emanate from and give symbolic expression to the wounding that has occurred. Therefore, we are, paradoxically, obliged to thank our symptoms, for they catch our attention, compel seriousness, and offer profound clues as to the deep will or intentionality of our own psyche. In the end we will only be transformed when we can recognize and accept the fact that there is a will within each of us, quite outside the range of conscious control, a will which knows what is right for us, which is repeatedly reporting to us via our bodies, emotions, and dreams, and is incessantly encouraging our healing and wholeness. We are all called to keep this appointment with the inner life, and many of us never do. Fortunately, this insistent invitation comes to us again and again.

The Freedom of This Contemporary Hour

Before the last century, we could not have been sharing the conversation this book invites. In 1900, the average life expectancy of a North American was only forty-seven. While some individuals lived longer, the statistical majority lived out their mortal transit in service to what we would now call the agenda of the first half of life. (Even today, if any of us is run over by a truck on our thirty-fifth birthday, we will have most probably lived according to the limited consciousness of the first half of life exclusively, the only script available, the only agenda we knew.) Additionally, social institutions powerfully burdened the past, in the form of family, social, ethnic, and gender values, as well as the defining sanctions of marital and religious institutions. Before we wax nostalgic about the past, please remember that many souls died within those constrictive roles and scripts. How many women's souls were squelched, how many men crushed by expectations and roles that offered each no expression for the infinite varieties of the soul?

Today, with the erosion of those normative roles and institutions, as well as our enormous life extension through better sanitation, diet, and medical intervention we often take for granted, other, larger questions necessarily emerge. In this new century, we have twice the length of adult life than our forebears were granted. Thus we are faced with an unprecedented opportunity and responsibility to live more consciously. In ways not possible in the past, we are now able to ask: "Who am I apart from the roles I have been playing—some of them good, productive, and consistent with my inner values, and some not?" Or we may wonder, "Since I have served the expectations of my culture, reproduced my species, become a socially productive citizen and taxpayer, what now?" What, in short, is the second half of life about—the time today between thirty-five and nearly ninety years—if it is not to repeat the script and expectations of the first half of life?

Two things seem to have to happen before these questions become conscious to us. First, we have to have lived awhile, long enough to develop enough ego strength to be able to step back, examine our history, and be willing to deal with whatever disappointments or failed expectations have come to us. The younger we are, and the less formed our sense of conscious self, the more intimidating and destabilizing such probing questions seem to be. A young person can't afford such questions, which threaten to erode the ego's fragile structure. But by midlife, one may finally be strong enough, or desperate enough, to ask these questions in a committed fashion—for perhaps the first time. Secondly, we need to have lived long enough to see that we have constructed patterns in our lives—patterns in relationships, patterns at work, and, so often, self-defeating patterns, which undermine our best interests. We are obliged to acknowledge that the only person who is consistently present, in every scene of that long-running drama we call our life, is ourselves. It stands to reason, then, that we might bear some responsibility for how this play, or soap opera, is turning out. We are clearly the protagonist of the drama, but is it possible that we are also the author, and if not us, who then, or what?

Tom Stoppard wrote a wonderful play about this question of life authorship, titled *Rosencrantz and Guildenstern Are Dead*. The title comes from a line in *Hamlet*. We all know the story of *Hamlet*, in which Rosencrantz and Guildenstern are minor characters who have a brief moment on the stage and then are slain. But what if we are Rosencrantz or Guildenstern and not Hamlet? His story is the stuff of high tragedy, but what if ours is the stuff of banality and obscurity? In Stoppard's play, the two title characters wander around in a fog, much as we, and try, much as we, to figure out what is going on. Some guy named Hamlet occasionally crosses their path, but he is some other dude in some other play. What their lives are about is never clear, until they are victims of forces set in motion by agents they don't know, leading to ends they don't desire. If we shift uncomfortably in our seats, it is because the play feels very uncomfortably close to home. What role do we play in our own dramas? Are we the protagonist, or a bit character in someone else's script? And if so, whose script, and what is that story?

The Silent Passage into the Second Life

Even in my first months as a therapist, I began recognizing a pattern in the lives of virtually all of my patients. Each presented a different history, a different family of origin, and a variegated set of external problems and emotional distresses. Their age varied from thirty-five to seventy-plus, but what seemed common to all, and brought them to my office, was that their understanding of themselves, and their attendant strategies in the world, was undergoing some sort of sea shift. Whatever "the plan" of their lives was, conscious or unconscious, it progressively seemed not to be working too well.

None of them had come to therapy as a first choice. Their initial line of defense against the eruptions of the unconscious into their lives was denial. (This is our most understandable, most primitive defense, which, if continued indefinitely, proves to be the only truly pathological state of being.) Typically, their second strategy was to revivify their efforts in service to the old plan. Their third choice was to strike off toward some new projection—a new job, a better (different) relationship, a seductive ideology, or sometimes to drift into some unconscious "self-treatment plan" such as an addiction or an affair. Their fourth choice, after having tried all of the above, was to admit futility and reluctantly come to therapy, feeling frustrated, sometimes angry and defeated, and always, always humbled. This shaky beginning marked the onset of the deepest inquiry they had ever undertaken, the risky adventure of getting to know who they really were, often quite apart from whomever they had become.

The Midlife Crisis?

There is some debate in professional circles about whether the so-called "midlife crisis" exists. This professional debate has not prevented the public from co-opting the term to disparagingly categorize the distress of their fellow humans as only "a momentary madness," without deeper implications for that person's entire life, and their own as well. Others have used the term to describe a wide range of errant behaviors, while continuing to dismiss the possibility that it might have meaning, namely: why has this disturbance occurred, and what might it mean for the life of the person suffering it? No matter the debate, there is little doubt that various agitations and confusions occur in the mid-thirties to mid-forties for many, even as some deceptively seem to cruise through the midlife shoals and sail unvexed into the calmer seas of later life.

There are reasons why these disturbances frequently manifest at what we typically consider "midlife." One has to have separated from the parents long enough to be *in* the world, to make choices, to see what works, what does not, and to experience the collapse, or at least erosion, of one's projections. By this age, the ego strength necessary for self-examination may have reached a level where it can reflect upon itself, critique itself, and risk altering choices, and thereby values as well. (I have also encountered many for whom this core strength is lacking, and they find ways to sabotage this invitation to recover their lives. Seldom do they stick to, or even enter, therapy.) This more radical examination of one's life, this more compelling engagement with the soul, cannot be undertaken on a whim, or finessed through a weekend workshop. To engage with the summons of our souls is to step into the deepest ocean, uncertain whether we will be able to swim to some new, distant shore. And yet, until we have consented to swim beyond the familiar lights of the port left behind, we will never arrive at a newer shore. For some the entry is gradual; others are pushed suddenly into deep waters.

How It Begins

Joseph came to his first hour of therapy convinced that it would be a quick lube job—in and out like a franchised chop shop along the interstate. After he presented the argument he and his wife had been having, I asked, "If you had to choose between your marriage and gambling, what would you choose?" He smiled and said, "Well, you can always get married." I knew then that we were in deep water. He had not come to therapy for healing. He had come to comply with his wife's ultimatum. As a working professional, he would slip away from the office and drop up to a thousand a day on the green felt tables, and be back as lunchtime ended, with no one the wiser. Only when his first child turned eighteen and the college tuition fund was looted was anyone aware of this habit. Joseph had no intention of confronting the habit, its effect on his family, or what inward agenda brought him to this daily brink. As anyone who deals with any form of addiction knows, we have to acknowledge that there is a world of hurt inside these persons who are desperately trying to "medicate" their distress with increasingly costly medication.

In my professional analytic training society, trainees, after extensive personal analyses and many exams, have to write up five major cases, two of which must be considered "failures." In these so-called failed cases, they are expected to analyze their own shortcomings and discover what is to be learned for the next time. With Joseph, I knew that I was dealing with a deep anxiety, in reaction to which he steadfastly steered toward the iceberg of disaster from the bridge of conscious life. He was confessing, without knowing fully what he was saying, that he would sacrifice all to continue to treat his deep anxiety. While such a person creates an untenable situation for others, his anguish is much to be pitied. After the third session, with no magic bullet available, no strategy for having one's cake and eating it too, he departed. I never saw him again. The appointment with his own sad history was not kept, and I can only surmise that the ship of life wrecked shortly thereafter.

It has been my experience that such midlife distress, while driven from inner engines, often presents itself first to consciousness in the outer context of intimate relationships, then in career, and then in more personal symptoms such as a depression. Intimate relationship, which will be the subject of a later chapter, is especially freighted, because it is the carrier of our deepest expectations for home, for confirmation of our identity, for nurturance and protection. As time goes by, our partners prove flawed and mortal, as we are to them, and we blame them when our projected scripts erode and deteriorate into conflict.

Similarly, we frequently have enormous expectations that careers will provide satisfaction in our life, and, however well or unwell our jobs work for us, in the second half of life we often find ourselves working for *them,* with decreasing satisfaction even as we accomplish our goals, collect our paychecks, and invest in a 401(k). If the soul could so easily be bought, then our culture would really work. Only the unconscious think it does. Look around you; look within you. Be honest. How well does material affluence work? And what is the price?

The psyche is always speaking, and its urges will manifest first as ennui, then more conscious boredom, then inner resistance to our conscious scripts, and, as we continue to turn deaf ears, finally, an eruption of invasive feelings and behaviors: interrupted sleep or eating habits, the lure of an affair, troubling dreams, self-medicating addictions, and so on. What is common to all of these seemingly disparate phenomena in so many different lives is the exhaustion of the scenarios that one has ostensibly chosen and expected to be served by in return. We find ourselves asking, "I have done the expected things, according to my best understanding of myself and the world, so why does my life not feel right?" These are painful questions, and all of us, *all of us,* sooner or later, experience this discrepancy between what we sought, served, and accomplished, and what we feel in our private, honest moments.

Yet, though these collisions of external expectation and inner reality frequently reach the surface in chronological midlife, I would suggest that each of us experiences a summons of the soul not once, but many times in the course of our lives. Either way, a substantial crisis of identity occurs whenever we experience the unavoidable conflict between the natural Self and the acquired "sense of self," with its attendant attitudes, behaviors, and reflexive strategies. Sometimes this conflict occurs when we go through a divorce only to find our problems continuing into the next relationship. Sometimes it rises out of the traumatic loss of a partner, which reveals to us a dependency we did not know lurked beneath our seemingly independent behaviors. Sometimes it manifests in the departure of our children, who have been carrying more of our projections and unlived life than we imagined. Sometimes it emerges in the context of a life-threatening illness or some other brush with death. (All it takes is a lump in the breast or an elevated PSA for the bottom to fall out of our well-planned life.) Or sometimes it simply comes to us as a sudden shock, as an occluded storm front sometimes passes over a sunny field, and we realize that we do not know who we are, or why we are living, or begin to sense that how we spend our now limited, precious time on this planet might really be up for grabs.

Thus, no matter their age, I saw that client after client was undergoing some sort of passage for which their conscious life was unprepared, leaving them confused, frustrated, disoriented. Such substantive passages have been universally observed. Traditional cultures evolved communal rites to support a person's passage through such times, and provided a vibrant set of mythological images that relocated the loss of the old in a larger, transcendent realm of meaning. In our era, however, such support, such rites of passage, are generally missing, or weakened, and these periods leave the individual adrift, disoriented, alone. These multicultural rites of passage were always grounded in the transcendent images and sacred histories of the tribe; thus, one was told in so many words, "We do this, or understand this, or practice this, as first modeled and ordained by our gods and our ancestors, and our reenactment today mirrors and reenergizes their meaningful paradigms for us." Compare that historic sense of the larger meaning of our natural deaths and rebirths with how today, when a person's personality structure deconstructs, he or she may be shamed, ridiculed, or pitied, and nearly always distanced, by friends and coworkers. For such isolated persons, the only supportive community may be found in the company of a therapist.

The most common characteristic of this kind of passage, despite the different story we each embody, is the deconstruction of "the false self"—the values and strategies we have derived from internalizing the dynamics and messages of our family and our culture. Yet each person is invited to a new identity, new values, new attitudes toward the self and the world, which often stand in stark contrast to the life lived prior to this summons. In the absence of the tribe, the weekly ritual of analysis becomes the supportive rite of passage for some. Although this transition from the old life and received values may prove frightening and disorienting, it is stunning, and ultimately transforming, to discover that something larger wishes to emerge. At this point in the journey, one is invited to experience deeper meaning in one's suffering, and to learn that something transcendent to the old way of being always comes when one has the courage to continue this journey through the dark wood.

I cannot help but think on Julia at such moments. She had spent her life keeping one step ahead of rage and depression by serving others. She felt that, from her impaired parents to her narcissistic husband to her needy children, she had never been loved for herself. Working with her dreams, which she began to do as a curiosity recommended by her therapist, led her to the inevitable encounter with a vast world within. Her dreams spoke to her history, her daily dilemmas, and her unlived life. From this ongoing dialogue she experienced love, finally, from some source within her that cared for her, loved her unconditionally in a way she had never experienced. Naturally, it took a while for the old ego, driven by anguish to serve others in order to feel valuable, to let go of the old agenda. If in fact Julia was loved, from some deep place independent of the ego, then her former sense of self, and the exploitation by others it invited, had to go also. This reorientation of the personality took time, took trial and error, but led to a larger life in which Julia's own needs became valued as much as those of others. We cannot underestimate how even a change for the better is a searing passage, a death of an older understanding, and its gradual replacement by something larger still.

Some of us, understandably, do not wish to hear even this message of hope and personal growth. We wish to have our old world, our former assumptions and stratagems, reinstituted as quickly as possible. We are desperate to hear: "Yes, your marriage can be restored to its pristine assumptions; yes, your depression can be magically removed without understanding why it has come; yes, your old values and preferences still work." This understandable desire for what is called "the regressive restoration of the persona" merely papers over the growing crevice within, and off we go in search of another palliative treatment, or another less demanding view of our difficulties. It is quite natural to cling to the known world and fear the unknown. We all do—even as that crevice between the false self and the natural self grows ever greater within, and the old attitudes more and more ineffectual. Most of us live our lives back-ing into our future, making the choices of each new moment from the data and agenda of the old—and then we wonder why repeti-tive patterns turn up in our lives. Our dilemma was best described in the nineteenth century by the Danish theologian Søren Kierkegaard when he noted in his journal the paradox that life must be remembered backward but lived forward. Is it not self-deluding, then, to keep doing the same thing but expecting differ-ent results?

For those willing to stand in the heat of this transformational fire, the second half of life provides a shot at getting themselves back again. They might still fondly gaze at the old world, but they risk engaging a larger world, one more complex, less safe, more chal-lenging, the one that is already irresistibly hurtling toward them.

Paradoxically, this summons asks us to begin taking ourselves more seriously than ever before, but in a different way than before. Such self-examination cannot proceed without, for instance, more honesty than we have been capable of. In most cases we come to this point in our life serving a diminished view of ourselves. As Jung once put it humorously, we all walk in shoes too small for us. Liv-ing within a constricted view of our journey, and identifying with old defensive strategies, we unwittingly become the enemies of our own growth, our own largeness of soul, through our repetitive, history-bound choices.

Taking oneself seriously begins with a radical acceptance of some truths that seem evident to those who stand outside us, but which are intimidating to that insecure ego through which we manage the tenuous conduct of daily life. A recent example comes to mind. A man I know attended his thirtieth high school reunion and came home to tell his wife that he saw his childhood sweetheart and that he wanted to live his life with her. He was caught in a powerful projection onto this comparative stranger, and sought to recover youth, the hope and vitality of the past, and feed the fantasy of emotional renewal. These are not bad goals, as such, but the fantasy that romance with an old flame will bring this about is a profound delusion. All who stand outside know this, but the person in the grip of this unconscious agenda cannot see that the outer woman is a surrogate for his inner life, which has been neglected these many years.* The problem with the unconscious is that it is unconscious. How many of us know enough to grasp that we really do not know enough?

The second half of life is a continuing dialectical encounter with divergent truths, truths that are generally quite difficult to bring to consciousness until we are forced to do so. These truths include the recognition that this is *our* life, not someone else's, that after our thirtieth birthday we alone are responsible for how it turns out, that we are here but a fleeting instant in the spinning shuttle of eternity, and that there is a titanic struggle going on within each of us for the sovereignty of the soul. To grasp this reality, live with it, accept its summons, is already to enlarge the frame of reference through which we see our life. No matter how humble our circumstances, it is necessary for us to step out onto center stage, where large issues are at stake and where we are involved in a divine drama. In his memoir Jung spoke eloquently of our struggles:

> *I have frequently seen people become neurotic when they content themselves with inadequate or wrong answers to the questions of*

---

*To serve the reader's interest in knowing endings: The high school sweetheart, similarly swept up for a while, changed her mind. The man, having ended his marriage, is now is adrift out there, somewhere.

life. They seek position, marriage, reputation, outward success or money, and remain unhappy and neurotic even when they have attained what they were seeking. Such people are usually contained within too narrow a spiritual horizon. Their life has not sufficient content, sufficient meaning. If they are enabled to develop into more spacious personalities, the neurosis generally disappears. *

Surely his words speak to the most pervasive yet seductive delusion of our time, that we can find something "out there"—some person, some social stature, some ideological cause, some external validation—that will make our lives work for us. If this were true, we would see the proof all around us. Instead of widespread satisfaction, we see the frenzies of popular culture, the distractions of the idle, the rage of the dispossessed, and only rarely a person who moves through this life with a sense of transcendent purpose, deep psychic grounding, and a spiritually enlarged life. Developing a more spacious personality, to use Jung's felicitous phrase, sounds pleasant, but seldom do we grow toward one without the old order being called into account. It is generally through the experience of unsolicited suffering that we grow larger, not because the unexamined life proved easier.

In order to enhance this passage toward a more authentic existence, it is useful to become more knowledgeable about how the psyche works. We are invited to take a different view of our symptoms. Our first, natural desire is to suppress them, but we must learn to read them as clues to the wounded wishes of the soul, or as the autonomous protest of the soul over our mismanagement. We learn to exercise a form of discipline that requires the daily scrutiny

---

*Jung, *Memories, Dreams, Reflections,* p. 140.

of life: "What did I do, and why, and where did it come from within me?" We engage our soul's agenda, which requires a humbled attitude, and a wary watchfulness. It requires that we understand that our lives, even when fraught with outer difficulties, are always unfolding from within. (Jung disturbingly observed that what we have ignored or denied inwardly will then more likely come to us as outer fate.) "So, where did this outcome, this event, come from within me?" is a most critical, and potentially liberating, question. To ask it consistently requires a daily discipline, increased personal responsibility, and no little amount of courage. It means that no matter how nervous we may be, we have to step toward center stage in that play we call our life, the only one we get.

The rest of this book will illustrate some of the many things we can learn about ourselves during this time: how the psyche works, how we can cooperate with it, and how we can enlarge our journeys, find their various meanings, and ultimately live them to the betterment of our world. This work upon which you embark is far from an exercise in narcissism or self-indulgence. (And don't let anyone tell you that it is!) The quality of our relationships, the quality of our parenting, the quality of our citizenship, and the quality of our life's journey can never be higher than the level of personal development we have attained. What we bring to life's table will be a function of how much of our journey we have made conscious, and how much courage we were able to muster to live it in the real world that life has presented to us. This more conscious journey, which demands a life of spiritual and psychological integrity, is the only journey worth taking. After all, the diverting, addictive alternatives are all around us, and their sad evidence suggests that a more effective route must lie in the risk of looking within for a change.

This book may itself become a sort of passage for the reader, asking that you leave old assumptions behind, risk living amid the real ambiguities of life for a while, and move toward a larger role in the conduct of your life than ever before. It is a journey across that most archaic, most daunting, most inviting of seas—our own souls.

Chapter Two

Becoming Who We Think We Are

"I shall now try to look calmly at myself and begin to act inwardly, for only in this way will I be able as the child in its first consciously undertaken act refers to itself as 'I,' to call myself 'I' in a profounder sense."

Søren Kierkegaard, *Papers and Journals*

H OW DID WE EVER COME TO BE who we are in this world, in this particular way, a way now known to those around us as who we are, or at least who they think we are? And just who do *we* think we are, we might ask as well. What does the ego know, and what does it not know? And doesn't what it does not know play a large role in the conduct of daily life? Again, what is unconscious owns us, and brings the weight of history into our present.

Our lives hang always by a slender thread. Before consciousness, that thread was the umbilical cord to our mother, our source. We floated through time and space, before either category of consciousness existed for us, with our elemental needs met, and our home secure. And then we were flung into this world, violently—and it has never been so safe since. All peoples have had their tribal account of this event, and almost uniformly image it as a loss, a decline, a fall from a "higher" estate. In the Eden story of the Judeo-Christian tradition, we are told that there are two trees, one from which we may eat, and the other forbidden. Partaking of the Tree of Life is to abide forever in the world of instinct—whole, connected, and living the deepest of rhythms without consciousness. Partaking of the Tree of Knowledge brings the mixed blessing of consciousness. The phenomenon of consciousness is both traumatic *and* the great gift, and these apparent opposites forever remain comrades. Out of the separation of child from womb—consciousness, based always on splitting and opposites, is born. The birth of life is also the birth of neurosis, so to speak, because from that moment on we are in service to twin agendas—the biological and spiritual drive to develop, to move forward, and the archaic yearning to fall back into the cosmic sleep of instinctual subsistence. These two motives are at work within each of us always, whether we consciously attend them or not. (If you are the parent of a teenager, you see this titanic drama every morning. If you are mindful, you see it in yourself as well.)

Yet our being inevitably depends upon repeated separations, repeated developmental departures, ever farther away from the archaic, safe place. Drifting as we do through the gossamer dance of life, we are flooded with *nostalgia,* a word whose Greek origin means "pain for home." We need to remember that these twin agendas of progression versus regression war within us each day. When the desire to "go home," prevails, we will choose not to choose, rest easy in the saddle, remain amid the familiar and comfortable, even when it is stultifying and soul-denying. Each morning the twin gremlins of fear and lethargy sit at the foot of our bed and smirk. Fear of further departure, fear of the unknown, fear of the challenge of largeness intimidates us back into our convenient rituals, conventional thinking, and familiar surroundings. To be recurrently intimidated by the task of life is a form of spiritual annihilation. On the other front, lethargy seduces us with sibilant whispers: kick back, chill out, numb out, take it easy for a while . . . sometimes for a long while, sometimes a lifetime, sometimes a spiritual oblivion. (As a friend advised me in Zurich, "When in doubt, administer chocolate.") Yet the way forward threatens death—at the very least, the death of what has been familiar, the death of whomever we have been.

This fundamental ambivalence may be seen played out in a poem by D. H. Lawrence titled "Snake." In the poem the narrator goes down to the village well to draw water there and meets a serpent, sunning itself regally, in high disregard of the speaker. They eye each other. On the one hand, the narrator admires the majesty of the creature; on the other hand, he fears him. An intolerable tension rises and the speaker throws his bucket at the serpent. What convulses him into action is the recognition that the serpent is *choosing* to enter the depths, the same depths the speaker fears. He tries to kill his fear by attacking the animal, much as people attack gays for stirring unconscious insecurities about their own sexual identities, or minorities for simply being other than what falls within the ego's narrow purview. The narrator's fear of depth is understandable, but, in a harsh self-judgment, he believes that he has met one of the lords of life, has been terrified by the summons to a larger encounter, and now has to live forever with a petty soul.

The daily confrontation with these gremlins of fear and lethargy obliges us to choose between anxiety and depression, for each is aroused by the dilemma of daily choice. Anxiety will be our companion if we risk the next stage of our journey, and depression our companion if we do not. Like Baba Yaga, whose head nods at the crossroads in Russian folktales, bobbing this way and that, we are obliged to choose, whether we wish or not. (Or, as that noted American philosopher Yogi Berra reportedly said, "When you come to a fork in the road—take it.") Not to consciously choose a path guarantees that our psyche will choose for us, and depression or illness of one form or another will result. Yet to move into unfamiliar territory activates anxiety as our constant comrade. Clearly, psychological or spiritual development always requires a greater capacity in us for the toleration of anxiety and ambiguity. The capacity to accept this troubled state, abide it, and commit to life, is the moral measure of our maturity.

This archetypal drama is renewed every day, in every generation, in every institution, and in every decisive moment of personal life. Faced with such a choice, choose anxiety and ambiguity, for they are developmental, always, while depression is regressive. Anxiety is an elixir, and depression a sedative. The former keeps us on the edge of our life, and the latter in the sleep of childhood. Jung spoke most eloquently of the role that intimidating fear plays in our lives:

> *The spirit of evil is fear, negation . . . the spirit of regression, who threatens us with bondage to the mother and with dissolution and extinction in the unconscious. . . . Fear is a challenge and a task, because only boldness can deliver from fear. And if the risk is not taken, the meaning of life is somehow violated.* *

The "mother" to which he refers was once the literal parent for the child, but for the adult "she" now symbolizes the safe and shel-

---

*Jung, *Symbols of Transformation*, CW 5, para. 551.

tering harbor: the old job, the familiar warm arms, and the same unchallenged, and stultifying, value system. Domination by our "mother complex," which has little to do with our personal mother, means that we are in service to sleep, not the task of life, to security, not development. This archetypal drama plays out in every moment of our lives whether we recognize it or not. These choices create our patterns, the values of our daily lives, and our variegated futures, whether we know we are making choices or not, and whether those choices are fed from the deep springs of the soul, or from our fated, repetitive psychological inheritance. The struggle for growth is not for us alone; it is not self-indulgent. It is our duty, and service, to those around us as well, for through such departures from the comfortable we bring a larger gift to them. And when we fail ourselves, we fail them. The Prague-born poet Rilke expressed the paradox this way:

Occasionally someone rises from evening meal,
Goes outside, and goes, and goes, and goes . . .
Because somewhere in the East a sanctuary stands.

And his children lament as though he had died.

And another, who dies within his house,
Remains there, remains amid dishes and glasses,
So that his children must enter the world
In search of that sanctuary, which he forgot.*

How scary is it that what we don't do in the surprising adventure of this journey, our children will need to do, for they will be limited

---

*Rilke, "Occasionally someone rises . . . ," author's translation.

by our sad example, or overwhelmed by having to do it for us? In my last conversation with my dying father, the best, gentlest, good man I ever met, I said to him, in an irrational, unplanned moment, "Dad, I went out and kicked ass for you." I meant it as a thanks, and a blessing. He looked at me quizzically. I thought for a moment then he understood and was proud. But as I reflect on that spontaneous moment, I have reservations. How much of what I did in pushing limits and traveling to unknown lands was a compensation for his unlived life or, more precisely, an overcompensation to help redeem the oppression of his life?

Despite that good man, I have to ask how much of my life has been truly mine, and not some spectral agenda derived from his. I recall the time in a college football game when I deliberately kneed an end who came down to block me and, failing, rolled his legs into me and kicked my shins. When the referee threw the yellow flag and gave my team fifteen yards for unsportsmanlike conduct, I was proud of the moment. How much of that perversely proud penalty owes to compensating for the passive, unlived life of my father? When my adult life has been spent empowering others through education, writing, therapy, teaching—how much of that is overcompensating for the unrealized potential of my father's life? Why would my child self have become so identified with the task of empowerment if he did not conclude in some deep place that healing his environment was critical to his own survival as well? How much of it is a natural talent, in service to a natural calling? I am still trying to sort all this out. Differentiating the various levels of psyche that are at work in all that we do takes time, patience, and often courage. These questions are troubling to us all, but the reader needs to ask them in order to gain a measure of freedom for the precious moment that is now, this moment which, for a short time, is yours.

Why the Tragic Sense of Life Matters to Us

The word *tragic,* like *myth,* has been debased in our time. It has come to mean something horrible, calamitous, as in the newscaster's phrase, "Tragedy tonight on the West Side Expressway—five killed in collision of cab and SUV." (The Greeks did have a word for that sort of occurrence: *catastrophe.*) But we have much to learn about our lives from recalling what our ancestors intuited twenty-six centuries ago, and embodied in their "tragic vision" or "tragic sense of life." Their imaginative rendering of the human dilemma, the dialectical play of fate, destiny, character, and choice, remains the best paradigm for how life's permutations play out on this finite plane.

Our predecessors discerned that we often intend a certain outcome, work diligently toward its achievement, and yet wind up in an entirely different place than expected in our lives. And, most disturbingly, this altered course derives in substantial measure from the choices that a presumably conscious being made. How could this be, that we could be our own enemy? They understood that there were forces in the cosmos to which even the gods were subject. Such forces they named *moira,* or "fate," *sophrosyne,* or "what goes around comes around," *dike,* or "justice," *nemesis,* or "consequential retribution," and *proerismus,* "destiny." These forces might be translated by us today as the organizing, balancing, structuring powers of the *cosmos,* a word which itself means "order." When we are ignorant of these forces at work, as frequently we will be, we most likely make choices that run counter to the principles and energies of our own deepest nature, and will then suffer compensatory and restorative activity.

Moreover, our ancestors believed that we often "offend the

gods," that is, violate the energic designs of which they are the dramatized personifications. Thus a wound to Aphrodite will show up in one's intimate relationships; or one possessed by Ares will act out of unreasoned anger, with all its attendant consequences. Accordingly, they believed that by "reading" the texture of one's life, one can identify the ignored or repressed archetypal powers, the gods offended, and offer homage and compensatory behaviors to them to restore the balance. (This ancient practice is not too far from the modern idea of therapy, which attempts to read the texture of one's life, identify the locus of wounding, and outline the program to which the ego consciousness submits in order to provide correction, compensation, healing, and right relationship to the soul.)

Added to the mix, our predecessors acknowledged the role of individual character, which repeatedly plays a role in the creation of our choices and patterns. What they called *hubris,* often translated as "pride," might more pragmatically be defined as our tendency toward self-deception, especially the delusion that we are in possession of all the facts when we make decisions. What they called the *hamartia,* sometimes translated as "the tragic flaw," I would prefer to call "the wounded vision," the inherent biasing of our choices as a result of our own psychological history.

Our tendency toward wrong choice, or unintended consequences, is fueled by these two liabilities. The first is our temptation to believe what we wish to believe, the assumption that we know all we need to know about ourselves and the situation to make wise choices. (In fact, seldom do we know enough even to know we do not know enough. Any person at forty or fifty years of age who is not appalled by some of his or her choices in the earlier decades is either dumb lucky or remains unconscious.)

Moreover, there is a second element here, namely the biasing of our vision by the profound influence of our personal and cultural histories. Our experience subtly alters, even distorts, the lens through which we see the world, and the choices we make are based on that altered vision. At birth, each of us is handed a lens by our family of origin, our culture, our Zeitgeist, through which to see the world. As it is the only lens we have ever known, we will presume we see reality directly even as we are seeing it colored and distorted. How could we ever choose wisely, when our information is biased, even inaccurate? Only the corrections of others, or the corrections from our violated psyche, may oblige us to consider that our fundamental way of seeing and understanding is suspect. When I was young, I fantasized that I could learn all that was needed to know to choose rightly; today I know that I can never know enough, that there are always unconscious factors at work, which will only become apparent down the line, if then, and that the old powers, "memory's unmade bed," are far stronger than I had ever given them credit for. What once was the confidence of youth, albeit often just whistling in the dark, I now see as a combination of hubris, hamartia, and unconsciousness. From this encounter with our limitations the wisdom of humility comes: to know that we do not even know what we do not know, and that what we do not know will often make the choices for us.

The classical prototype for humbled knowledge was Sophocles' Oedipus. Gifted with intelligence, he nonetheless drifted into the fulfillment of dark prophecies, that is, the unfolding tendencies of history, which overruled reason at critical junctures of choice. How different is the semicomic tone of the more recent film *Peggy Sue Got Married,* which shows a mature woman who, possessing the knowledge of later years, revisits the past, marries the same jerk, and repeats the same bad choices as the first time, and thereby sleeps anew in "memory's unmade bed." And yet how similar the message. (If only we could live in the greater possibility of the film *Groundhog Day,* replaying one day over and over and making better choices. Even then, however, the capacity for ineffective choices in any given day seems infinite, so we might never get through the first twenty-four hours.)

Such humbling wisdom feels like a defeat for the arrogance of our assumptions, but it is also ennobling and healing, for it brings us into right relationship with the gods again. "Right relationship with the gods" as a psychological concept means that we harmonize our conscious life with the deepest powers that govern the cosmos and course through our own souls. Such moments of congruence will be felt as a sense of well-being, a reenergized relationship to self and world, and a feeling of "home" in the midst of the journey. (Is not this deepened journey of the soul, in fact, our "home"?) The tragic sense of life, then, is not morbid but rather heroic, for it is a summons to consciousness, change, and humility before the awesome powers of nature and our own divided psyche. Who ignores this summons will suffer the wrath of the gods, the splitting of the soul we call neurosis. The tragic sense of life is an ongoing invitation to consciousness, which, when accepted, is paradoxically enlarging through the humbling restoration of our place in the larger scheme of things. The traditional admonition to walk humbly and in fear of the gods has continuing meaning for us all.

Existential Wounding and the Programming of Our Sense of Self

Recall that our life's journey begins with a traumatic separation, a shock to the system from which we never wholly recover. The core message that we derive from this event called our birth is that we are expelled from home and are set adrift in an unknown world with many intimidating powers. We all received this same message: the world is big and you are not; the world is powerful and you are not; the world is inscrutable but you must discern its ways to survive. The presence of loving parents and sustained reassurance in a child's life goes a long way toward moderating the severity of this message and activating the natural empowering resources that are latent in each of us. Other children, less fortunate, experience disempowering messages and feel even more overwhelmed by the world. And all of us, to varying degrees, experience two categories of existential wounding that affect the rest of our lives.

The power of these primal, formative experiences in programming our sense of self, our sense of the world "out there," and how we are to relate to it can hardly be overemphasized. In the initial years of our life—unsupported by the development of an ego that surveys the world and its alternatives, learns parallel possibilities, learns to differentiate cause and effect better—we all are limited to a modality of experiencing, which anthropologists and archetypal psychologists call "magical thinking." Magical thinking results from an insufficient ability to differentiate self and world. The child concludes that "The world is an encoded message to me, a statement about me, about how I am valued, and how I am to comport myself." Another way of putting this is: "I am what happens, or happened, to me." Decades later we may begin to differentiate better. We learn that Mother's anger, or Dad's aloofness, or the impoverishment of imagination that haunted our tribe, was the limitation of *another* and not about ourselves at all. But this recognition comes late in life, if at all, and after many painful turns and returns. Long before then, this primal internalization of life's encrypted messages, this identification of self with a contingent and demanding world, has been embedded as a paradigm for our core sense of self.

Lacking other "readings" of the world, it is natural for a child to conclude: "I am as I am treated." As one woman said to me, coming from profoundly limited parents who were indifferent to her needs, "I have never been loved. I have always believed it is because I am not worth loving." She internalized how she was held, treated, addressed, as a de facto statement about herself, as all children do. Children internalize the psychological atmosphere of the parents, as well as their outer environmental conditions. General family dynamics, socioeconomic resources, and other cultural conditions, reinforce the primal messages about the self and the world. Only decades later, if even then, are we able to differentiate that powerful "other" from ourselves.

Additionally, the child observes the behaviors of the big people as they struggle to adapt, to survive, as statements about the world. Is my world safe, nurturing, reliable, or absent, hostile, problematic? (As a child during World War II, even though I was personally safe, I reasonably concluded that the world was an anxious, dangerous place, for I felt that troubled atmosphere all about me.) Fundamental values are framed in this primitive fashion, and are internalized in a way we may be serving decades later in quite different settings: trust/distrust; approach/avoidance; intimacy/distance; vitality/depression; and so on.

It is sobering to consider how fortuitous these causal events are. Rippling outward from the spinning cycles of fate, they have nothing to do with the essence of that child, and yet they are so often internalized as a set of statements about self and other as to dominate the relationship the adult has with the world. Yes, the *Self* is active, producing symptomatic protests at its submission to such a fate, but the power of our earliest messages is extraordinarily difficult to confront, especially when it is at work unconsciously. What we do not know does indeed hurt us, and others, and has the potential to guide our choices in directions quite different from those the soul desires.

Let's examine the general categories of existential trauma and see the ways the psyche reacts to them. Each of us will have enacted each of these unconscious strategies at some time in our life, although one or two may prove more familiar than the others. If we do not see their employment in our lives, perhaps we are not yet conscious of the manifold ways in which they weave our histories, and are weaving them still. It is truly sobering to reflect on the possibility that so many of our life choices, and their attendant consequences, may be based on something so primal, which has such lasting impact on the outcome of all we do.

The Wound of Overwhelmment

The first category of inevitable existential, childhood wounding we may call *overwhelmment,* namely, the experience of our essential powerlessness in the face of our environment. That overwhelming environment may consist of invasive parental presences, socioeconomic pressures, biological impairment, world events, and so on. In the face of this overwhelmment, the central message is, again, that one is powerless to alter the course of the outer world. How that message is internalized, and extended into our coping strategies, is a matter of almost infinite variety. However, it is possible to see three major categories of reflexive response.

It's important to remember that everything we do as adults is "logical," if we understand the unconscious psychological premise from which it emanates. A reflexive behavior or attitude is the expression of a state that is preconscious, derivative, and the cause of our reactions. Thus, we are never acting "crazy"; we are surreptitiously expressing the logic of our internal experience, even if the premise is profoundly flawed, incorrect, derived from another time and place, and completely ignores what the adult knows to be true.

What are these three categories of reflexive response to the existential wound of overwhelmment? See what seems familiar, for all of us have explored these logical strategies in our lives, and may still be employing them today.

First, given the message that the world is larger, more powerful, we may logically try to evade its potential punitive effect upon us by *retreating, avoiding, procrastinating, hiding out, denying, dissociating*. Who has not avoided what seemed painful or overwhelming? Who has not forgotten, postponed, dissociated, repressed, or simply fled? We all have. And for some, this primitive defense becomes a deeply programmed pattern of aversion to life's large demands. For the child who has profoundly experienced the overwhelmment of the world, experienced the devastation of psychic invasion, the motive to avoid may come to dominate life in a so-called personality disorder named "the avoidant personality." Avoidance, dissociation, repression become the first line of defense for those who lacked the resources to otherwise defend the fragility of their condition. The problem occurs for all of us, however, when such reflexive responses make the decision for us, and usurp consciousness, with its wider range of alternatives. I have seen people marry someone they did not love because they felt unable to approach the one they did love, because they had reflexively imbued that other with such transferred powerfulness that they were afraid to approach them. Others avoided going to college, or seeking the more challenging career, or risking their talent in the face of a world they experienced as too powerful to take on.

The second logical response to overwhelmment is found in our frequent efforts to *seize control of the situation*. In its most primitive form, the child who has been profoundly abused may evolve into the sociopathic personality in service to the core message he or she internalized: "The world is hurtful and invasive. You must hurt or invade it first, or be hurt and invaded instead." Most of us learned other, less extreme, coping mechanisms. We may pursue education as a means to understand, because to understand is to be in control . . . perhaps. For example, some experts have asserted that the fear of death and dying is stronger in medical professionals than in the average person. If so, it could be argued that physicians—who enter the arena of threat, attempt "heroic measures," and conceive death as the enemy rather than a natural process—might illustrate a reflexive response to the existential message of overwhelmment.

At any rate, all of us have endeavored, with greater or lesser success, to get in control of our environment, lest it control us. Many have sought overt power in life, from petty dictators to insecure, bullying spouses. Their urgent desire for power is a measure of their inner powerlessness. How little they realize that their behaviors are a continuing confession of what they fear. One of my patients chose to be a police officer, for the gun and badge granted him an authority he had lacked in childhood in the face of a sexually abusive mother. In his serial marriages he was a bully, given to verbal and physical abuse of his spouses. Others, giving up on the notion of gaining power overtly, resort to what we commonly identify as "passive/aggressive" behaviors. Such a person appears to cooperate, even be congenial, but surreptitiously sabotages, turns up late, inserts the chilling, critical remark, fails to carry through, and thereby gains power through apparent powerlessness. Somerset Maugham's short story "Louise" dramatizes a woman who presents herself as an invalid in order to control others. Every time they act independently, she has a heart spell, and yanks their chain.

Fragile soul that she is, she runs through two husbands who precede her into mortality, and finally, after her daughter's long acquiescence ends with her deciding to marry and move out, Louise has the last word by dying for real. We can only imagine how her daughter's life will continue to be psychologically dominated by this passive–aggressive, controlling ghost. Such logical controlling behaviors, based on early and overly generalized conclusions, can come to not only dominate our lives, but also hurt those around us.

Thirdly, with the power of the world inordinately impressed upon us, there is another category of logical response, surely the most common: "Give them what they want!" Beginning with Mom and Dad, most children learn to get love by providing others with what is demanded, expected, or merely implied. *Accommodation* is a learned response, sometimes even necessary for civilization to survive. But when repeated accommodation overrides the desires of our inner life, becomes a violation of personal integrity, the results are ugly. Notice that there are so many polite words we have learned to accommodate our accommodation. We say someone is "sweet," "personable," "amiable," "easygoing," and most often, "nice." When these labels repeatedly apply to someone's behavior the consequences to the person's inner life may in fact be ugly. We are conditioned to be nice, yet if we find ourselves repeatedly, reflexively being nice, we have not only lost integrity through reflexive responses, we have lost the power to conduct our own life. (Indeed, the stakes are even higher, for studies of totalitarian systems, or any society with strong collective pressures, show that through intimidation, most, if not all, citizens become "nice," which is to say, docile, compliant, and ultimately complicit in evil.)

In recent years, this adaptive response has become so common as to earn its own pathologizing name, "codependence." Recently, the American Psychiatric Association, which writes the book on psychological disorders and their diagnoses, seriously considered including codependence as a diagnostic category. Finally, it was not included, at least for now, because this adaptive behavior would prove so common as to flood insurance companies with claims from so many, and because its very ordinariness makes it suspect as a mental disorder. Codependence may or may not be a psychiatric category, but it is certainly an estrangement from our souls.

Codependence is predicated on one's reflexive assumption of powerlessness and the inordinate power of the other. Whenever that disempowering lens of history falls over our eyes, the present reality is subverted to the dynamics of the past, and one remains a prisoner of fate once again. Learning to find one's own truth, hold to it, and negotiate with others seems easy enough on paper. In practice, it means catching reflexive actions while they occur, suffering the anxiety aroused by acting more consciously in integrity, and tolerating the assault of anxiety-driven "guilt" thereafter. (This guilt is not genuine; it is a form of anxiety aroused by the anticipated negative reaction of the other person. Such reactions for the child were enormously distressing, and are still debilitating in adulthood. One man, when answering machines were first coming out for general use, discovered that he could simply not answer any request on the phone for twenty-four hours, long enough for the old, compliant pattern to resettle and for him to more truly decide what he wanted to do.) Becoming conscious in the midst of such a psychic reflex is a tall order, and thus the old pattern of powerlessness is far more likely to be reinforced one more time. Over the years, we tend to believe that such an old, familiar system is who we really are, and, by and large, such a system so frequently presented to the world becomes how others view us. Being nice has, however, ceased being nice.

The Wound of Insufficiency

The wound of *insufficiency* tells us that we cannot rely upon the world to meet our needs. It may have been that a parent was repeatedly not there for us, perhaps caught in his or her relationship difficulties, his or her depression, distractions, addictions, or real world pressures. Even insufficiencies outside parental influence, such as poverty, contribute to this sense of scarcity. At worst, we have the experience of literal abandonment. Those children abandoned in reality usually suffer what is called "anaclitic depression," which can manifest as physiological, emotional, mental, and psychological problems, including vulnerability to opportunistic diseases and, commonly, much earlier death. The "failure to thrive" paradigm is based on the fact that the resources that are genetically present in us at birth require positive mirroring reinforcement to develop. What is not fed will starve. A child who experiences absence, actual or psychological, will twist in an unfulfilled desire to be fed, comforted, and engaged by another, or turn off and die. And even for those of us who had a modicum of nurturing, who among us has not often felt, in the words of the old spiritual, "like a motherless child"?

Again, from this preconscious experience, a wounding and biasing message comes to each of us, and we evolve at least three major categories of response to protect our fragile psyche.

The first category of response to the insufficiency of nurturing derives from the magical thinking of the child ("I am as I am treated"). For some, the absence of the supportive other is internalized as "I am not met halfway because I am not worth being met." Such a person has a tendency to *hide out from life, diminish personal possibilities, avoid risk, and even make self-sabotaging choices.* One takes the lesser opportunity as a confirmation of one's apparent worth. One chooses the safe option, be it in work or relationship, rather than one that challenges and opens new possibilities. Through the power of this internal program, one repeatedly makes self-defeating choices, believing each time that they have come from outside and are but further confirmation of an impaired self-worth.

Such self-defeating repetitions are an example of Jung's perturbing insight that what is denied inwardly will seem to come to us from our outer fate. We may continue to curse fate and fail to recognize that after childhood, we are the ones making the choices, serving the old program. One patient, Gregory, having grown up in abject poverty and considerable neglect, continually undermined his gifts. When he lost most of his savings through repeated unwise investments, his reaction was "It was only money, and I was never to have any. That I know." His constricted, but carefully chosen circle of friends confirmed his self-image, even as his range of life choices kept him within the old, familiar diminishment. As a child, he had unavoidably read the limited affirmations of his family and their impoverished social conditions and identified with them. Deficits had once been brought to him by an indifferent fate, but his subsequent adult choices subtly reinforced his diminishment as a steady state of being, indeed the "story" of his life. An even more sinister example of this phenomenon will be found wherever one has been subjected to the denigration of bigotry. Either one will be filled with hatred toward others and the compulsion to overcompensate, or one will identify with the denigration and live a life of self-hatred and self-sabotage. The sad catalog of hurt brought to those who suffer discrimination includes not only the original hurt, but the frequent, unconscious collusion with this deficit definition of self. Again, the unconscious equation is: "I am as I am treated by others."

Just recently I received the following dream from a patient. Harold grew up decades ago in abject physical and emotional poverty in Arkansas. As a teenager he made his escape from desolation by joining the merchant marine. On board those many voyages around the world, he educated himself. Finally, he got off ship in Houston, began his own business, and gained some material affluence. Improbably, he later registered for a post-graduate business program at Harvard, was accepted, and graduated, even though he had never been to college. Still, for all his achievements, he remained haunted by the sense of deficit:

> I am at the Harvard Club for a meal. Strangely, everyone is unable to be fed because their tie is in a strange knot. I am able to touch my knot and it is released and everyone can eat now. I realize that the club is halfway up a mountain. I climb up the rest of the mountain, go over the top. I then run down the other side in joyous leaps and get to the bottom. I see a peasant with a cart, and the cart is empty.

In the dream, the Harvard Club embodies his sense of dispossession and the lifelong need to "arrive." He is there at the club, as he had in fact been in life, but cannot be fed until some knot is released. Yet the psyche is ready for release from this constraining history. He possesses the capacity to release the knot while realizing that he has been climbing this mountain for a long time. His psyche tells him that he is over that hump and he is then able to effortlessly gambol down the hillside. His association with the peasant was with his own agrarian origins, but now without "baggage" in the cart. All his life, Harold had identified with deficit and deprivation, and either succumbed to it, or was consumed by the need to compensate through acquisition. In his seventies, by learning to value his often painful journey, which brought him to many interesting ports of call, and learning to value himself as the traveler who had made that journey, he got over the hump of history. Then he could for the first time value his origins without that baggage. Again, who would ever dream this stuff up consciously? Yet something in us does dream, and brings an invitation to consciousness, to risk embodying a larger sense of self.

The second pattern we may elect in response to the insufficiency of our early environmental setting is to *overcompensate* and seek power, wealth, the right partner, fame, or some form of sovereignty over others. In this pattern, what one lacks within one will seek in the outer world. The power complex may be found in all of us. It may propel one to the heights, hurting others along the way, and may also lead one to reconstruct the very conditions that bring the restoration of the old deficit. Consider the life and times of Richard Nixon. From his childhood of deprivation in Whittier, California, to the most powerful office in the world, he was driven to ever higher acts of will to prevail. Yet, even after achieving a landslide victory, he drew other insecure worthies about him and together they set in motion the compensatory choices that brought about his forced resignation. It was no accident that his tearful farewell in the East Room of the White House focused on his abandoned mother and the hard times of long ago and far away. In another era, Nixon would have been the subject of a Sophocles. Gifted, driven, paranoid, he achieves the throne, and then obliges himself to return to the old worst place, the place of absence.

The power complex may be found in many if not most human exchanges. How many marriages are in service to the hidden agenda of the less psychologically evolved of the two? Another of the saddest, and most destructive, of these power stratagems is that employed by the narcissist. Narcissists works very hard to conceal their inner poverty from recognition by others. They may boast, inflate their reputations, swagger and belittle others, or they may fall apart at the first hint of neglect and criticism, making others feel guilty for the alleged injury done to them. All of these behaviors are designed to deflect us from the central truth, that their sense of self is predicated upon emptiness, and derives from early childhood neglect or insufficient mirroring. The will to power of narcissists is, however, a fearsome thing, and wreaks havoc in their psychological domination of their own children, usually abetted by a compliant spouse, or in workplaces where others are obliged to cooperate and comply. As Pearl Bailey reportedly said, "Thems whats thinks they is, ain't." But their lives are consumed by trying to fool you, and themselves, into thinking that they believe they really do matter. And given the impairment of their ego strength, any argument or disappointment with them will always prove to be your fault and not their responsibility.

I have seen so many adult children whose lives are tormented by the conflict between the pressure to marry the kind of person who would reinforce their parent's narcissism and the person whom they would choose on their own. It is too facile, even if accurate, to say that if one cannot make such an important choice for oneself then one is not ready for marriage. This truism ignores the fact that that person lived as a child in narcissistic energy field. The core message of that field was that their well-being depended, as indeed it did, on serving the impaired parent. Thus, to choose freely in the present often evokes a disabling anxiety in the adult child. (If even the Bible spells out that marriage was best seen as leaving mother and father, then this dilemma must always have been a problem.) Such adult children typically either run off and marry the person they love, and suffer the guilt and loss of their parent's approval, or accede to their parent's desire and live depressed and angry marriages. Some even fantasize waiting until the parent dies, so great is their inner anxiety. The damage wreaked by the narcissistic parent is awesome, and typically ripples into the grandchildren, who are the carriers of the unhappy tensions in their parent's lives.

The third, and most pervasive reactive pattern to the experience of deficit is embodied in *the anxious, obsessive need to seek the reassurance of others*. This pattern shows up in the repeated heartbreak of the lovelorn, who forever feel let down by their beloved, after they have escalated their hidden agenda for fulfillment and driven the other away. Paradoxically, such a person will frequently be drawn to someone who is relationally impaired as well, hence ensuring the comforting misery of the familiar. We tend to get what we unconsciously expect, and may even go to great lengths to bring it about. This is why greater consciousness is so critical to healing, and to new life choices.

Every therapist will attest to receiving many clients who complain about their relationships. They think all the good men are gone, or there are no woman without disturbed agendas. They meet and mate with someone and quickly begin to hector them and demand continuous reassurance from them. In time they grow weary of the other person, for the other can never fill the vast void within them. They are quick to find fault and they bitterly blame their partners for being so inadequately present. Even in normal marriages this sort of disappointment arises, for each of us has a lifelong need for fulfillment that no other person can ever meet. For the more mature, this insufficiency is perceived as the nature of life itself, and not the fault of their partner. For those whose history is especially charged with insufficiency, this intractable wound is larger than consciousness, and leads to a familiar, heartbreaking round of repeated disappointment, frustration, anger, disillusionment, and the desire to cast off in a new direction in hope of better results through the "magical other" over the next hill.

Susan is a much loved schoolteacher, bubbly, vivacious, always on with her students . . . and doing coke and serial sex each weekend. Her many talents are assembled to entertain others, while she anguishes within. The child of two narcissistic parents, she never felt seen or valued in and for herself. Initially idealizing her boyfriends, she comes soon to denigrate them—none of them is up to fulfilling the magnitude of her need. Her archaic deficit feels unfillable. Similarly, she cycles through therapists. "You understand me," she gushes, "unlike my previous therapist." But when she learns that there is no magic, that her hurt will follow her, and that she alone is charged with the responsibility of filling her own emptiness in more durable ways, she glides on to the next therapist. She changes boyfriends at a rate twice as fast as she changes therapists, but the dynamic is the same. The "other," upon whom she once depended as a child, now carries an inordinate weight of responsibility to take care of her. No relationship can withstand this urgent agenda. To watch Susan's tragic drama repeat itself over and over is painful to all who care for her. Fate dominates destiny; history dictates the future; what Freud called "the repetition compulsion" prevails. Sadly, Susan is unable to assimilate the insights she obtains in therapy, because of the desolation within, and therefore nothing changes.

In addition, one can see the psychodynamic birth of addictive behaviors in this deficit setup. As Susan demonstrates so boldly, most addictive hopes will be played out in relationships, because relationships can offer so much more and at an unconscious level more fully reactivate the original parental dynamics. But other venues will also receive this hunger for connection. Food, for example, is especially prone to receive the projections of perceived loss and gain. We have to eat every day, and one can scarcely argue that food does not nurture, yet the emotional baggage imposed upon food is something else indeed. The United States is the most obese country in the world, and that is not just because of the ready availability of food, or the want of exercise; this obesity intimates something far deeper: that psychological hunger does not abate in the midst of plenty. Susan is surrounded by those who might care for her, but she is starving. In her adolescence she was, predictably, bulimic. Other patterns—work, gaining power for reassurance, obsessive-compulsive repetitions, even personal rituals—compulsive prayer, news junkies, zoning out through television—to hold back the dark—are all addictive stratagies to fill the want within.

Almost everyone has some addictive pattern. Any reflexive response to stress and anxiety, whether conscious or not, is a form of addiction. The chief motive of any addiction is, of course, to help one not feel what in fact one has already been feeling. Breaking the tyranny of the addiction will require one to feel the pain that the addiction defends against. No wonder, then, that addictive patterns have such staying power as flimsy, faltering defenses against primal wounds.

• • •

REMEMBER THAT EACH OF THESE six patterns of response, to overwhelmment and insufficiency, may be found in each of us, though in widely varying degrees of prominence and autonomy in our lives, and each is frequently called upon in turn by differing external stimuli. Some may have been more prominent at a past stage of our life than now, but they lie just below the surface still.

Whenever we are fatigued, stressed, or whenever conscious control is lessened, these old patterns are especially prone to reactivation. (If the reader cannot see personal examples, with many variants, of each of these six adaptations to a powerful world, then he or she is hitting a blind spot, which will show up sometime soon in one's outer life.)

In addition to finding all six patterns in our habitual behavior at different stages of our emotional history, it is likely that one or more of these stratagems is presently dominating how we do business in our daily life. We may, for example, be one of those nice people, always cooperative and compliant, and we will be "rewarded" for this strategy by being asked to serve on still another committee. But what will the psyche say to the repeated violation of being asked to do this sort of thing over and over and over again, a violation in which we are wholly complicit? Or perhaps much of one's life is caught up in a drive for power or recognition from others, but having attained what one seeks, one still feels empty and lacking enduring value. Or which of us has spent life hiding out, hoping not to be summoned forth to largeness and living meanwhile in a safe but small world, in which the soul knows it has been shortchanged?

It is not our intention here to judge these stratagems we develop, even though we are responsible for their consequences to ourselves and others, especially in the second half of life. For all of us suffer from the unavoidable "fallacy of overgeneralization." What was once experienced in powerful ways is internalized, provisionally interpreted, and institutionalized within, and the dynamics of that fated early environment are re-created over and over. How else can we explain our patterns, our self-defeating behaviors, our sense of the same-old, same-old without these unconscious programs, these archaic overgeneralizations at work? Seldom are we wholly present to this moment, this ever-new reality, without the interference of the past. Whoever denies this invasive power of history is living unconsciously, sleeping still in "memory's unmade bed." Who acknowledges it is humbled, and opens the door to the genuine possibility of change.

After all, these adaptive stratagems experimentally evolved to help us survive, and without them we might not have gotten out of childhood. But can we readily give our lives over to these conditioned reflexes now that we know they are there? Can we abdicate adulthood because we have that archaic childhood vision of self and world to care for and defend? Go ahead, defend that child as one should, but do not give it the power of choice in your adult life. Remember that the place of origin for all these patterns is (1) in the traumatic past, (2) from the disempowered world of the child, and (3) confined within the limited range of choices and values of that world. Understandably, the internalization of these values, roles, and scenarios as the reflexive way to live a predictable, safe life once made sense, but today they condemn one to an iron wheel of repetition. Do not judge this history, for it was as it had to be, but do not abdicate the possibility of the present either. Learn the reflexive patterns, see where they show up, what activates them, what damage is done to self or others, and learn anew that the adult can manage so much more than the child. The tyranny of the past is never greater than when we do not recall. Faulkner once opined that the past is not dead; it is not even past. Forgetting the presence of the past, we may live still in Shakespeare's unconscious prisons.

When we ask the question "How did we come to be who we think we are?" a significant part of the answer is found in the conscious, learned influences of our family and the environment we were born into, but much more of our lives will be deeply governed by the powerful patterns we adopted in order to survive in the larger world. These instruments of adaptation allowed survival, for which we are grateful, but their autonomy in our lives binds us to a disempowered past and the cycle of repetition. We are summoned to leave them behind and endure the anxiety that always accompanies transcending the predictable securities of the past.

No freedom is possible, no authentic choice, where consciousness is lacking. Paradoxically, consciousness usually only comes from the experience of suffering and the flight from suffering is why we often elect to remain in the constrictive yet familiar old shoes. But the psyche is never silent, and suffering is the first clue that something is soliciting our attention and seeking healing.

Chapter Three

The Collision of Selves

"He has a terrible fear of dying because he has not yet lived. . . .
What is essential in life is only to forgo complacency, to move into
the house instead of admiring it and hanging garlands around it. . . .
But why do such nights leave one always with the refrain: I could
live and I do not live?"

Franz Kafka, *Letters to Friends, Family and Editors*

DESPITE WHAT WE SAY TO OURSELVES about
wanting to know who we really are, there is a very
strong chance that we will steer clear of decisive meetings with ourselves for as long as possible. It is far easier to walk in
shoes too small for us than to step into the largeness that the soul
expects and demands. Can we really bear to know who we are, with
all those contradictions, all those other energies and agendas that do
not conform to our ego ideal of ourselves? No one I ever met began
a serious, sustained therapeutic conversation simply in order to have
a good chat with a stranger. They made the first call because the
strategies that had worked, or that they'd fantasized worked,
theretofore had clearly played out. Most of us are brought into

therapy on our knees, or at best in a state of disorientation. The old map, the presumptive guidelines, the clear points of reference are not, for whatever reason, working anymore. An exception to this generalization comes to mind. One young man, in his late twenties, decided early on to come to therapy in order that he might "know himself" more fully. In his initial dream he found himself allied with a nefarious, manipulative con man. Together they were conceiving and executing schemes to bilk others. While he consciously repudiated these values, I reminded him that his own dreammaker had brought this shadow partnership to his attention. Abruptly, he canceled all future sessions. His youthful ego had claimed to wish to "know" itself, in order that he might gain even greater control of others. While we all have such shadow dimensions to our personality, how many of us are really willing to bring them to consciousness and accept responsibility for them in our relations with others? Yet why would we expect anything to improve in our lives if we do not?

A formal, committed therapeutic relationship provides a deeper, more objective, more informed conversation with oneself, through the engagement of another person who has our interests at heart. Many, however, fear the accountability that therapy asks, and seek their own path, or avoid getting on the path of self-discernment, and the damage to themselves or those around them continues. Either way, the invitation to meet oneself is seldom if ever solicited; it is rather brought on by outer or inner events that force one to question who one is, and in service to what values. A death in the family, the loss of a relationship, a termination at work, a serious illness, or an encounter with the 3 A.M. terrors, the so-called hour of the wolf—all or any may bring us to meet the stranger in the mirror for the first time.

What we initially see in the mirror is what we wish to see, the persona, not the instinctually grounded self. What we are seeing is sometimes called the "provisional personality," the acquired behaviors, attitudes, and reflexive strategies through which we learned to manage the world the best we could. The provisional personality, an interwoven fabric of adaptations, may be far removed from the inherent Self, but, "for good or ill, it brought us this far," so we are afraid to let go of it now. However, life has a way of calling this provisional personality into question. For most of us, this fated encounter is a shocking and confusing appointment. One woman in her early sixties, whose husband was delayed by heavy traffic and torrential rains, experienced the first panic attack of her life, thought of selling the house, moving somewhere else of unknown location, and encountered her secret fears of abandonment in that two-hour period. She began to explore her dependencies and her secret terrors more honestly. A man, still on the career track, still invested in the notion that burdens most men, that their worth is a function of their performance, realized that he had topped out in his corporation, that there was no more "up" up there, and spiraled down into depression. Both had had an unexpected meeting with themselves, and found that their otherwise well-functioning lives were actually quite fragile, that their provisional personalities were gossamer floors over an abyss of doubt and dread. Still another man, struggling throughout his life to overcome the shame he felt he had inherited from his father's misdeeds, was driven to adopt an impossibly high moral and professional code. He never thought of it as a compensation for someone else's life, or a reactive burden that he had heroically carried, until he began to ask why his sons had grown alienated from him. Having sought to redeem his own life from the apparent "received shame," he rolled over the same impossible set of expectations onto his children and drove them away. All of these good souls were living as strangers to themselves, colluding with the power of early wounding and remaining captive to adaptive strategies.

Whoever has not discovered this truth about the fragility of our journey, and the pervasive power of our necessary adaptations to this vulnerability, is living in a form of self-delusion that psyche, fate, or the consequences of our acts will sooner or later bring to the surface. What we do then will make all the difference in the rewriting of history. None of us is pleased to encounter the false self, the necessary fictions in which we invest, until even we can no longer believe them. Naturally, we will avoid these unpleasant truths as long as possible, and will enter a deepened dialogue with ourselves only when exhaustion or failure or disorientation is no longer deniable. But our long-delayed appointments with the soul are meant to be taken seriously, and treasured, for the level of consciousness we bring to such moments will make all the difference for the rest of our lives—for ourselves and for our loved ones.

As we noted in the last chapter, we inevitably take provisional readings of whatever world fate first brings to us. Inevitably, we misread the world, overpersonalize it, and fall into the fallacy of overgeneralization. This "misreading" is of course based on the child's or youth's limited range of experience, constricted imaginative alternatives, and limited capacity for experimentation outside the range of the family or tribal sphere. This is how a child may be scarred by poverty, drug abuse, social discrimination, and so on— all forces that have nothing to do with the inherent potential of that soul, and have everything to do with fate, social inequities, and the thin membrane that separates our soul from the world around us. Even though we might later come to recognize that these influences had nothing to do with us, nothing to do with the infinite, precious soul that lies within us, the damage is done and we are invested in the mythologically charged value system called the provisional personality with all of its misreadings of self and world.

And all of us suffer from such fallacies of overgeneralization.

Certain core experiences quickly become precepts, attitudes, readings of self and world, and through repetition and reinforcement are, over time, "institutionalized" within and begin to govern how we reflexively function in the world. The key word there is *reflexive*. Perhaps 95 percent of our daily functioning is reflexive. External stimuli, or internal promptings, activate those old "readings" of the world and we respond in familiar ways. How else do patterns occur? None of us rises saying, "Today? Why, today I think I will repeat the same dumb things I did in the past." But that is precisely what we do because so much is on automatic pilot, giving credence to the old saw that we are our own worst enemies.

Again, the wisdom of Greek tragedy cannot be overemphasized. All of them dramatize this universal confession: "I created my life; I made these choices; and, stunningly, this flood of unimagined consequences are the fruits of my choices." From such humbling recognition comes wisdom at last. Mary, the mother in Eugene O'Neill's autobiographical play *Long Day's Journey into Night*, puts it this way:

> *None of us can help the things life has done to us. They're done before you realize it. And once they're done, they make you do other things until at last everything comes between you and what you'd like to be, and you've lost your true self forever.* *

Mary is voicing the regret of many who come to face the world they have unwittingly created through the power of these unconscious forces at work. Sadly, it is sometimes only at the end of life that these fruits of unconscious choice come home to us. One of the most telling examples is found in Tolstoy's nineteenth-century

---

*O'Neill, *Long Day's Journey into Night, Complete Plays*, p. 212.

novella "The Death of Ivan Ilych," whose name might loosely be equivalent to the English John Johnson, or Everyman. Ivan lives strictly by the codes of his day; he has learned to adapt to the world's values rather than find his own. He expects thereby that life will continue to flow evenly and pleasantly. Then he is stricken with a terminal disease. He goes through the familiar sequence of denial, anger, bargaining, depression, and finally acceptance, but not without being obliged to question the meaning of his whole life. Only in those last days, in the midst of humbling suffering and regret, does he come to live his life as a conscious, self-examining being. Though he is dying, such a turn to living with large questions, large perplexities, is what saves him by bringing him a more meaningful encounter with the mystery of his life. It would seem that creating our life is nearly impossible without coming to some kind of consciousness about these matters. Yet few if any of us really come willingly to that which is humbling. We are usually dragged there, along with our brother Ivan.

A mystery so profound that none of us really seems to grasp it until it has indisputably grasped us, is that some force transcendent to ordinary consciousness is at work within us to bring about our ego's overthrow. No, it is not some malevolent demon, though we often project our search for such a slippery spirit on our partner or our employer or even on our children. That force, paradoxically, is the *Self,* the architect of wholeness, which operates from a perspective larger than conventional consciousness. How could the ego ever come to understand, let alone accept, that its overthrow is engineered from within, by that transpersonal wisdom that has our being's interests at heart even in our darkest moments? This idea of beneficent overthrow is preposterous to the ego, for overthrow embodies the greatest threat to it, through the loss of sovereignty and the summons to live an agenda much larger and more demanding than the agenda of childhood adaptation and survival. No wonder the biblical admonition "Unless ye die, ye shall not live" strikes terror in every conscious being, yet offers a larger path.

These two force fields of conscious life, with its attendant repetitive stratagems, and the natural inclinations of the Self, with its goal of wholeness, compete with each other within each of us. The ego wishes comfort, security, satiety; the soul demands meaning, struggle, becoming. The contention of these two voices sometimes tears us apart. Ordinary ego consciousness is crucified by these polarities. Again, the paradox emerges that in our suffering, in our symptoms, are profound clues as to the meaning of the struggle, yet the path of healing is very difficult for the apprehensive ego to accept, for the ego will be asked to be open to something larger than itself.

Accordingly, stronger souls seek therapy; the more damaged seek someone to blame. Allen, a man with a marital gun at his head, snickered at a box of tissues in my office, so threatened was he by the possibility of his own unshed tears. His prognosis was not good, obviously, because he was so separated from his emotional life. The truth is, I could sympathize greatly with a person who felt so deeply that he had to scorn feeling, but sooner or later we have to be willing to face our lives. He had come to complain about his wife, not look at himself. As a result, he shortly terminated therapy and aborted his chance to have a real conversation with himself. If we shun this conversation, we will likely not be able to have a conversation in any depth with anyone else.

Another woman, in her forties, whose husband died suddenly, asked me the question, who would take care of her now. I said to her, gently, that *she* would take care of her, that unwanted as this traumatic loss was, she was at the beginning of her real journey. She got up and walked out. I presume she looked long enough to find someone to take care of her. Another woman, grieving the loss of her marriage, asked the same question. I replied that it was her marriage she'd lost, not her life. She got it, began work on herself, and thereafter entered the most soul-satisfying time of her life. These are not made-up examples; these are real people who were hurting, who naturally wished protection, perhaps the arrival of the good parent surrogate, or some magic, but who had to face the truth that the real work required was a deepened conversation with their journeys. Some will accept the conversation, and some will not, and some will come back years later when they are strong enough to ask large questions and dare to live larger lives.

Depression's Therapeutic Gift

What are the symptoms that help us identify that we are undergoing this kind of summons? Arguably the most common, and perhaps most telling, symptom is depression. There are many kinds of depression. There is *biologically based depression,* which typically slides in and out of family histories. Almost all studies indicate that this kind of depression may best be treated with antidepressant medication, especially when combined with some form of short-term therapy. And there is *reactive depression,* which is appropriate to a significant loss in our lives and tends to vary in intensity in proportion to the amount of energy we invested in who or what was lost. The child going off to college, the end of a relationship, downsizing at work or retirement—all can occasion a reactive depression, as the psychic energy that was once invested externally loses its object or container and reverts to the personal psyche. Only when this sort of depression lasts for too long a time (more than a few weeks or months) or substantially interferes with the person's capacity to function in daily life does it become pathological. Grieving is an honest affirmation of the value of the original investment of energy. No grief, no true investment occurred.

But even with reactive depression in grief there is always a task that awaits us, namely the invitation, indeed the necessity, to examine where we may have been overinvested in the lost other, where it was carrying too much for us. When that energy returns to us, it is ours to carry, and ours to invest in ways that serve the developmental agenda our souls always wish from us. When our relationship leaves us, we may grieve its loss, and yet we are responsible for whatever aspects of our personality that relationship was asked to carry. For example, when our child leaves—the famous empty nest syndrome—we need to say: "Job well done." Children are supposed to leave; if they didn't, it would mean you had failed to empower them, ask enough of them to develop the wherewithal to conduct their lives without you. We may miss them, but if we cling to them we are not loving them; we are revealing our own dependencies. To love them is to empower them to live without us, as surely they will be obliged to in any case.

To grieve the loss of an intimate relationship is to celebrate what was received as a gift, but it may also raise the question of what we were asking of the other person that we need to do for ourselves. If we were, like Jack Spratt and his spouse, expecting the other person to carry a part of reality that we find onerous or difficult, then whose job is that, really? Even though together a couple may have licked the platter clean, each partner will be in a difficult place if they do not learn to cover the broader range of life's tasks themselves. Even amid the grieving, a reactive depression is always going to bring home to us an agenda for growing up. It takes a great deal of psychological honesty to be able to look directly at our sorrow and take responsibility for what personal task has now emerged.

But the sort of depression we most commonly think of when we use the word *depression* is not that generated by our biochemistry, or the reactive withdrawal of energy in the face of outer loss, it is a phenomenon of intrapsychic dynamics that has huge therapeutic significance. (Actually, this garden variety of depression is today called *dysthymic disorder* in the psychiatric manuals, namely, an absence of or disturbance of strong affect for the conduct of one's life.) This form of depression is a manifestation of the autonomy of the psyche. The ego, the conscious sense of who we are, wishes to invest energy in a certain direction, perhaps in service to economic goals, but the soul has another agenda. It autonomously withdraws the invested energy, inverts it, and as it withdraws into the psyche it often pulls the ego in after it. We have each experienced this kind of depression from time to time, for there is a certain ebb and flow of energy that is common to us all. Indeed, a close cousin to this form of depression is boredom, or ennui, which means that the object or the goal that has carried our projections of psychological energy thus far no longer sustains the agenda of the soul. Even what may have been a good choice at one point has now been served, the task exhausted, and the psyche demands renewal, or greater balance, through investment in other values.

Invariably these experiences of loss will feel like defeats for the sovereignty of the ego. Wise is the ego, strong is the ego, that can stop reinforcing the old investments and ask, "What is going on here, why does the psyche not cooperate; what might its desire be?" Many people in therapy have learned that the way out of a depression is *through* it, asking not what I, the ego consciousness, want, but what the soul wants. Only the reorienting of conscious energies in service to other values will lift the depression.

In the course of our developing lives, we are all in service to certain norms, certain expectations—ours, those of our family, and those of our culture—and moreover, we are obliged to choose every day, this but not that, and can never realistically meet the full range of the soul's desires. For these reasons, our choices are necessarily biased by our own security needs, insufficient permission to live our own life, constricted imaginative alternatives, and the limited options actually available at any given moment in our history. This biasing, this partiality, this limitation is frequently, and unintentionally, wounding to the soul. I think of a woman who, the child of two psychiatrists, grew up to be a psychiatrist in order to win their approval, neglecting the fact that her soul had another plan. Her true talent and calling was found in the arts, and while she was a caring and competent psychiatrist, her midlife depression deepened with each passing year. One might say that with each year her soul was further exiled from her constructed world, her depression grew as a sign of the psyche's protest. She was living in constrictive service to parental complexes, as we mostly do, and not in service to the larger summons of her talent. Why would she not be depressed? She was very good at dispensing medication to others who suffered biochemical depressions, but was so close to her own problem that she could not recognize intrapsychic depression when she saw it.

Sometimes these depressions take us over and leave us prostrate. At the bottom of this well, and there is always a bottom, there is a clear task and a summons. The task is to ask what the psyche wants, not what the parents want, not what the parent complexes want, not what the culture wants, not what the ego wants. The summons is to respond from the depth of one's being and risk giving the soul what it always wants—a larger journey.

Most of us did not receive permission to take our journeys so seriously. Seldom if ever can we go back and obtain that permission.

We have to seize it today from the depths of despair and doubt. When we do, the depression lifts. All of us, even while functioning at a high level, will carry pockets of depression, for parts of our psychological nature will have been thwarted, remain unfed, unacknowledged, unloved. All of those pockets will, of course, be part of our ongoing agenda, for they will come to the surface in different ways at different times, as various dimensions of outer or inner reality activate them. Each encounter offers the possibility of healing and growth, as we make conscious what has been left behind, repressed, or given no investment of energy.

Even when we bring these pockets of depression to consciousness, so often the way forward is fraught with anxiety as it takes us into new territory, asks more of us than ever before, and causes us to grow up by demanding full responsibility for how our lives turn out. But, as we noted earlier, this anxiety must be chosen over depression, for it is developmental, and depression is regressive. Anxiety is the price of the ticket to life; intrapsychic depression is the by-product of our refusal to climb aboard.

We can see hereby the huge therapeutic potential lying within depression. So often we experience depression as a dark herald with a grim countenance that tells us something in us is dying, has reached its end, is played out, and yet it really is announcing something new, something larger, something developmental that wishes greater play in our life. Clearly, a person, often with the help of a therapist, needs to differentiate the forms of depression; namely, does it come from a biological base, a reaction to loss, or an intrapsychic conflict that, becoming conscious, has great information for us about the next stage of our journey? Under every depression there is a still lower level waiting for us; it is the place in which we find the agenda of growth hiding. Rather than deny the pain, over-medicate, and flee the challenge of growth which it asks further of us, we need to discover where our soul wants to go, long after the ego has exhausted its resources.

Relationship As Field of Fire

Similarly, the field of intimate relationship almost always suffers disturbance when the psyche grows agitated. Intimate relationship is prized so highly by so many, and everywhere is broken and in disarray. Relationships have a tendency to disappoint because so much— too much—is asked of them. We seldom appreciate how much freight is imposed on us by our partner, or by us upon them. In the many agendas of our histories, the deep desire to heal old wounds, to repeat them, or to find the good parent in the other person rises to the top. Naturally, no one consciously sets out to find the parent in the partner, but the dynamics of those first, primal relationships are always present as we engage each other. Freud noted that when a couple goes to bed six people are present, for psychologically the couple brings along their parents as well. One might just as accurately consider fourteen present, for the parents' internalization of *their* parents, which came through to the couple in psychological transmission, are present as well. It gets rather crowded in such a small space, and quickly complicated. While more on the dynamics of interpersonal relationship will be discussed later, the field of outer relationship is always troubled when we are troubled within. Even if we can hold it together at work, who can do that the other hours of the day, every day? Intimate relationship offers the possibility of so much, and is therefore especially vulnerable to whatever is working unconsciously through us. What is not faced inwardly will play out in our external world; whatever burdens within will, sooner or later, burden without.

For relationships to survive this freight one needs luck, grace, patience, and an enormous devotion to personal growth. The conflict and suffering that rises in relationship at midlife is an invitation to examine what agendas, dependencies, expectations, and sabotaging complexes are at work. Rather than accept this very onerous responsibility, it is much easier to blame our partners, or try to reform them, or leave them.

Projections Eroded, Projections Renewed?

Similarly, we find in other symptomatic patterns—the onset of an affair, the nervous switching of external interests, the use of substances or overwork to anesthetize feelings, depression, turbulence in the relationship—that there is one common denominator: the erosion, if not the collapse, of projections. A projection rises from a neglected but dynamic value within us; usually it is essentially unconscious, but has a certain energy, which, when we have not attended it consciously, escapes repression and enters the world as a hope, a project, an agenda, a fantasy, or a renewal of expectation. No one rises in the morning and says, "I will make a projection today," but we all do. What is unconscious, charged with meaning, has a certain dynamic autonomy, and is denied inwardly will appear in some guise in our external environment. Thus, we project our vision, or our parent's vision, or our culture's vision of the good life onto our jobs, our partners, our children, homes, and possessions, without knowing how much we are asking of them. We are counting on them to make us happy, bring us success, fulfillment, meaning, and perhaps even allow us to remain naive children a bit longer. Nothing external can carry such a burden of expectation for very long. The job for which we prepared and sacrificed proves demanding, repetitive, boring; our partner is cranky, controlling, fractious, limited, and mortal; our child is intent on becoming him- or herself rather than making us feel better about ourselves by replicating and endorsing our values.

Our projections rise from issues, values, tasks we have not yet made conscious, so they spontaneously arise from the unconscious and enter the world in seductive ways. Thus, we jump from job to job, believing a promotion, a new title, a fresh start will do it; or the companion at the gym is suddenly surrounded by a celestial aura and magically promises the fulfillment of an archaic agenda while one's actual partner proves flawed, limited, demanding; or the child within us, confused with this outer child we have borne, this *other* who has come into but is merely passing through our life, forces upon him or her the additional burden of being asked to carry our unlived lives, achieving what we could not, and continuing our narcissistic agenda for us.

Projections always pass through five identifiable stages. At the onset they feel magical; they literally alter our sense of reality and have a compelling power over us. This compelling power is understandable only later, if at all, as the power that some vital energy or value within our own unconscious has for us. So we are always, always, projecting some vital, meaningful aspect of ourselves upon the other, whether the "other" be career, partner, or child. In other words, we are seeing some unknown part of ourselves in the exterior world—no wonder it has such compelling power. (I have had people read my books and write me and say they want to become Jungian analysts, even though they have never undertaken a single hour of personal analysis, let alone sustained several years. This desire is understandable, for they are wanting a deeper relationship with the soul, but it is projected onto a particular job that has its virtues and its costs as does any other, and a very onerous training process. There are many other ways in which one can undertake a deepened dialogue with the soul, and with greater fidelity to the particulars of the individual psyche.)

After the luminescent power of a projection does its work upon us, the second stage begets disillusionment. The other does not carry through as expected. The other is not behaving or producing as we prefer. Then, thirdly, we begin to do whatever we can to reinforce the projection, to recover its pristine attraction. We redouble efforts at the job, seek further advancement. We start cajoling, hectoring, nagging, controlling, or withdrawing from our partner or child to bring them back into line with our projected expectations. Since this stratagem is doomed to defeat because the other is never the same as the content and agenda of our projection, this stage invariably leads to further conflict, confusion, alienation, and often wounding behaviors.

The fourth stage is to suffer the withdrawal of the projection. This stage almost never occurs voluntarily because we did not recognize that we were projecting in the first place. We withdraw the projection because we are forced to do so; the reality of the other simply will not conform sufficiently to our fantasy agenda. The discrepancy has become painfully evident, no longer deniable. The other is finally, and always, *an*other, and not our intrapsychic content. (Often, this recognition occurs after the affair, after the job change, after the plastic surgery, or other precipitous choice.)

The fifth stage of a projection, if we reach that point at all, is to become conscious that a projection has occurred. This sounds easier than it usually proves to be. Usually, we will just renew the projections, for these agendas run deep and have a lot of energy attached to them. The erosion of a projection follows this predictable trajectory of discrepancy between the intent of the projection and the reality of the other, confusion or dissonance, disappointment or anger, renewed effort, and the experience of failure. In such moments we are invited always to become more conscious. If I grow depressed after having achieved, or failed to achieve, my goals, what has the ego projected upon the world around me? Where does the soul wish me to go? If my partner disappoints me, can I look at my disappointment with myself and attend realistically to my own repair? Can I free my children from carrying the burden of my unlived life, as I wished to be freed by my parents?

Every failed projection is a quantum of energy, our energy, an agenda for growth or healing, and a task that has come back to us. Can we bear to take the step to own the projection, see that its agenda may not be realistic, may be infantile, may not have legitimacy when flushed out of hiding, and then redirect our lives more fully, more responsibly?

Talk is cheap. We seldom know ourselves well enough, are seldom strong enough, or conscious enough, to attend this task on a permanent basis. There are many places in the psyche of each of us that seek aggrandizement, healing, reinforcement, or even satisfaction of what Freud called "the repetition compulsion," the magnetic summons of an old wound in our lives that has so much energy, such a familiar script, and such a predictable outcome attached to it that we feel obliged to relive it or pass it on to our children. Thus we look for jobs that confirm our doubts about ourselves, partners who collude with our self-denigration, and so on—all in the face of reason and common sense—so great is the power of this split-off energy. Yet every projection is something important, something powerful *in us* that has come back to us. What will we do with it? Addressing the content and the issue raised by an eroded projection will initially feel defeating, but it is the chief way to become responsible for our issues and for addressing the possibility of a genuine change of course in life.

Being accountable for the content and issues embodied in our eroded projections is probably the chief service we can bring to our jobs, our partners, our children. As we lift the burden of our unconscious traffic off the other, we free them to be whatever or whomever they are meant to be when we are not interfering with them. This principle of cleaning up our own backyard can as much apply to the conflicts between faiths, between nations, between social systems as it does to those between individuals. And just how many leaders of nations, ethnic groups, religious bodies are wise enough, brave enough, to take on the question of projection, summon followers to personal accounting, and free the unknown but feared other from entanglement in their unconscious dynamics? How many wars are generated by the power of what we will not face in ourselves? And who among us is strong enough, or ethical enough, to say that we are our own problem?

Job's Abrogated Contract

Twenty-six centuries ago, an unknown Hebrew poet took a story quite familiar in the ancient Near East and worked it into his own version, a version which challenged the orthodox understanding of his people. His struggle produced the archetypal drama we have come to know as the story of Job. Job is a good person, who, having done no harm to others, has a ton of grief fall upon his head. Naturally, he asks why, and how justice, as he perceives it, and the restoration of the old comforts, as he desires them, might be reclaimed. He is visited by so-called comforters who represent the orthodox tradition, which maintains that humans have a contract or covenant with God. If humans behave properly, God will bless them, they assert; since Job has been so severely visited by hardship, if there is a contract with the Divine, then it is only logical to conclude that Job has sorely erred, sorely sinned. When Job contests these accusations and proclaims his innocence, the comforters accuse him of either ignorance or dishonesty. Job even summons

God to be his chief witness that he has not done wrong, and therefore does not "deserve" such hardships. When God does appear to him, as a voice out of a metaphoric whirlwind, He tells Job that He does not have to answer to Job's idea of the agreement between them. It seems that the God of the universe will be bound by no contract, at least not one struck by humans. Job experiences a revelation, a transformation of perspective, and declares that his widely proclaimed piety was based on a hubristic assumption that his compliant behavior compelled God to treat him well. Job realizes that there is no deal, that such a deal is a presumption of the ego in service to its now familiar agenda, which promotes its own security, satiety, and continuity.

Job moves from being a good little boy in the face of a stern but predictable deity, to a man who has been shaken to his core. He experiences a radical revisioning of self in the world, a crisis of assumptions that awaits all of us, in so many different venues. Each of us, from childhood on, engages in magical thinking similar to Job's, believing we can strike deals with the world and with the divinities. These "deals" are part of how we attempt to protect our vulnerable selves in an omnipotent and often inscrutable universe. (As a youth I believed that right conduct, right intention, and a lot of learning would bring control into one's life. But the psyche had other plans. Being so humbled by the psyche was the beginning of discerning the difference between knowledge and wisdom.) But such deals with the universe are our fantasy alone, and have little to no bearing on reality. Just as we try to live in smaller fictions in order to feel more secure, so our "deals" unwittingly diminish the world and those around us by seeking to contain and control their autonomy.

There are many modern versions of this presumptive contract we have with the universe. For some, the presumption begins in a compliant interaction with parents, and later their surrogates in social institutions, who have explicitly imposed a code that promises reward when one behaves according to the rules. (Thus, we expect that the company for which we labor so diligently will not let us go when downsizing.) For others, it appears in the assumption that if one acts with goodwill, always, one will be met by goodwill, always. For others, the presumption takes form in the expectation that right practices, right spirituality, right diet, right analysis will spare one from cancer. Yet, sooner or later, life brings each of us not only disappointment, but something worse, a deep disillusionment regarding the "contract" that we tacitly presumed and served to the best of our ability. Who does not occasionally feel betrayed by the universe, though it is hard to identify a source of the "betrayal"? Who has not felt disoriented, when the plan which they presumed was in place, the map of reality, the directions on how to live, the expectations of productive outcomes—all seemed abrogated? As deep as the suffering may prove in our outer world, this other, spiritual suffering, this loss of one's fundamental understanding of the world and how it works shakes the foundations of beliefs even more.

Periodically, all of us lose our understanding of the world, our means of coping, our plan for prevailing. Each of these nodules of negation will be experienced as a crisis; it is a crisis of a belief system. Such a crisis is an existential wounding and a spiritual wounding as well. Not only do we suffer in the outer world, but we suffer in our very personal sense of meaning, and in our sense of relatedness to the mysteries of this world. The friendship we counted on, the protection we assumed would be there perpetually, the comfort that someone would pick us up and make it all right when we fell— in a hundred, thousand permutations, all these presumptions are brought to earth. Robert Frost expressed our collective dismay at this turn of events in his sardonic couplet:

Forgive, O Lord, my little joke on thee,
And I'll forgive thy great big one on me.

This betrayal by the other—by God, by our lover, by our friend, by the corporation—is a betrayal of our hope that the world might be manageable and predictable. As we grow older, we find repeated affronts to our sense of self, our capacity to control outcomes, and our presumptions of omnipotence. As the child once fantasized that its wishes governed the world, and the youth fantasized that heroism could manage to do it all, so the person in the second half of life is obliged to come to a more sober wisdom based on a humbled sense of personal limitations and the inscrutability of the world. How easy it is, then, for some to give up risking their lives in anything meaningful, or how easy it is to slip into cynicism and criticism of hope, or to numb out to avoid the pain of losing one more delusion.

Once again, out of the experience of suffering, an invitation is found. As our brother Job learned, our presumptive contracts are delusory efforts by the ego to be in control. We learn that life is much riskier, more powerful, more mysterious than we had ever thought possible. While we are rendered more uncomfortable by this discovery, it is a humbling that deepens spiritual possibility. The world is more magical, less predictable, more autonomous, less controllable, more varied, less simple, more infinite, less knowable, more wonderfully troubling than we could have imagined being able to tolerate when we were young.

Competing Agendas

On his fabled journey home across the wine-dark sea, Odysseus had many obstacles to surmount. One was the Symplegades, the clashing rocks that threatened to crush his fragile ship. We, too, are frequently caught between competing forces, opposing values, which we fear will sink our fragile souls. Even the elemental stages of life present us with competing agendas. We can see that the agenda of the first half of life is predominantly a social agenda framed as "How can I enter this world, separate from my parents, create relationships, career, social identity?" Or put another way: "What does the world ask of me, and what resources can I muster to meet its demands?" But in the second half of life, the worm turns, the agenda shifts to reframing our personal experience in the larger order of things, and the questions change. "What does the soul ask of me?" "What does it mean that I am here?" "Who am I apart from my roles, apart from my history?" These questions necessarily raise a different agenda, and oblige us to ask questions of meaning. If the agenda of the first half of life is *social,* meeting the demands and expectations our milieu asks of us, then the questions of the second half of life are *spiritual,* addressing the larger issue of meaning.

The psychology of the first half of life is driven by *the fantasy of acquisition:* gaining ego strength to deal with separation, separating from the overt domination of parents, acquiring a standing in the world, whether it be through property, relationship, or social function. But then the second half of life asks of us, and ultimately demands, *relinquishment*—relinquishment of identification with property, roles, status, provisional identities—and the embrace of other, inwardly confirmed values.

About Schmidt, the film starring Jack Nicholson, traces the plight of an Everyman who hits a wall when all the roles and people that supported his sense of self are removed. He is forcibly retired by his company, his wife dies, his daughter moves away, marries, and begins her separate life, and he is left utterly empty. He thrashes about like a zombie. At the end of the movie, he realizes that his only spiritual or relational connection is a very tenuous link to an orphan he supports in Africa. This connection is very fragile, but it implies that he has to find new ways in which his soul may be expressed, or he will drown in depression and succumb earlier to death. To the film's credit, the creators do not provide a typical Hollywood ending; rather, they make clear that his former life has ended, and the task of forming a new one is just beginning. Was Schmidt ever really here, apart from the supportive structures he spent decades constructing? Did they not help him avoid the radical, necessary questions? Will he ever really be here, and find what he is now to do and be in this world? Those are the themes for another film than this one. What we delay addressing will, sooner or later, bite us in the rear, as *About Schmidt* so well portrays.

Beneath the symptoms, the variety of our stories, such a turn is occurring for all of us in the second half of life. The old sense of self wears thin, and the new is yet uncovered. Such moments of crisis are typically very painful, but they constitute an invitation to the ego to reorient its priorities, an invitation that the ego will resist until it is forced to do otherwise.

These continual "defeats" of the ego may finally, perhaps, bring it to the point where it begins to ask other kinds of questions. When the ego gets conscious enough and strong enough, or battered enough, it will be begin to say: "What new thing do I have to learn about myself in the world?" "Since I can no longer manage all this perplexity by my former understanding, what does the soul ask me to do in the face of this overthrow?" While the ego seldom frames these questions in quite this conscious way, it is usually led, through suffering, frustration, and defeat to demanding questions. If we stop running and turn to these questions, renewal, not defeat, emerges and we grow larger, often against our will. After all, who or what is asking these questions? If they are not asked

by the ego, or presented by our culture, they must be asked by
the soul.

These "collisions" we experience periodically are in fact collisions between the natural, instinctual self and the provisional personality, with its attendant attitudes and adaptive strategies. As we
have identified ourselves with the latter, the meeting with the former will be unwanted at best, and usually feel defeating and de-
meaning. Such collisions occur not only at midlife but repeatedly,
throughout the course of our lives. If we can bear to acknowledge
this, such collisions indicate that *the soul is in charge,* doing its
work, whether we like it or not, and is always urging us toward a
larger life. What made sense of the world before frequently no
longer applies, or is found inadequate to contain the new level of
opposites. Yet from this dialogue between different identities, enlargement invariably arises. We may not want to grow, really, but
we are really forced to grow, or we will regress and die, because the
soul, the eternal dimension of our quite mortal lives, demands
growth.

When the ego prevails, change is forestalled, and spiritual stagnation, even regression, sooner or later occurs. Even though we consciously resist change and cling to the familiar, when the soul is at
work, we will change, quite apart from our conscious desires. As
twelve-step groups say, "What we resist, will persist," and sometime
later impose itself on us, or on those around us. Something else,
some larger energy, is at work in the universe, about which we
know very little at all, and it has very little interest in our cautious
plans, or our conscious understandings, as Job found out.

Chapter Four

Barriers to Transformation

"We would rather be ruined than changed.
We would rather die in our dread
Than climb the cross of the present
And let our illusions die."

W. H. Auden, *The Age of Anxiety*

IF OUR PSYCHE is programmed for growth, why is it so difficult to live these lives with their developmental agendas? Why do we stumble all over ourselves, repeat ourselves, recreate the pattern of parents whom we thought we'd fled? Why do we ignore the wishes of the transcendent that courses through each of us?

For starters, we must recall that the central, universal message of the world to the child is: "I am big and you are not; I am powerful and you are not; now find a way to deal with that." Whatever stratagem we evolve—approach/avoidance; trust/distrust; fight/flight; control/placate—has a tendency to get locked in as a core relational paradigm for self and world, a reflexive strategy for survival, and a means for getting one's needs met. The more unconscious these readings of self in the world, the more autonomous they are, and so we repeat ourselves, create patterns, replicate old setups in ever-new forms.

In later life, it is frequently shattering to our ego's pride to realize that we have been in servitude to these adaptive patterns throughout our presumed adulthood. I recall a nurse at a workshop on the psychological history of professional caregivers crying out, when she examined the exercises she had completed in our workshop: "My god, I have wasted my entire life!" Perhaps her reaction was an excess of the moment, for her life had been full of good works, but it was also clear that her need to heal her family of origin had rolled over into the unchallenged assumption that continuing to play that role throughout her adult life was her destiny. Just as she had confused what happened to her with who she was, so we all have a tendency to confuse fate and destiny, between what life presents us and what we are meant to become. It is essential that we not judge ourselves, for we cannot be blamed for choices we made as children, but it is even more important that we learn what autonomous core ideas have been operating, lest we remain their captive. After midlife we are truly on our own, morally and psychologically responsible for the conduct of the journey, and not only the outer world but our own psyche will hold us accountable. In the outer world we will have to deal with the consequences of our choices, clean up the mess perhaps, and in the inner world, we will suffer the dis-ease that arises from violating the agenda of the soul.

History writes messages upon us and through us. They may be found in our neurology, in our behavioral patterns, in our repetitive choices, in our value systems. We are our history, yet we are also something more. The power of historic influence at work within and through us cannot be overemphasized, as so many of our predecessors have recognized. The tragic imagination of the Greeks is once more informative. They observed that certain patterns of choice and consequence rippled down through the generations and had horrible repercussions. How to account for this? The Greeks metaphorically concluded that some god had been offended generations before and pronounced a curse upon the family, a curse that played out from generation to generation until, through suffering, someone came to recognize the casual factors, paid compensatory homage to the neglected values, and broke the chain. Today, in their work with clients, some therapists utilize genograms, or outlines of familial patterns as far back as they may be traced. Genetic predispositions, recurrent addictions and medical problems, marital patterns, and other repetitions—all reveal themselves the more accurate and more complete the genogram is. Those of us who wish to pride ourselves on autonomy, on the self-made life, on freedom of choice are often humbled by the recognition that archaic patterns are playing out through us. Who is in charge of our lives if we are not? Why these self-defeating repetitions?

We have all heard the word *complex* before, but few of us appreciate the importance and the daily utility of this idea, which Jung brought to our attention. A complex is cluster of energy in the unconscious, charged by historic events, reinforced through repetition, embodying a fragment of our personality, and generating a programmed response and an implicit set of expectations. (Jung even called them "splinter personalities.") We all have complexes because we are all historically programmed beings. Some of these programmed, reflexive responses can be helpful, as they defend us and preserve our psychological territory. If we did not have some positively charged clusters of relational experience, we could not trust, could not love, could not make interpersonal commitments, could not operate in the world without divisive distrust and distancing from others. We would not love music, esteem justice, or treasure our values if we had not had deeply felt positive experiences of them.

On the other hand, these splinter personalities are shadow governments and usurpers of ego's powers, frequently subject us to the same old, same old, and may make us prisoners of that history. Even when we bring a complex to consciousness, we may still fall captive to its accumulated power. Why is it that a person falls so easily into moods? A complex has been hit and its unexamined, unprocessed contents flood the conscious life. Why do drunks grow angry, or sentimental, or funny? The normal inhibitory powers of the ego are chemically relaxed and the unlived life below floods the field of the present with its historic agenda.

An extreme example of a complex at work will be found in the antisocial personality disorder. He or she has always suffered early and sustained abuse. This overwhelming suffering becomes a lens through which he or she views others. This reflexive filter carries a message: "You are here to hurt me, and so I must, through power or manipulation, gain control of you first." The earlier, the more powerfully repeated the message, the less susceptible it is to consciousness and to repair. This archaic message thus contaminates every new relationship and brings only dreary repetition of dismal outcomes.

Folk wisdom has long recognized the presence and power of complexes in such homey sayings as, "Count twenty before you say something," or "Write the letter but wait a week before you send it." We have long recognized that we can do strange things, fall in love, grow quickly enraged, slip into the old slough of self-disdain, and then, later, the mood state shifts. Who are we, really, during these interruptions? If I am not my ego state, then who am I?

Unfortunately, while we are in the grip of a complex, we seldom know it. The energy expended through a complex always proves excessive, although the person who is possessed by the complex usually feels that the energy generated is appropriate to the situation at that moment. (The example of road rage is a noticeable revisiting of an old grievance: "You cut me off, just as others have disregarded me in the past, and the anger I feel toward you is justified." In fact, the emotional discharge is "referred anger" and disproportionate, but the consequences are real.) Moreover, when a complex is at work, there is always some seizing up of the body—a constricted throat, a flutter in the stomach, sweating palms—but such a signal is only recognized, if at all, in a reflective mood later. Learning to recognize such signals in the rush of emotion and the bodily disturbance can help one avoid the tyranny of history, but learning to be reflective while history is happening is difficult indeed. Nietzsche once wryly wondered why bad music and bad reasons sounded so good when one is "marching against the enemy." Not only individuals, but whole nations may be gripped by a complex, and brew devastation for generations to come.

A complex takes place when an unconscious stimulus is received. You may be driving to work, not really listening to the music on the radio, and then arrive at the office in a mood, not knowing that a song on the radio hit an old spot. You might be melancholy, lighthearted, irritable, distracted, without any outer reason. Little do you know that the stimulation of that song has activated your unconscious and produced a quantum of energy sufficient to flow into the present moment and dominate your consciousness. (Our word *influenza* derives from the medieval notion that Luna, the moon, produces illness when one falls under its malevolent influence. So we are frequently gripped by a psychic flu, a mood possession,* when we succumb to a complex. It may also make us, temporarily, *luna*tics).

Once the stimulus has occurred, the psyche, as befits the historic organism that we are, reflexively asks the questions: "When have I been here before?" "What does this feel like?" "What do I know from my past that could be playing its old tape here?" Even though we are not consciously aware of it, this historic filter alters the actual stimulus and distorts it in service to history.

All of us may occasionally look back and be able to identify our possession by a complex, though at the time we were unable to recognize this state of "possession." For example, you frequently attend meetings and leave berating yourself for not speaking your mind. What blocked you? Unbeknownst to you at the moment, the old fear of judgment, devaluation, even punishment from another time, another place, rises up and shuts you down. (I had a patient who routinely, and unwittingly, brought her hand to her mouth as a physical screen when she was about to say something emotionally charged.) Or you are strongly drawn to a total stranger. How little you may grasp that his silver hair recalls you to the father who is no longer present. And how many marriages avoid being the battleground of these splinter histories, which, activated in the moment, bring the jealousies, the hurts, the longings of the past to this present and replace conscious engagement with the archaic dramas of history? As we mature, and seek consciousness, we can begin to identify the most commonly recurring complexes, and even iden-

---

*An emotion is a neurological discharge of energy. A feeling is created when that energy passes through our psychic filter and takes on enough power to possess the ego. A mood is a feeling state that, often unconscious, has pooled up, and has power to occupy the ego for a prolonged length of time.

tify what we must do to oppose their sovereignty. But many, perhaps the deepest, complexes will remain unknown to us.

When a complex is activated, not only does this stimulus trigger the stored affect tied to that issue, but it also extrapolates it into the wider range of experience, especially the fields of overwhelmment and abandonment we spoke of before. In this broadening influence, not only are specifics of our personal history present to us, albeit unconsciously, but so, too, is a generalizing into wider values, such as trust/distrust, approach/avoidance. This quantity of unprocessed affect begins to flood the field of consciousness and reaches the surface as a behavioral, physical, or attitudinal response. This circuitry takes only an instant to activate and complete its cycle! From the autonomous activity of these core ideas, these charged perceptions of self and world, these once accurate understandings or overgeneralizations or false readings, patterns emerge. We do not consciously intend such repetitions, but for good or ill, they have a life of their own, and bind us to the narrowness of our history rather than our capacious future, the more so because we are unconscious of their presence and their power. That of which we are not aware, owns us.

Even when we bring complexes to consciousness, we find that the old, archaic histories form subpersonalities as it were, splinter identities who often have a tendency to act out contrary to our will or best interests. We who prize our conscious autonomy are dismayed to learn that there is a shadow government at work within us. We think we are the CEOs of our personal corporation, but there are other members of the executive committee, various invisible partners who are present and voting all the time, whether we acknowledge their presence or not.

It is because these historically generated but invisible clusters of energy are activated over and over that patterns form in our lives, patterns which seemingly have a life of their own and are seldom consciously chosen. For this reason, our ancestors speculated that the hand of an offended divinity was at work. The modern individual, having dismissed the gods, is more likely to see such repetitions as accident, as rationalized cause/effect, or as something other than his or her own choice. But don't we have to ask: "If we are not choosing our lives, who is?"

No one begins to really exercise conscious life until he or she has some inkling of what complexes have been acquired up till now, what splinter personalities are making choices independent of ego consciousness. Clearly, the adolescent passage from childhood into adulthood does not do the job of freeing us psychologically from bondage to childhood, as we once hoped. A person in the first half of life is so swarming with the power of these unconscious forces that he or she is inclined to remain in the field of the family of origin even when he or she has put many miles between. (As the Zen saying has it, "Everywhere you go, there you are.")

If this secretive governance by history is at work for so long, why should we expect the second half of life to be any different? What I have elsewhere called "the middle passage" occurs only when a person begins to discern that his or her repetitions, compensations, and treatment plans for life have their origin not in conscious life but in unconscious history. Such a discovery is always humbling, for all of us are deeply invested in the fantasy of freedom. We think we are autonomous, self-made persons, and more and more we prove to be what we did not expect. We thought we were in charge of our lives.

Wisdom begins when we recognize that there are these split-off parts of the personality that have a life of their own. They rob energy from our conscious life, oblige us to serve historic patterns rather than be in the present with all choices open, and bind us, like the mythic Ixion, to the wheel of repetition. Until we bring these fragments of charged history to consciousness, dialogue with them, and observe them at work in our lives, we can never create our lives as we wish them to be.

We can never afford to underestimate the power of these splinter personalities, these subgroupings of will and history, for they will reassert themselves in ever-new form, with many disguises, amid shifting settings. This is why we have a tendency to repeat our parent's marriage, or remain defined by it as we seek to do the opposite. This is why we often turn out to be and do other than our conscious value systems would seem to suggest. Occasionally we have moments when we see ourselves and do not like what we see. Who was steering the ship? Who was at the driver's wheel during those critical moments of choice? (As St. Paul observed, while we may intend the good, we seldom do it.) Only with insight can the second half of life have any real capacity for choice and for development beyond these recalcitrant powers of our history.

Consciousness, however, is wrested from the enormous powers of the unconscious only after some considerable pain. No one can be conscious all the time, or even conscious of very much, regrettably. The ego, the central complex of consciousness, can only focus fleetingly, and then narrowly, on what summons its attention. All the while, the rest of our lives course onward, often in programmed, reflexive ways. When we step into that shower in the morning, when the water hits us and we shudder, we are conscious for an instant, fully present to the moment. But most of the time, we are only dimly focused on the objective character of the moment, even as the field of choice is flooded with these old subjective energy clusters.

Frankly, we only begin to recognize complexes and their sabotaging effect when we have suffered their consequences, or those around us have suffered, and now call us to account. We begin to realize that we are not alone in our psychic house when we begin to acknowledge the presence of these other psychic specters. In these moments of defeat or repetition, we may begin to ask: "When have I been here before?" "What does this feel like?" "How is this tied to my history, my patterns?" Then we have taken giant strides toward the possibility of more conscious choices, but only after acknowledging the presence of these unconscious partners. It is when we ignore their inner presence that they are most present in our outer lives.

Rather than accepting responsibility for whatever went wrong, we claim we have bad luck, bad karma, bad genes, someone else is at fault, and continue to ignore the demand of consciousness. Previously I mentioned the grinning gremlins of fear and lethargy at the foot of the bed. Fear governs so much of our lives, and produces all sorts of defense strategies. Standing up to our fear is perhaps the most critical decision necessary in the governance of life and the recovery of the soul's agenda in the second half of life. The subtlety with which fear can govern us is extraordinary. Its effect is found not only in the patterns of avoidance, which are so common in our lives, but also in denial, splitting (separating our lives into simplistic good-and-bad choices), or projection onto others.

One of the most common ways fear can be in charge will be found in our flight from personal responsibility. We project authority onto other people, certain offices, institutions, traditions, ideologies, and defer deciding what is really true for us. As long as we resist deciding what works for us, what is confirmed by our experience rather than external authority, what opens rather than narrows our life, then we will never grow up. As scary as living can be, stop and think how you will feel if, on your deathbed, you look back on your life and conclude that you never really showed up because you were afraid. Isn't that grim prospect more frightening than facing the fear itself, up front, now? Making choices without the support of others may be intimidating, but since we are here to carry out the soul's agenda rather that of our family, or our neighbors, or our peer group, doesn't it make sense to treasure personal authority over a fearful, childhood-driven defense in the choices of one's life?

We recall that the other grinning gremlin at the foot of the bed is lethargy, the torpor of the spirit. It is no accident that this word reminds us of Lethe, the river of forgetfulness in the classical topography of the underworld. Forgetting that we are summoned by each moment to make life-defining choices is rather easy to do. It is always tempting to pull the blanket over our head, fall back asleep, and wait for another day, having successfully avoided the responsibility of conscious life. Lethargy is a part of our nature. It is testimony to the enormous sucking power of the unconscious, which can, without our concerted effort, pull energy for conscious life back down into darkness. Does anyone really believe the old saying that "what I don't know can't hurt me"? We are hurt every day by what we do not know, and we in turn hurt others. Staying conscious is a difficult task, and none of us is up to it all the time. Being able to reflect upon oneself and take responsibility proves more difficult than we thought when we originally set off into life.

Spiritual lethargy is further abetted by the many distractions of our time, especially those of popular culture. We are a wired society, with all sorts of seductions of the senses. Our children can hardly read anymore because they have grown up with a passive visual culture where someone else does most of the work. They have lost the power for critical thinking and imaginative interaction and are easily seduced by visual images, whether they sell products, lifestyles, or political agendas. Perhaps the two greatest addictions in our culture do not include street drugs, which make for easy scapegoating by politicians, but are television and food, both of which are readily available on a twenty-four-hour basis. Even as far back as the seventeenth century, the French philosopher/mathematician Blaise Pascal noted that popular culture had become a vast *divertissement,* a diversion from the engagement with the Self. Even the king had to have his jester, Pascal noted, lest the bejeweled potentate brood too much and, perhaps, have an encounter with the soul. One wonders what Pascal would think of our age, where lethargy of the spirit is merchandised by very intelligent people and lulls all of us into the sleep of reason, and the slumber of the spirit.

This image of sleeping one's way through life recently appeared in the dream of a patient. She had heroically wrested her life away from her insecure mother and her jealous father to become a working professional with her own business. But her business languished. She missed appointments, failed to market her talent, and sabotaged job after job. Unwittingly, she remained in service to the old denigrating complexes. ("Leaving home" is always more difficult than just leaving home.) In her dream she found that she was watching a number of young businesswomen like herself moving about with vigor, in eye-catching clothing. She then curled up on the floor and fell asleep. One of the women (who in the subjective language of the dream was also a part of her, albeit still foreign to her consciousness) yelled at her, "You are sleeping. Wake up!" She got the message. Interestingly, once she'd "awakened," her good brain readily told her all the steps necessary to build her practice. She outlined them in the next session of therapy. Today she has so much work, good work, that she has to turn clients away.

Growing up, leaving home, requires two practices. First, we must take responsibility for ourselves, and stop blaming others: the society, the parents, the partner, the malevolent gods. Secondly, we have to look within to see the repetitive core ideas, the complexes, and the historic influences where the true enemy lies. Growing up sounds easy on paper, but how many of us really grow up? If I take responsibility for my life, I lift the burden off others, but I then have a whole ton of stuff to carry myself; moreover, I will find myself very much alone when it comes to the critical decisions of life. If I look within, then I have to stop blaming and acknowledge that I am the party responsible for these outcomes that I deplore, and even these symptoms that rise to annoy and trouble consciousness. Growing up is difficult, and one's powerful position in life, whether as a parent, or a CEO of a multinational corporation, has absolutely no correlation with one's emotional maturity. In fact, a person who voraciously seeks outer validation through social position is one most likely to have large, unfinished business within.

While it is easy to be intimidated by the largeness of life, seduced by lethargy, diverted by popular culture, and assimilated into collective fantasies that have little to do with our soul's agenda, we still have to face ourselves in the end. The various ways we have to numb out, to flee into our work to avoid our real job, to get exercised over trivial issues, to rationalize our choices are virtually infinite. Life has a way of bringing these moments of choice back to us in ever-new venues. We only move through the middle passage, only truly begin to grow up, when we begin to confront these questions more consciously, these questions that have already come to confront us. We are more than our history and conditioning, but not if each remains unconscious. Whatever is not addressed by consciousness will play out in our lives somewhere, and we and others will have the butcher's bill to pay. And, worse, we will not have remembered why we've come to this brief, fragile, precious life. As the Persian poet Rumi mused,

A King sent you to a country to carry out one special, specific task. You go to the country and you perform a hundred other tasks, but if you have not performed the task you were sent for, it is as if you have performed nothing at all. So man has come into the world for a particular task and that is his purpose. If he doesn't perform it, he will have done nothing. *

---

*Rumi, *Fiha-Ma-Fiha Table Talk of Maulana Rumi*, p. 84.

Chapter Five

The Dynamics of
Intimate Relationship

"Sometimes I forget completely
What companionship is.
Unconscious and insane, I spill sad
energy everywhere."

Rumi, "Sometimes I Forget"

TURN ON THE CAR RADIO tomorrow morning, to
something other than the local news or sports station.
Listen to the music. What is it about invariably? Why,
"love," of course, and the search for the one who will make your life
work. Is that not the deepest of our fantasies, the one that infiltrates
so many other levels of our lives? Is not the hope that we can find
him or her who will make it right, who will heal our history, who will
really be there for us and resolve our strongest private need? I recall
one woman, who was in an impossible relationship, saying, "I will
not let go of this hand until there is another hand there in the darkness." I knew what she meant, and yet I also knew that it was her
challenge to face the darkness, without rescue, and that the journey

of her soul depended on this courageous act. But what self-help book or well-intentioned friend recommends facing darkness, rather than offering ways to flee it? The flight from the darkness will drive one into someone's arms, any arms . . . but the darkness only grows.

I have had the privilege of speaking to many groups in many states and several countries, and invariably, no matter what the announced topic, the question of relationship always comes to the surface. Why is this so? The obvious answer is that relationships are important, as indeed they are. But is it also possible that we make relationships too important? How could relationships be too important? Perhaps the clue may be found in noting that whatever comes up repeatedly, perhaps obsessively, is charged from another time, another place and has gained an autonomous foothold in our lives. In other words, relationship evokes powerful complexes. Since all insistent, obsessive desires are first fueled by an anxiety of some sort, what then is the hidden agenda behind our preoccupation with relationships?

Of all the ideologies that possess the contemporary soul, perhaps none is more powerful, more seductive, and possibly more delusory than the romantic fantasy that there *is* someone out there who is right for us, the long-sought soul mate, what I call "the magical other," the one who will truly understand us, take care of us, meet our needs, repair the wounds, and, with a little luck, spare us the burden of growing up and meeting our own needs.

This fantasy is in us all, and is the most virulent ideology of the modern world, even more powerful than its chief rival: the fantasy that material goods will bring us happiness. Perhaps the combination of romance and affluence are surrogates for belief in God.* In

---

*Indeed, Robert Johnson has written, "Romantic love is the single greatest energy system in the Western psyche. In our culture it has supplanted religion as the arena

earlier epochs the notion that one might find fulfillment in this life was considered laughable, even impious. This world, our predecessors believed, was a "vale of tears" and could only be compensated for by an afterlife. Today there is less clarity about an afterlife, and despite the uncertainty that sells popular theologies, just as many distracted souls have scant interest in spiritual questions, and romance and material abundance are therefore served religiously. As an ideology, the compulsive preoccupation with sex and love stands virtually unchallenged and is not only embraced by our popular culture, but has a special place in the heart of all of us. After all, the ancients considered Eros a god, sometimes described as the oldest of the gods because he was the foundation of all things, and sometimes as the youngest since his presence was felt anew in all moments. So it is not that we can ignore Eros, for, as Jung metaphorically suggested, a neurosis is an offended or neglected "god." The question, then, is not avoidance of the demands of desire, or the more complicated question of relationship, but how to live with them consciously.

As a therapist, I have worked with so many broken relationships, so many "soul mates" who were discovered—surprise—to be merely human after all. What is going on here? Why this obsessive fantasy? Why do we, longing for relationship, repeatedly sabotage the few we have? These are questions too important not to ask. And yet, in asking these questions about relationship, I find many who, while agreeing with the logic of the questions, stoutly resist the necessary conclusions and the agenda for personal responsibility that they ask of us.

It is far easier to be disappointed in the other than to call ourselves

---

in which men and women seek meaning, transcendence, wholeness, and ecstasy." (*WE: Understanding the Psychology of Romantic Love*, p. xi.)

to account. Indeed, recent statistics indicate that traditional marriage is in significant decline. Currently, only 56 percent of adults in America are married, compared to 75 percent thirty years ago. Some are divorced, some are gay (and blocked by ignorance and prejudice from legal marriage), but many more are choosing not to get married. Married or not, in my view the two chief causes of relational discord are imposing inordinate expectations on each other and transferring old baggage into the present, thereby burdening the fragile new relationship with too much history. In both cases, whatever history we bring to the relationship occasions the attraction, the pas de deux, and thereby the often predictable outcomes.

The Psychodynamics of Relationship

At least two psychodynamic stratagems are present in all relationships, at all times, though in varying degrees, namely *projection* and *transference,* phenomena therapists are trained to identify, but as fellow human beings we are no more inoculated against their toxins than the next person.

All relationships begin in projection. While each moment is wholly new, one of the ways in which we are able to function without having to reinvent ourselves over and over is to reflexively impose past experience, agenda, and understandings onto each new person, each new situation. These are projections. Unfortunately, as we look to each new situation, each new person through the lens of the old, we risk compromising its unique character with our historic experience and distorting its essential reality in service to the unfinished agendas of the past. And as projection is an essentially unconscious phenomenon, we do not know that we are externalizing our internal experience onto the other person. Through projection, our inner life plays out before us as psychodrama, a magic lantern whose phantasms simulate reality and repeatedly bewitch consciousness.

The second psychological mechanism employed in relationships is *transference*. As historically charged creatures, we have a tendency to transfer those historical patterns, and their predictable outcomes, into every new relationship. Fundamental values are always brought into the new setting and impose themselves on the relationship: attraction/repulsion; love/hate; passivity/aggression; trust/distrust; approach/avoidance; intimacy/distance; and many others. As one has experienced the primal relationships of childhood, so those core ideas and reflexive strategies, with their predictable outcomes, are brought into the present.

Initially, we are incapable of recognizing that we are experiencing another person reflexively through the refracting screen of our history, especially those parts that are similar to the new situation. This is why we see so many repetitions in our relationships. These fated relationships occur and reoccur, often with a tragic sense of inevitability and a strange familiarity.

If projection recognizes a familiar profile in the other, a set of characteristics that derive from us not them, then transference is the script, the old drama, the programmed repetition that is most likely to follow that projection. Initially, we are incapable of recognizing that we are experiencing the other person reflexively through the refracting screen of our personal psychologies. This is why we see so many repetitions in relationships. Incredibly, the abused child will unwittingly seek out either an abusive partner or one who has no spirit whatsoever and is easily controlled. Either choice is dictated by the unmetabolized events of childhood. Or the person who grew up with an impaired parent will be drawn to another troubled soul and reenact the familiar role of caretaker or enabler. These kinds of patterns are repeated in so many lives with so many variations and, because they are unconscious, produce such tragic inevitabilities.

If we are sincere, and really do wish to improve relationships, as so many popular books and magazines claim, we may usefully ask: "What do we project, and what do we transfer onto the other person?" What is projected and transferred most is our *intrapsychic imago* as charged and programmed by our history. An imago is a very deeply charged image. An image becomes an imago when it activates an archetypal energy field, and thereby touches on not just this present occasion, but activates our whole history as well. Our intrapsychic imago of the beloved other will most commonly have been shaped by our most primal experiences of relationships. This imago most likely derives from our experience of our parents, although other experiences, traumatic or healing, can affect this primal data. A common misconception about therapy is that it obliges endless, reductive discussion of one's parents and an unsparing dissection of their alleged failures. Far from it, most therapy is reality-based, present-oriented. Nonetheless, our first experiences of relationship, our messages about security, trust, predictability, expectations, and other strategic dynamics, will derive from these archaic experiences with our primary caretakers and role models.

Because of the magnitude of the parent/child relationship—since every child's sensibility is so dependent, so malleable, and so unaware of alternatives—these archaic, childhood messages about self and world have enormous purchase on our souls, and astonishing staying power. As we recall the twin categories of our universal wounding, feeling *overwhelmed* or invaded by life, or insufficiently met, even *abandoned* by life, so all the varied strategies ingrained in our deepest imago of self and other will likely show up as the prevailing style, the pattern-generating dynamic of the present relationship. In the face of the core trauma of being overwhelmed, one will have a tendency toward avoidance of intimacy, be caught up in the need for control or, even more likely, be overly compliant and accommodating to the other. Carrying the imago of abandonment, one is likely to elect a self-denigrating or self-sabotaging role in the duo, exercise inordinate power over the other to wring what one desires from them, or be caught in an anxiety-ridden search for the impossible and overburden the relationship with expectations. It is not that we consciously choose these strategies, but that they have an opening through the unconscious to insinuate themselves whenever we are not wholly conscious, wholly in the present, which is much if not most of the time.

Of the tens of thousands of persons whom we will meet in our lifetime, only dozens, perhaps, will activate this powerful imago enough to produce strong attraction or repulsion. But all relationships will carry some imprint of these first, most influential messages about self and other, and how we relate to each other. The earlier and more powerfully charged the script, the more archaic and less susceptible it will be to consciousness. All of these behavioral stratagems rise from the archaic power of history, and are stoutly defended by rationalizations when challenged. In fact, the surest evidence that a complex-ridden imago is in charge is the ready availability of a rationalization to justify it. These dynamics show up most powerfully in the field of intimacy. In other arenas we are likely to have more filtering devices in place. One does not show one's undefended self very often at the factory or office for it might prove costly, though even there it leaks out from time to time. And, of course, intimate relationship comes closer to our original, primal experience than more distanced, filtered relationships will.

I am not asserting that we are only prisoners of childhood history. Many other experiences of relationship in the course of our life have the power to modify this intrapsychic imago of self and other. If this were not so, we would remain infants, and could not mature, or experience healing, and would remain victims of fate. On the other hand, the power of those old imagoes cannot be ignored. When they remain unconscious, we are most likely consigning our choices of partners to history not present reality, enacting a familiar pas de deux, and repeating the dynamics of our family of origin.

Our programmed, psychic radar is on at all moments, scanning the world and identifying those persons who can attract or activate a projection and perhaps for a while carry the burden of our unconscious agendas and transferred history. This search, this fantasy, is the chief fuel for our culture—the fantasy of romantic love, the fantasy that there is this *other* who will make our life work for us, heal us, protect us, nurture us, and spare us the world's trauma. At the same time, the other transmits his or her historic material onto us as well. No wonder that relationships get so complicated, and are so easily sabotaged. If we could see all the imagoes we project onto each other, and the transferential histories with their predictable outcomes as well, it would look like an air traffic controller's screen at O'Hare at rush hour.

When person A meets person B, say on an airplane or at a party, each is able to relate to the other from conscious intentionality. Sometimes this is the sole level of relationship engaged, as occurs in most of our superficial social transactions. But each has brought his or her history, "memory's unmade bed," to the party as well. The mere presence, appearance, action, or context of person B can activate the unconscious of person A, triggering a projection, with its attendant transferential history. When this engagement occurs, powerful emotion, be it attraction or repulsion, is activated. Person B may or may not know that he or she is receiving all this energy, but it will affect both parties nonetheless. Remember, the unconscious screens the exterior world constantly, and asks of all new encounters: "What do I know of this other person?" "When have I been here before?" "How do I react to this person?" Once two people have met, each of them is already affected, already changed, though neither may be conscious of such a transformation of the space between them. Not only do individuals relate to each other in these powerful but unconscious ways, but so do groups and even nations, often with tragic, repetitive outcomes. How much historic horror has come about between religions, ethnic groups, and nations because of what each has not faced within? What we do not know about ourselves nearly always proves a terrible burden on others.

When two parties are caught in a mutual projection they may have strong repulsion to each other or strong attraction. One woman I worked with reported a strong negative transference to a professional football coach whom she had only seen on television. After months of this confusing emotion generated by a total stranger, she finally recognized that his curled lip reminded her of her mother's grimace when she belittled the child. Here is one stranger disliking another stranger, and all because of the amazing power of history to impose itself unconsciously upon the present. When, however, the projection is of attraction, a strong desire to merge with that other occurs. This projective identification is called "romance," and people everywhere intensely desire its effect on their spirit, their slumbering endorphins, and their deeply resonating agenda for repetition.

Who does not seek "love"; who does not wish to "fall" in love? Moments of projective, romantic history, from Dante first espying Beatrice on the banks of the turgid Arno in Florence to "some enchanted evening," when one meets a magical stranger, are highly celebrated. People even fall in love with movie stars whose only reality for them is a spectral two-dimensional image on a screen. John Hinckley sought to murder a president so that a movie star might pay attention to him and find him worthy. And we think we do not live in the world of symbols! Folk wisdom observes that lovers are fools, lovers are blind; we also speak of a folie a deux because in this mutually projective state, the person is acting not out of a conscious relationship to reality, but out of the archaic and often overwhelming power of personal history. Such behavior, as we know, often leads to disaster. Yet note how this disaster is desired, as expressed by Rumi, centuries ago:

> *I would love to kiss you.*
> The price of kissing is your life.

> *Now my loving is running toward my life shouting,*
> What a bargain, let's buy it. *

I recall a client who indulged in a series of romantic escapades with dangerous outcomes. In hoping that she might more consciously weigh the costs of her decisions, I suggested that she watch the movie *Damage,* which depicted a French diplomat who brought ruin to his life, his career, and his family through a compulsive affair. She came back to the next session and said, "That is exactly what I want." High passion, great cost, great damage: "let's buy it."

For the faithful, even in the face of multiple disasters, it still seems blasphemous to the popular religion of romance to suggest that it is fueled almost wholly by fantasy through the mechanism of

---

*Rumi, "Two Poems by Rumi," in Bly, *et al., The Soul Is Here for Its Own Joy,* p. 139.

projection. And we all know the next chapter of this story. Behind our projection is, surprise, surprise, a mere human being like us. Whoever they are, whatever they are, their imperfect reality will inevitably wear through the projection until a different picture emerges. "You've changed; you're different; you are not the person I thought you were," we hear, and so they are different, as they always were. They are always something different than what our projections and our psychological agenda presumes. (It is possible, of course, that something profound, something for which we might rightly reserve the word *love,* may survive the collapse of a projection. But this happy discovery is no sure thing.)

The erosion of the projection's power causes it to fall back into the unconscious, after which each person experiences confusion, disorientation, and irritation, and perhaps ramps up controlling strategies to sustain the projection as long as possible. Rarely does one truly analyze the phenomenon and discern the humbling truth, that some dynamic, script, expectation, or project from our consciousness has been unwittingly projected onto the other. In reality, whether they are a celebrity seen from afar, an office mate, or perhaps a neighbor—all of us are truly strangers. If we so barely know ourselves, how can we know the other? Yet the almost supernatural power of the projection is fascinating.

Who would not be drawn to a missing part of their psychological life, for that is what a projection carries, and who has not felt the power of this phenomenon? (No wonder the phrase *soul mate* has become such a cliché, for aspects of our soul *are* involved, but we can mistakenly think we actually see them in the other.) The weaker the consciousness of a person is, the more he or she is likely to get fixated in the projection, even when the reality has long departed from it, and he or she will remain captive to the power of history, the agenda of longing, and the wheel of repetition.

These possessions by our unconscious history are the stuff of movies and romantic theater, but their outcomes are seldom benign. A compelling enactment of this projective power is found in the phenomenon of stalking. I once had a client, an officer of the court, who stalked his beloved after she had rejected him and his possessiveness. Even in the face of disbarment by the court for violating a restraining order, he continued his obsessive pursuit. Spousal violence similarly derives from the failure to honor the reality of the other when it does not conform to projective expectations. A weak ego can only tolerate discrepancy by resorting to violence. Each city has its women's shelter, and the sad phenomenon of violence, physical or verbal, haunts too many breakups. Violent men don't have the strength of consciousness and character to own responsibility for what is missing in their own psychological life. They pummel others for not carrying their own anguished souls.

In a similar vein, I saw a patient drive his loving wife away because he could not believe that she would be faithful to him. Despite her professed and apparent fidelity to him, his capacity to appreciate her was undermined by the memory of his mother leaving with a stranger in front of his eyes when he was eight years old. He never saw her again. That imago, programmed by the actual experience of abandonment, was so powerfully charged that it was transferred to his wife, and sure enough, history was repeated. She had no choice but to leave this obsessive doubt and distrust, and the childhood imago was tragically confirmed. For my patient, neither reason, nor interpretation, nor medication proved stronger than this archaic imago.

The most critical element in this dynamic is the relationship of our conscious life to what is unconscious within us. What we do not know can and will undermine the presumptions of conscious life, and will provide the content of the projection. Who wishes to hear this admonition, especially since falling in love is so easy and so pleasant? How often are we willing to pay attention to our processes working in the moment? How often can we see what we are asking of this unknown other, and own that agenda as ours not theirs? Typically, only when the projections fall away is one likely to begin asking this question, if even then. And many, even those in therapy, having explored their relational history and understood the dynamics of their past relationships, still easily walk into the same blind place all over again. In fact, it is virtually impossible to do therapy with a person "in love," just as one cannot work with a drunk. Often, they suffer more than an intoxication; they are temporarily psychotic and cannot reflect, own, and sort through their lives until enough of the projection has worn away that the ego consciousness resumes its proper function. The fantasy of "love" has everyone in its grip, especially the person who is lacking resolve to look within and to take responsibility for meeting more of his or her own needs. Moreover, and this is seldom noted while in the throes of desire, our projections depersonalize the other whom we profess to love. They become objects, artifacts of our psyche, and in those moments we are no longer in ethical relationship with them.

We have mutual effects upon each other whether we are conscious or not—sometimes for good, sometimes not. Sometimes, the mere presence of the other can have a healing effect, as therapists and hospice workers, or parent and child especially have observed so frequently; sometimes, the mutual unconscious activity can have a pernicious effect as what is hidden has a strange and compelling power over an otherwise conscious being. We find ourselves repelled by a stranger, a character in a sitcom, and for what reason? For the moment that unknown other carries aspects we wish to repudiate in ourselves or dilemmas we wish to distance as much as possible. Generally speaking, whatever moves us, whether consciously or not, will somehow be found as touching a deeply buried aspect of ourselves.

The secret goal of "falling in love" is fusion with the other, and the obliteration of the individual consciousness is the outcome most desired. (*Le petite morte,* the French expression for orgasm, is, after all, "the little death)." While the desire for obliteration is an inescapable by-product of the rigor and hardship of our journey, when it prevails we are infantilized, regressed, and dependent, and secretly wish to be so. But in the light of day, it does not seem so pretty. The much greater risk of truly loving the other presents a quite different agenda, a more demanding summons, as we shall see.

When we look at this problematic question of falling in love, we see a number of implications emerge. First, what we do not know about ourselves, or do not wish to know, has a tendency to be projected onto our "beloved." Second, we have a predisposition to project our childhood agendas, our infantile longing, and the burden of our assignment for personal growth onto the other. Thirdly, since the other cannot in the end, and should not ever, carry responsibility for the task of our life, the projections inevitably wear away and the relationship has a tendency to deteriorate into a power struggle. When the other does not conform to our relationship agenda, we often seek to control them through admonishment, withdrawal, passive/aggressive sabotage, and sometimes overtly controlling behaviors. We profess innocence when confronted, for we usually believe our own rationalizations, but the other whom we profess to love has in fact been victimized by us. An analytic colleague, Alden Josey, once employed the telling metaphor that secretly "we wish to colonize the other," and like most imperial powers, we are flush with rationalizations to justify our agendas of self-interest. And thus fourthly, it only stands to reason, that the best thing we can do for ourselves and for the other is to assume more of the developmental agenda for ourselves. In other words, to have a grown-up relationship, we have to grow up! How difficult that is when the unconscious relational "contract" may precisely be designed to help us avoid growing up. When we are able to sincerely ask the question "What am I asking of my beloved that I need to do for myself?" we have not only begun growing up, but may then be expressing a loving attitude toward that other after all.

This all makes sense on paper, but to work it out in concrete lives is another matter. Part of the difficulty of couple's therapy is getting each party to look rigorously at the psychodynamics they bring to their disagreements without continuing to blame the other. Even more difficult is bringing two diverse parties to the point where each can undertake that fourth principle by relinquishing their infantilizing agenda and taking on the full measure of their life's journey, with all its empowerment and nuturant tasks, rather than burdening the other.

As we saw earlier, every failed projection is experienced by the ego as a frustration and a defeat. But every projection is an aspect of ourselves that has come back to us. What are we going to do with that quantum of energy, that agenda of growth or regression? Asking this question seriously, and trying to live it, provides the possibility whereby a relationship can actually grow toward genuine intimacy, as well as support the growth of each person within it. The inescapable truth of any relationship is that it can achieve no higher level of development than the level of maturity that both parties bring to it. If I can bear to accept this truth, this challenge, I not only free the other whom I claim to love, but I begin to free myself from the shackles of childhood dependency. It is not a fault to have a childish region of our psyche, for we are all recovering children, but it is a culpable act to impose that disempowered, narcissistically driven history on the present beloved.

So then, one is obliged to ask, what would a mature relationship look like; what would promote an ethical, loving relationship, with a chance of enduring? Why, if we are exercising responsibility for our own journey, is there even a place for another person? Fortunately, there are persuasive answers to these questions. What another really can bring to us, their greatest gift, is not an imitation or confirmation of our limited vision, but the gift of their quite different vision, their otherness as otherness. The immature psyche needs confirmation to be secure, a cloning of interests and sensibilities, and there is no surer path to staying immature and undeveloped than seeking agreement in all things.

A more mature relationship is based on "otherness" itself, on the dialectical principle that demonstrates that my one and your one together create the third. The "third" is the developmental process that results as we influence each other in turn; we grow by incorporating that influence into our private sensibilities. We do not learn and grow by all subscribing to the same school of thought, copying the same values, or voting the same way.* We grow from the experience of our differences, although in insecure moments we quickly forget this. The capacity to include those differences, even incorporate them into an ever broader, more sophisticated range of choices, is the chief task, and gift, of an evolving relationship.

The "in love" state, great narcotic as it is, numbs consciousness, retards growth, and serves as a soporific to the soul. Consciously

---

*Søren Kierkegaard once observed that adults can be so like schoolchildren, copying answers from each other's slates, and never finding the solutions for themselves.

loving another obliges risk, courage in the face of ambiguity, and the strength of tolerance. Whoever lacks these qualities will never truly have relationship. Whoever lacks the capacity for a mature relationship will never fully be in his or her own life. In the encounter with the other, we begin to realize the immensity of our own soul; by encountering the immensity of the other's soul, including the parts we do not like, we are summoned to largeness, not the diminishment that our infantile agenda seeks. Like personhood, the gift of relationship is not so much a gift as it is an achievement to be earned.

When we are able to bring the mystery that we are to engage the mystery of another, then we are in a developmental, dynamic process that enlarges. As Jung expressed it, "The unrelated human being lacks wholeness, for he can achieve wholeness only through the soul, and the soul cannot exist without its other side, which is always found in a 'You.'"* What Jung is suggesting is much more subtle than we might see at first glance. He is asserting that wholeness only comes through relationship with another. Only in such fashion can the third appear. If we have only a conversation with ourselves, as a hermit might, we can easily get caught in the looping tape of our own madness, or our own stagnant, self-confirming neurosis. But Jung relates this paradox not only to relationships with others, but also to *our relationship with ourselves,* without which we have little to bring to the table. If we talk only with the other, we impose upon the other all that is unresolved, unconscious within us. The dialectical conversation with the other must include conversation both between our separate selves and within ourselves. If a relationship does not promote and support

---

*Jung, *CW 16,* para. 454.

the growth of each, even to risky, unpredictable places, it is not a mature relationship; it is a regressive folie à deux.

There is a telling paradox at work here. The more we wish another person to repair our wounds, meet our needs, and protect us from having to grow up, really grow up, the more dissatisfying the relationship will prove over the long haul. It will swamp in stagnation. If, however, we can see that the relationship is a summons to growth, in part by encountering the otherness of our partner, the relationship will support each person risking, stretching, and growing beyond the point where they entered.

Allison and Jennifer were two working professionals in a relationship where they were continuously angry with each other. They would pick fights over trivial issues and withdraw into sullen camps. When I saw them individually, I was struck by how remarkably similar their complaints about each other were. Each thought the other was depressed; each thought I ought to identify the other as the real patient; each thought she was unable to separate long enough to pursue her individual interests for fear of seeming to abandon the other; each was resentful at this apparently controlling behavior on her partner's part. With their separate permissions, I wrote two letters, each summarizing one partner's position, and presented them to the opposite partner in their presence. To their amazement, I gave each an identical letter, signed by the other partner. As they read the letters, they first expressed astonishment, then hilarity as the absurdity of their trouble hit them. Each felt inordinately responsible for the other's well being; each wished only to be supported in her efforts to be more and more individual; each was afraid this quite reasonable hope would be perceived as selfish; each sabotaged her own developmental agenda; and each had grown resentful, blaming, and withdrawn. Their stagnation was inevitable, given their failure to recognize that in fact they subscribed to the same idea of relationship. Thereafter, the bramble was cleared, and the relationship became much closer to what it was meant to be, a mature association from which both parties grew.

I wish it were possible to say that all therapeutic interventions could evolve toward such mutually developmental agreements. Too many, alas, continue to flounder on the recurring parentification of their partners. Projections and transference phenomena have enormous staying power, and continuously supplant the possibility of what we might oxymoronically term "disinterested love" with the unfinished business of childhood narcissism.

Yet, after the inevitable projections unavoidably fall away, we are re-summoned in a relationship to the immensity of our own journey. Romance may be replaced by something worth being called love, as a result of the humbling encounter with the challenges that our withdrawn projections bring home to us. This is why love requires big persons, not kids. Kids fall in and out of love at the moment's whim. Big people can ride the shifting tides of life, range between intimacy and distance, defense and openness, and grow through their mutual toleration of ambivalence and ambiguity. Love asks that we confer on the other the freedom to be who they most profoundly are, even as we wish the same for ourselves.

I have sometimes been asked what I have against romance. Actually, nothing. It is the confusion of romance with love that occasions our problems. If by romance one means sensitive attentiveness to the other, to the atmosphere in which the relationship transpires, and to those sentiments that form from aroused feeling life, then romance can well nurture and renew a relationship. But if by romance what is meant, as seems most common, is that one is swept off one's feet by the other, then it is only a matter of time, and intrusive reality, before one falls back to common earth. Sentiment in relationship feeds the soul. Romance as the gilding of the other may be a delightful deception, for a while, but will lack the staying power demanded of genuine relatedness. The problem is not romance, but what extra baggage romance is obliged to carry. As such, romance, which feeds on projection and hidden agenda, can actually obscure behind a rosy cloud the essential mystery we really are. While romance can arouse a psychic high, for it intimates the possibility of soul, it cannot sustain the connection, and inevitably leads to disappointment. A life lived only in a search for highs will prove in the end to have been a transient, superficial life. Romance, which frequently serves as a secular religion, does not serve for long. What person would consciously seek a short-term religious stance, yet as a culture we seem to rush to this temple of romance over and over, sleeping again and again in memory's unmade bed.

We can see that when a relationship is lived in the context of the soul, rather than that of the genitals, the complexes, or as a planned palliative* for the generalized anxiety disorder that is our human condition, we are asked to confront the essential mystery that we are with the essential mystery that our partner is. When we can tolerate this mystery, we are already becoming a larger person.

The chief disorders of our time are the fear of loneliness and the fear of growing up. The flight from loneliness drives people to mill amid malls, to stay in bad relationships, to abuse substances and worst of all, to avoid a relationship with the self. How can we ever have a good relationship with another when we cannot have a good relationship with ourselves? The flight from ourselves will always mean that we will be uncomfortable with another. What we fear in

---

*How many pop songs from "Help Me Make It Through the Night" to "I Can't Live If Living Is Without You" suggest that romance is the presumed antidote for dependency?

ourselves we will fear in the other; what we avoid addressing in ourselves we will avoid in the other; where we are stuck with ourselves we will be stuck with the other.

Growing up means taking psychological responsibility for ourselves, and not just economic and social responsibility—that is the easy part. Growing up means that we take spiritual responsibility for ourselves. No other can define our values, become our authority, or protect us from necessary choices. Until we accept this responsibility for ourselves, we are asking others to be a shelter for our homeless soul. As understandable, and universal, as that desire may be, remember that others will then be asking the same of us as well. How ingrown, and stagnant, such a relationship will prove to be. The immense soul that dwells within each of us will, in time, chafe and fret, and produce symptomatic messages of dismay. And in time, whether or not we stay outwardly bound together with a partner, we will psychologically leave the relationship by the diversion of Eros's energy to work, to another, to other projective possibilities, or invert it as depression or somatic illness.

An irony is found in recognizing that what our popular culture promotes as a solution can only result in our profound unhappiness. What passes for conventional love is fusion between two incompletes, both of whom are in service to a regressive agenda. How different this is from the poet Rilke's notion of a soulful relationship as the sharing of one's solitude with another. Loving will ask that we assume the burden of our fearful agenda, replace our tentative, timorous tread with a bold step into life, and spare the other the task of taking care of us.

Moreover, what the movies, the novels, the soap operas do not tell us is that the constant companion of Eros is pathos; desire and suffering are twins. If we risk loving, we will always open to larger suffering as well. (Perhaps that is why Cupid, the little guy in a diaper, shoots arrows, arrows that may pierce the heart.) To love another is to learn that we cannot protect them from suffering even as they cannot spare us. We will learn too soon that eventually one of us will lose the other. And we will discover that we, who can only barely begin to know ourselves, will never really know the mysterious other, even when we have learned their habits, their strengths, and their vulnerabilities. We will learn that the chief gifts of relationship are quite different from those offered by the movies and the top forty love songs. We will learn more about ourselves through the engagement with the other, sometimes more than we want to know; we will be asked for greater compassion in the face of the humanness of the other; but we may yet experience, in our aloneness, the community of those who have achieved solitude.

There is an old saying that the cure for loneliness is solitude. Solitude can be defined as learning that we are not alone when we are alone. When we have achieved the stature of solitude, namely achieving a conscious relationship with ourselves, then we are freer to share ourselves with others, freer to receive their gifts in return and not be infantilized by the mutual archaic agenda of childhood, the agenda that covertly uses the other to provide for us.

Mature relationship requires sacrifice, and not just the daily sacrifice of setting aside our narcissistic interests in service to the other—no small achievement in itself. If that remains the only sacrifice, virtuous as it may be, then the relationship will breed bitterness and a corrosive martyrdom over time. The toxins of such compelled sacrifices have poisoned many a relationship. Rather, the sacrifice asked of each partner is to the dialectic, to the developmental idea of the relationship. It requires a willing suspension of our understandably common regressive agenda in order to remain open to the otherness of the other—also no easy task. As Stephen Dunn reminds us:

No one should ask the other
"What were you thinking?"

No one, that is,
who doesn't want to hear about the past

and its inhabitants,
or the strange loneliness of the present.*

This sacrifice is not codependence, not an excess of superego oughts and shoulds, but is an investment in the development of the souls of both parties. In so many couples I witness one person resist the growth of their partner, for they fear that growth will divert energies from them, or will lead the other in a divergent path; however, growth denied by one party to another will only breed resentment and ensure that both parties live in a sour stew.

The permutations of Eros, the declensions of desire, take us to many places on this earth, and many places within the unfolding mystery that we are. Without Eros, the life force, pulling us into the world, we would all stay home and perish, and there would be no big persons available to take on the world, or even be big enough to rise to the challenge of relationship. But intimate relationship, when it is in service to the summons of the soul, is only one of many engagements with the mystery. Relying on it to replace the many other realms we, as spiritual beings, are meant to travel will not only burden the other with our unlived life, but will keep us from that appointment which the soul consistently solicits for us.

---

*Dunn, "After Making Love," *Loosestrife*. p. 21.

Companionship, mutuality of goals, sexuality, and supportive endeavors are great possibilities in any relationship, but when we learn that engagement of the soul's agenda is our real task, that this journey is our real home, then we'll see that how we use relationship will either serve, or hinder, that prospect. Accepting the journey as our home will free the relationship to serve the agenda of life, the agenda of growth, and the agenda of the soul. When we have accepted this journey, truly accepted it, we will be flooded with a strong, supportive energy that carries us through all the dark places. For this energy we have an appropriate word. It is called *love*. It is love not only of the other, but love of this life, this journey, and love of this task of soul.

Chapter Six

The Family During the Second Half of Life

"What usually has the strongest psychic effect on the child
is the life which the parents . . . have not lived."

Carl Jung

ISTORICALLY, the family evolved as a necessary
institution, including not only blood kin, but also all
those who were present to carry on the work of sur-
vival, essential chores, and the transmission of tribal values. Gathered together, a group could better defend itself, differentiate roles
and tasks, protect their young, and ensure their continuity. If the
social biologists are right, the males were genetically programmed
to spread their sperm in service to the survival of the species, and
the females to seek continuity of partnership to ensure the protection of themselves and their vulnerable young. This dual agenda
was perhaps best served by the creation of the idea of marriage,

with sufficient sanctioned powers to govern and channel the wild swings to which Eros is so often prone.

As cultures evolved, the family became the one stable unit in a world of change, hostile invasion, depredations of nature, and constant search for food and shelter. That stable unit further evolved as a critical carrier of culture, that is a vehicle to sustain the tribal mythology, social role functions, and the linkage to both tribal and transcendent values. But family was always more, and remains more, whether fractured or intact, whether localized or far-flung. It was and remains an archetypal force field in which all of us participate, long after we physically leave family in the first, easier, departure at the end of adolescence. Leaving family psychologically remains a separate, more critical, sometimes impossible task for the second half of life. This is why so often the farther away we move, and the more the years pass, the more we may stumble on the invisible family still quite near at hand in our psychic gestures and patterns after all. As Jung observed,

> *When a situation occurs which corresponds to a given archetype, that archetype becomes activated and a compulsiveness appears, which, like an instinctual drive, gains its way against all reason and will.* *

That is why Father forever walks on one side, and on the other is "Dark Mother always gliding near with soft feet."[†]

On the other hand, we all know that the normative power, the

---

*Jung, *CW 9i*, para. 99.
[†]Whitman, "When Lilacs Last in the Dooryard Bloomed," l. 143. *The Norton Anthology of Poetry*, p. 779.

ingrained authority, and the stability of all great institutions—the church, government, and the family—have undergone substantive, progressive enervation over the past two centuries, and are today most commonly attended by nostalgia, cynicism, habit, and rootlessness. The first, nostalgia, is epitomized by the now banal songs that assault one beginning in November, such as "I'll Be Home for Christmas." Most of my clients have unhappy memories of the holidays. Or they have inordinate hopes for what can be repaired in their families and are always disappointed, or they are re-exposed at holiday time to those familiar dynamics lingering with them as pathologies, or they miss those who have died or from whom they have been estranged. Not the pretty picture one would expect based on the commercialized versions one sees on television. As with the fantasy of romantic love, perhaps the idealized family fails because we ask too much of it.

This very afternoon I sat with a man in his late forties, just back from a holiday visit to his extended family of origin. His scattered tribe had gathered from distant places and brought all their familiar madness with them. This time, Father was dead. Mother was now, finally, benign, half-senile, half the viper she once was. One brother was drifting through an alcoholic haze, another addicted to video games. One sister was having affairs with two different married men. Only one sister was willing to talk with my client about his life. I told him that he was a survivor, and that he was entitled to echo the words of Job, "I only have alone escaped to tell thee." He asked, "How many of my family can I save?" "One," I said, "and I am talking to him." Battered as he had been by their substance abuse, their continual denigration, and their use of fundamentalism to batter him with guilt, he had in turn found intimacy with others so risky that, lonely as he was, he had never managed to commit himself to another. So much for over the river and through the woods to Grandmother's house we go.

What then, in this current era, with its mobility, its transience, and its anonymity, might family be, and what is reasonable to ask of it? How is family to serve the task of soul building? While the family as institution was historically necessary for survival, the protection of children, and the transmission of cultural values, I am not always ready today to venerate the idea of family naively, for I have seen where family can also be a vehicle of tyranny, a sanctioned mode of constriction, and the inhibitor of developmental needs in the individual.

As we ask tough questions of marriage, so we are obliged to question the sentimentality surrounding family as well. I would be much inclined to ask of any marriage: "Do these persons grow as a result of being in this relationship; are they prone to the infantilization of each other; has this vehicle taken them toward the incarnation of their larger selves?" How many souls have died in marriage; how many have flourished? Marriage as a measure of commitment to working things through, to not bolting at the first discord is a noble investment of soul. Marriage as a security zone, an economic agreement, a way of pleasing Mom and Dad and winning societal approval is execrable and soul-damaging. So, too, we have to ask these same tough questions of family in order to see if the institution in each particular instance serves the soul.

We have to ask of family, "Does each person receive affirmation and support in being different, or is the price of being in the family conformity, the subversion of the agenda for individual growth that each of us brings into this world?" Just as each marriage has the right to ask fidelity, loyalty to the task of marriage, and the willingness to work at resolution of discord, so every family has the right to ask the full participation of each member in the life of the family. Yet all marriage and family therapists know that family interactions are typically arrayed around its most damaged member. Except in the case of a catastrophic illness of a child, that damaged member is inevitably one of the parents, or sometimes both of them in their pas de deux. When I hear someone waxing sentimentally about family, I often detect nostalgia for what family is supposed to mean, rather than what they experienced. Those who experienced loving, supportive relationships in their family do not need to long for what they experienced, for now they carry with them an internalized stable and empowering ground to their being.

Don't suppose that I am negative toward, or cynical in approaching, the idea of family. Yes, it's true that as a therapist I am almost daily in the thick of trying to repair some of the hurt that family has brought to the life of the person sitting before me. But in my own family I have also experienced, and been immeasurably enriched by, being loved beyond my merit, having others sacrifice on my behalf, and knowing there were those who worried for me as I made my bumbling way through the world. My point is rather that I believe nothing can escape the realistic scrutiny of consciousness. Of every family we must ask, "How well did the soul flourish here; how much life was lost through the failure of modeling a larger life, granting permission to follow one's own course, or was constricted by the glass ceiling of familial fears and limitations?"

We recall the opening sentence in Tolstoy's *Anna Karenina,* that all happy families are happy in similar ways, whereas unhappy families find their unique ways of being unhappy. Each parent in a family is someone's child, and is a refugee from some other family, which in turn was governed by someone else's child, someone who has long faded into inscrutable history. We ask too much of someone else's child to be a perfect parent, and yet their psychological shortfall creates the burden of history for them and their children, which invisibly governs lives for decades to come.

What would happen to our lives, our world, if the parent could unconditionally affirm the child, saying in so many words: "You are precious to us; you will always have our love and support; you are here to be who you are; try never to hurt another, but never stop trying to become yourself as fully as you can; when you fall and fail, you are still loved by us and welcomed to us, but you are also here to leave us, and to go onward toward your own destiny without having to worry about pleasing us." How history would change! How each child would be freed by the parent's courage to sacrifice his or her narcissistic needs in service to that child's joint but separate journey! How each parent would then be free to address the questions that life brings to him or her, without living through the child! How each child could explore, experiment, falter, and regroup, without shame, without self-derogation, armed always by the experience of love and support, which one may carry as food for the soul in the times of desolation and defeat that come to us all!

But few parents are able to give this unconditional love to their children, having not received it themselves. And history repeats itself in maddening ways. Still, who makes babies? Young people just trying to separate from their parents, flooded by the dynamics of their families of origin, and often overwhelmed by the tasks of taking on both domestic and professional lives. So often grandparents, who lack the energy to keep up with the young, have so much to provide because they have been able, over the decades, to come closer to themselves, achieve their maturity, and may offer example and affirmation to the grandchild. Other grandparents, having not taken on the journey, remain narcissistic, demanding as always, and are shocked to find themselves unwelcome in their children's homes. I recall one woman who came to me inflamed that neither of her adult sons would invite her to celebrate religious holidays with them. It was their duty, she asserted, and I knew in minutes why she was unwelcome. She had not grown up enough to contain her own emotional needs. The only difference now was that the sons, who had been prisoners in her house as children, were now able to maintain their homes as fortresses against her overwhelming neediness. No one is served in this arrangement; no soul is supported.

As Jung once claimed, in words which properly should haunt all parents, the greatest burden the child must bear is the unlived life of the parents: "What usually has the strongest psychic effect on the child is the life which the parents (and the ancestors too, for we are dealing here with the age-old psychological phenomenon of original sin) have not lived."* What he means is that where the parent has stopped growing, is intimidated by fear, is unable to risk, then that model, that constriction, that denial of soul will be internalized by the child. Subsequently, the child who becomes an adult parent is most likely to roll that pattern over into another family with another child. If not repeating the essentially limiting pattern, the child-become-parent will be driven to overcome that unlived life, while remaining defined by it, or will have fallen into some "treatment plan" such as alcoholism or workaholism to assuage the soul's deep, secretive wound. Without consciousness of these influences, repeating the pattern, or trying to make up for it, will prove compelling.

As the classical imagination intuited, and analytic and family

---

*Jung, *CW 17,* para. 84.

therapists trace, these patterns play themselves out over the generations and reproduce themselves in an infinite number of variations.
How can we be other than realistic about family when we see this
ancestral mythos playing out all around us? How can one not be offended by sentimentality and demanding expectations of family,
without looking at the causal agencies at work within them?

Typically at midlife, one's children are maturing, beginning to
test the waters, standing up to their parents, and forming closer ties
to their peers than to those who are only paying the mortgage on
the roof over their heads. The adolescent rebellion derives not from
a whim, however, whereby the child suddenly desires one day to be
obnoxious and oppositional. Rather, some large energy pushes
them from within, beginning the separation necessary to effect the
maturation of the child. The body is changing; social role expectations are enlarging; and all the while these proto-adults are flooded
by vacillating hormonal and emotional influences, ambivalence toward responsibility, and a contradictory desire for the comparative
safety they enjoyed as a child. No wonder they are difficult with
others, because they are so conflicted themselves. My advice to parents is always the same: Hold your breath—they will finally grow
and leave, no doubt blaming you for everything until they find that
their problems have followed them. Try to model the fuller life,
and such ethical standards as you wish to affirm; give permission to
them to be different, to be, that is, who they are; manifest unconditional love while maintaining standards, boundaries, and reasonable expectations. Despite their protests, your teenagers also need
these statements of limit desperately, which they can hardly provide
for themselves amid their internal adolescent anarchies.

When they do leave, it is quite appropriate both to weep and to
breathe a sigh of relief as a part of your life comes back to you. I
certainly wept when my children left, but I also knew that if they

had not gone, I would really have failed them as a parent. Thank goodness the British psychiatrist D. W. Winnicott coined the phrase "the good-enough parent." We are not capable of perfection, and if we were, what a terrible burden that would be for our children. Yet those stuck in that depressive state so often called "the empty nest syndrome" are paying for confusing their own development with that of their children. We can see how the unlived life, the narcissistic needs, the fears of abandonment in the parent can be transferred to the child, and when that child leaves, the parent remains stuck with what is unaddressed in his or her own life.

It seems so evident that not everyone should be a parent. Perhaps at best only half of us are mature enough to undertake the role of caring for a child, a task which legitimately asks considerable sacrifice of our lives. Such sacrifice is well compensated because the parent-child experience can be so rewarding, and can powerfully charge our own developmental agenda through relationship with the intimate other. Still, for many, productive parenting is a task of which they are incapable, for they are unable to differentiate their own sense of self from the child's. Until they can be wholly responsible for their own journey, and not project it onto the child, such parents are not grown-ups either.

How often we see the burden placed on the child to emulate the parent's values, achieve some goal, be it attending the right school, marrying the right person, finding the right career. If the child does otherwise, he or she frequently feels contaminated by failure or guilt, and if the child complies with the parent's stated or implicit choices, then he or she has been diverted into living someone else's life.

What a terrible dilemma facing a child: "Please my parents and die within, or live my separate journey and lose their love." Such deformation of the child's unique journey is a kind of spiritual violence. And how many only come to realize this spiritual deformation of themselves years after the critical choices were made. Such demand for compliance cannot in the end be called love, for it is a harm of the deepest sort to those whom we profess to love. Yet how many parents do you know who are strong enough to free their child, to love unconditionally, to give ready permission to the child to be who he or she is? How many children have the genuine security to pursue the life they desire to lead, and know they will be supported, even if the parent might prefer other choices? How many parents, desiring this loving freedom from their own parents, still could not in turn bestow it upon their own children? What remains unconscious in the parent, however well intended the parent is, is what will be transmitted to the child and remain a continuing obstacle to a fuller life.

Frequently, too, at midlife, as we have seen earlier, the growing gap between the parent's natural self and the acquired, provisional self that he or she assembled widens to the point that the parent's psychology, the marriage, the stability of the family is jeopardized. This is a painful time for everyone. As one adolescent said to me as his parents divorced, "I thought I was to leave home, not home leave me." The tears were just below the surface of his joking. Approximately half of our children will experience the fracturing of their family. In many cases this fracturing is helpful to them for it may remove some of the sources of conflict and discontent that trouble their days. In some cases, it merely makes matters worse. In all cases, there is a deep ache for the parents, both of them, for the fantasy of a stable, predictable home, and for the security it seemed to promise in an uncertain world. As one forty-year-old, who is herself a mother and a practicing therapist, said to me the other day, "I wish I could talk to my dad now." I replied that I certainly understood that desire. "I wish I could talk to mine, too. And I do.

Every day, and I think I know what he would say to me." I suggested that she talk to her dad, and that she might be surprised when she felt something within respond to her. No wonder there is such nostalgia for home. As the word implies from its Greek etymology, we feel a "pain for home," the home which is a respite from life's buffeting, a sanctuary in a conflicted and intimidating world. Robert Frost once said that home is where you go and they have to take you in. That is some small comfort, and sometimes that comfort disappears as well.

Similarly, parents in the second half of life experience the aging of their own parents, the diminution of their powers, and finally their death. Many a patient I have seen has felt freed, albeit with a sense of guilt, when their parent died, for they no longer had to try to please them. Others suffered guilt for things undone, words unspoken, relationships that now could never be repaired. Some suffered despair because now all hope for working things out was irrevocably gone. Still others suffered anxiety attacks as that tacit, invisible, protective layer that the parent always constituted, even through times of estrangement, was now removed, and with it the buffer against the inscrutable world. Now it is their turn to stand directly, nakedly, before the universe, next in line in the mortal procession. As Thomas Hardy once wrote to a friend of his, over the death of a mutual friend, "Now the thin red line is disappearing before us." His metaphor reminds one of the ranks of British soldiers marching off against an ultimately unconquerable foe.

Sometimes called "the sandwich generation," the person in the second half of life who is raising teenagers and caring for parents at the same time, however willing to do so, will find his or her own developmental needs neglected. The only way in which one can avoid resentment, a resentment that is seldom brought to the surface and therefore festers in the unconscious, is to try to do all the above caregiving more consciously. This means that one exercises caregiving responsibility for children and parents while also sequestering time for oneself. The long-term neglect of the self will manifest somewhere, perhaps in physical illness, or depression, or more commonly in that crankiness that is the leakage of repressed anger. The difficult task is to balance one's own need for personal freedom and personal growth with the needs of others. It is never easy to find such a balance, but the failure to try will ensure burnout, resentment, and depression, which is typically anger turned inward. However great one's sense of responsibility, no good fruit comes from such a contaminated tree.

If the aging parents never took responsibility for themselves as younger adults, they may prove especially demanding of their adult children. Why would we expect narcissistically oriented folks to suddenly grow up? As a matter of fact, rather than mellowing, most people become more of what they already were. Those who whine now will whine more; those dependent now will become children; those in denial now will blame others; those who neglected growing up and assuming full responsibility for their emotional well-being will expect you to carry it when their powers decline.

Double-burdened midlife adults, however functional they may be in other parts of their lives, will find it especially difficult to find a healthy balance with these demanding parents. They will either overcompensate by distancing themselves, or remain powerless to resist the parent's expectations and find it virtually impossible to draw self-protective boundary lines. If they say no to their children, or their parents, they are riven with guilt. But of what are they guilty? So frequently what appears as debilitating guilt is really a form of anxiety, the anxiety learned earlier in life as the cost of asserting oneself against the potentially abandoning or punitive parent. Parental complexes do not go away; they simply go underground and infiltrate other regions of the personality.

Many of our lives are governed by guilt. If one can be conscious enough to recognize that attending one's own needs is healthful and honest, and that drawing a boundary on someone else's demands is often necessary, then where is the offense? Guilt induction may be used by that dependent parent, even as they employed guilt earlier in life to control their offspring. If one is further conscious enough to recognize that guilt that compels compliant behaviors is really anxiety management, then perhaps one can stand up to the anxiety and be the only adult on the scene, the only one capable of knowing when enough is enough.

I have already told my adult children that I do not expect, nor do I wish, them to take care of me should I become dependent, or even mentally incompetent. I wish to free them for that approaching day, and wish them not to divert their lives, no matter how needful I might be. This freedom may take some courage on both our parts, but courage is always demanded of those who wish to live a life with some integrity. Just as they knew they always had my love, so I know that I always have theirs. We do not have to prove that through some compliant acts. Only in such freedom can love prevail, and genuine balancing of service to others and service to self be possible.

Recognizing that the family as institution often served many culturally cohesive functions historically—religious and cultural values preserved, children protected and nurtured—so it is also true that family is the chief arena for the pathologizing of the child. The healthy family certainly helps mediate and buffer the pathologizing experiences of the world, but the unhealthy family renders the child all the more vulnerable to them. Today, given our access to diverse values, our geographic mobility, and our economic, lifestyle, and cultural choices, the family has lost much of that cohesiveness and sometimes the child has suffered. However, lest we romanticize the past, wherein many souls were trapped in constrictive and abusive families, we are driven now to redefine the role of the family in the context of the care of the soul.

The modern family is more than a division of labor, though it is that, more than a protective environment for raising a child, though it is that, more than an economic unit, though it is that. The modern healthy family posits the nurturance of the individual as its highest value—all the individuals in that family. The family, as with the intimate relationship of the parents, is to support the growth and individuation of each of its members, parent and child alike. None is there to serve the narcissistic needs of any other. Each is there to support that growth and feel that support in return. This is not an idealistic view of the family. It is a functional goal, an eminently practical plan that serves the society by presenting it with more mature, evolved citizens. The more the family can be a holding environment in which differences are valued rather than suppressed in service to the anxieties of a parent, the more each person will flower. The more the family can tolerate divergence, and separate summonses to a larger destiny, the more each person will feel freed for his or her own growth. The more the family can affirm each member, child and parent alike, the greater the likelihood that love rather than perversions of power will prevail.

The lessons of history reveal over and over that the struggling family will be dominated by its least conscious parent. The parent's first task is personal growth, allied with the conscious assumption of responsibility for the growth of the others. When this growth prevails, each will be encouraged through outer modeling and inner assent toward individuation. In short, the modern family can be created, even if one has come from a family of origin in which these values were not affirmed. Why, if these matters become conscious, must one be bound to the iron wheel of repetition? By now, surely, we have learned what works for us, and what does not. Why can we not create the values in our familial settings that best serve the agenda of the soul? The modern family is one in which the divergent values of our separate souls are supported, valued, encouraged. Diversity is not just tolerated, it is affirmed as the radical gift of relationship. Conflict is mediated with accepting love despite disagreement, and no one carries the assigned burden of becoming something other than what they are. What a freedom that would be! What a place for the soul to thrive! Such a valuing of the soul is a rediscovery of one of the oldest truths, found in all the great religions, namely that one treats the other as one would wish to be treated in return.

To create a modern family requires maturity, courage, and personal risk, for as one accepts that one is on one's own, despite the presence of loving others, so we support each member in their solitary journey toward themselves as well. Then the family can be an agent of the soul, not a function of the unfinished business of the past.

Recently, a patient in his late fifties was flooded by the following dream themes in a single week. His family of origin had been dominated by his mother's emotional agenda and her will imposed on everyone else. First he dreamed that he was in New York City and that he was lost. The dream ended with a man who felt like his father (from whom he had wished more support and guidance when he was young) now giving him directions to help him find his way. He also dreamed of inheriting a blue Chrysler sedan, not unlike the one his father had once proudly driven. And in the third dream he was in the backyard of his childhood home, and while an adult in the dream, he was enjoying singing with other children and banging a set of drums. This play was interrupted by a phone call from his mother indicating that she had a problem and wanted him to come solve it for her. Once again, he was taken from the free field of play to serve his mother's demand.

Both of his parents are long deceased, yet they remain alive in his unconscious, and the unfinished business of the past persists. Is it not amazing that our psyche continues to bring these issues to the surface in order that we might continue to heal and to grow? Even in his sixth decade this man is still feeling the pull of the mother complex to take care of other people's problems, as he was forcibly enlisted in taking care of hers. He is still wishing to recover the childhood spontaneity and play, and to do so he was alerted by the dreams to the task of recovering more energy and insight from his father/mentor to guide him and to help compensate for the mother's psychic control.

How many of us will be capable of creating the soul-based family will be directly proportionate to how many of us have truly accepted responsibility for our own lives. Until we have assumed such a responsibility, we will lack the strength, and the consciousness, to support that process in others. Notice that the responsibility always comes back to us: we cannot ask of the other what we should do for ourselves. When we do what we need to do for our own enlargement, we serve others, and achieve the moral enlargement to support their development as well. Such relationship, whether the intimate marriage, or the effective family, is in service not to selfish agenda but to the Self, which is in turn in service to the soul. The ultimate test of the family is not whether it provides safety and predictability, but whether or to what degree each person can leave it, freely, and return, freely, as a larger person.

Chapter Seven

Career Versus Vocation

"I chose what I was told to choose:
They told me gently who I was . . .
I wait, and wonder what to learn . . .
O here, twice blind at being born."
David Wagoner, "The Hero with One Face"

HOW MANY TIMES have we asked the question: "What am I to do with my life?" So often the question is answered by the grim necessities of economic reality, or by the internalized voices of Mom, Dad, or culture. When I was a college professor, I heard student after student say, in so many words, "I want to study X, but Mom and Dad said that they would only help if I was a business major." When I suggested that they could find a way to pay for their own education, they resisted, and not because they were lazy, but because they feared the loss of parental approval. I always wondered if such parents really thought they were helping their children by enlisting them in their own security needs, and by ensuring that the children they professed to love would be miserable in their work lives. Freud once noted that two requisites are necessary for sanity: work and love. Surely he meant the right work, just as much as the right love.

By midlife the limits of what intimate relationship can provide are typically evident, as are the evolving roles in the family. For many, next in line as a carrier of projected satisfaction is career. More of our conscious energy is directed toward our work than any other venue. Stand on Main Street on a Monday morning and observe what mobilizes such frenetic, purposeful energy—economics, the unquestioned deity who dominates our culture. While all of us have to find a way to support our material existence, our work also carries a larger invisible burden, the presumption that it will provide our lives with meaning and energize our spirits. Sometimes it does. By midlife, however, many find that their work drains rather than energizes them. They suffer vague discomfort, find themselves bored, wistful, longing for something else.

The sham we perpetrate when we insist on our young people preparing for a lifelong career means that we wish them to arrive at midlife about as unhappy with their lives as their parents. I strongly advocate the study of a liberal arts curriculum for all persons, because we can always learn the tools of a trade on the job, and in this era of constant change we may practice many trades before we're done. Making a living is the easy part, but far more critical is what liberates us from the limits of our family and cultural history. What values, what ways of critical thinking and discerning evaluation do we possess to enrich our lives? What understandings of history allow us to escape its binding repetitions? What personality development and differentiation will we carry with us through all the days of our journey? These rich, intrapsychic companions will seldom if ever be served by the constricted aims of careerism and vocational narrowing. The liberal arts, however, contribute to the liberating art of a more considered, more thoughtful, more variegated sensibility, which in the end is necessary for more free choices.

As I reflect on those many troubled undergraduates, I have to wonder how those parents thought they were helping their children. As our paths crossed years later, almost none of those former students were in the field for which they'd prepared. Sometimes those parents wished their children to remain limited, though they would never openly confess as much, because they feared their child might acquire ideas alien to, which is to say larger than, the limited worlds of the parents. This is like the person threatened by new forms of art who says, "I know what I like." What he is really confessing is "I like what I know," or "I like what is familiar or comfortable to me." Friedrich Nietzsche once observed that the teacher is ill-served whose student does not surpass him. So our parenting is less effective if our children do not grow beyond us toward an enlarged vision of life's many possibilities for satisfaction of the soul.

Next in frequency to the minefield of intimate relationship, many persons enter therapy because they are facing a crisis of vocation. Perhaps they are unaware of that causal issue when they arrive, focusing on their emotional state rather than the source of it. So often the work of therapy, certainly not to be narrowed to career counseling, is to examine the forces that brought about the original choices, and to identify the affect-laden complexes that constrict a bold step and a change of life course.

Unexpectedly, I was led by a midlife depression to leave the world of academia for the world of the psychoanalyst. When I began therapy, I had no intention of such a career change, but in time, through therapy, I discovered that I had lost interest in much of the body of knowledge I had acquired and was more keenly focused on where it came from within us, what it activated for us, and what meaning it could have in the conduct of a larger life. I found that I was more interested in the symbolic life than the intellectual life—the symbolic engaging the soul, while the intellect engaged only the mind. These questions, and these distinctions, were not being pursued in academia, I found, but they were in depth psychology. Similarly, I longed for deepened, sustained conversation with adults with greater life experience, and with the questions that perplexed them, as opposed to the agitations of the late adolescent in most college classes. Beneath the wonderful task of learning, and the richness of the first half of my life, something disturbing was coursing, and demanding that I go deeper than the work of the mind alone, valuable as that is, and address the larger issue of meaning. A former mentor, Stanley Romaine Hopper, had once said to me, as a blessing, "May God grant your soul no peace." I came to accept as one benefit of that blessing the powers that moved me from a fine career to an even richer vocation.

Some of the most satisfying therapeutic work I have been privileged to conduct has focused on this powerful meeting point between work and vocation, career and *vocatus*. The Latin word is the source of our *vocation*, that is, our "calling," that to which the soul summons us. Yes, we need to earn a living, support ourselves and those who depend on us, but there is another call to serve, a summons to serve spiritual enlargement. And that is our true vocation. I think back on those college students laboring away, often in good faith, believing that their elders had their best interests in mind, that it would all add up to something in time. Many times I met them later, or people much like them, in the therapy room. Having achieved various successes in their work, they were beginning to tumble to the fact that we are more than economic animals. They began to suffer the difference between what we do and who we are.

Men in particular are conditioned to think of themselves as synonymous with their work. This is why layoffs, downsizing, and retirement almost always produce a profound depression in men after the first shock of anxious reckoning. The typical male will approach retirement as an opportunity to play a lot of golf. He may do so, but he will also hit a depression. Nothing has prepared him for re-visioning himself as something more than what he does. "A man's gotta do what a man's gotta do," we are told from childhood. Why? Because! Thus men cruise toward depression, a systemic loss of meaning, and an earlier death.

Women are usually far more emotionally differentiated—that is, they have a much keener awareness of their inner reality, have a range of friends who support their process of growth, and have already undertaken a wider range of personal exploration. Today's woman remembers a grandmother who suffered the horror of gender discrimination and had few professional choices. Her mother was caught in a changing world, whipsawed between motherhood and unprecedented opportunities for career. Today's younger woman sees models all around her, and is just as likely to define herself through her work as her grandmother did through home-making. But at least she has a choice today. Many choose to do both, and most struggle heroically to balance the world of domestic and professional responsibilities. And often without an understanding, and supportive, spouse.

At the same time, in speaking to women's groups, I have suggested that women look at men this way: if they took away their own network of intimate friends, those with whom they share their personal journey, removed their sense of instinctual guidance, concluded that they were almost wholly alone in the world, and understood that they would be defined only by standards of productivity external to them, they would then know the inner state of the average man. They are horrified at this notion. Having confused the wielding of outer power roles with identity and freedom, women assume that men have a better life. Certainly, they seem to have more outer choices. But most women do not recognize that men have fewer inner choices. And it is with the inner choices that we most define our lives, as almost all women know.

Whatever the source of the conditioning of our gender expectations, both women and men have a dual task today. We are called to be in the modern world in a way that is both productive and nurturing, *and* we are called to monitor our inner lives, which is the secret source of the wisdom for better choices. Both genders face the twin tasks: *nurturance* and *empowerment*. Empowerment does not mean power over others; it means that we experience, and can draw upon, our own capacities to choose our values and our mode of being in the world. We cannot ask a relationship, or the external, consensual world, to meet our deepest needs or give us a sense of personal worth. We cannot ask that our work satisfy all these needs without our having faced the reality of the soul's agenda in the process. In the end, we are alone responsible for our choices and for the acquisition of nurturing and empowering experiences in our life.

What was not modeled in the family of origin, what was not made available in the popular culture, becomes a personal task for each of us in the second half of life. Breaking the tyranny of history is a heroic enterprise and a task that confronts each of us, no matter how oppressive the past. I think of one man who was a gifted teacher. The weight of his family's history, and economic competition, obliged him to study and practice law for a number of years. He came to me in a depression in which he had repeated dreams of drowning or of struggling underwater. These images suggested that he was being flooded by his own unconscious. He described his daily life as spirit-draining, as if he were walking underwater all the time, even though he performed his work conscientiously. The burden of his summons was to discern over time how he had in fact left what he loved, in service to the expectations of parents and spouse, and grown miserable in turn. It took great courage for him to leave the more affluent world he had enjoyed to return to the far less lucrative field of teaching. He created his own charter school and flourished. His initial psychological task was to identify what sources had kept him from his vocation, chosen by the soul not by the parents, the culture, or the complexes he had internalized. His next task was to make the break, and carry the disapproval of family and spouse at this great economic change. One wonders how spouse and family could possibly believe that living with a depressed husband and son could be a virtue. If our work does not support our soul, then the soul will exact its butcher's bill elsewhere. Wherever the soul's agenda is not served, some pathology will surface in the arena of daily life.

We may choose careers, but we do not choose vocation. Vocation chooses us. *To choose what chooses us* is a freedom the by-product of which will be a sense of rightness and a harmony within, even if lived out in the world of conflict, absent validation, and at considerable personal cost.

Too often we remain in service to the agenda of the first half of life when the soul has already moved on to the agenda of the second. In the first half of life there is a place for ambition, for the driving powers of the ego, which compel us to overthrow our fears and to step into the world. As we have seen, the chief task of the first half of life is to build a sense of ego strength sufficient to engage relationship, social role expectations, and to support oneself. But we all fall into an overidentification with the ego and these various roles. No matter how successfully one has played out those roles, no matter how worthy they may be, and often they are not, ego identifications alone will not suffice to satisfy the soul over the long run. Even Plato recognized the risk of this confusion when, twenty-six centuries ago, he placed these words in the mouth of Socrates in the dialogue called *Crito:*

> *Citizens of Athens, aren't you ashamed to care so much about making all the money you can and advancing your reputation and prestige, while for truth and wisdom and the improvement of your souls you have no thought or care?*

As every depressed businessman or abandoned spouse or frustrated homemaker learns sooner or later, such investments as are imposed in the first half of life will ultimately betray one in the second, no matter how worthy their intent.

The ambitions of the first half of life are largely fueled by the charged images, that is complexes, one has obtained from one's family and one's culture, and often have very little to do with the support of one's personal destiny. While these powerful complexes may pull us out of dependency and into the world, they ultimately divert and distract consciousness from the care of the soul. Because of the grounding of these choices in complexes, with their origins in the disempowered past and their narrow frame of reference, lives are constricted and diminished rather than expanded. While we all must be weaned from the naive sleep of childhood, and the lethargy of dependence, the ego has a tendency to prefer security over development, and wind up with neither. What Paul Fussell has written of those in combat applies to the warfare of daily life:

The mind is not so capable as it pretends of producing trustworthy knowledge, so easily is it threatened by fatigue, pride, laziness, and selfish inattention. *

Usually, only when the symptoms of that split between security and risk are sufficiently painful, when we can ignore or medicate them no more, and when the ego's fantasy of sovereignty has been humbled will we begin to open to other possibilities.

Sadly, the majority of humanity remains trapped in the ego's identifications with such complexes, suffering from but also encouraging the avoidance of life's large possibilities. If the ambitions of youth, many of which we are able to achieve, truly served the soul, then we would see a lot more happy people. We would not have to deal with so much divorce, so much substance abuse, or prescribe so many antidepressants if the ambitions of the first half of life worked for the second half. Nor would we have evolved a culture that depends on ever-escalating sensations and daily distractions from its deep unhappiness. As Jung has concluded, "We cannot live the afternoon of life according to the program of life's morning—for what was great in the morning will be little at evening, and what in morning was true will at evening have become a lie." †

Ambition that drives the ego so often focuses on material things that even its achievement leaves us with the weariness and ennui of overindulgence. Why did Dante put the gluttons in their own circle of Hell? one wonders. Surely we all have overeaten at some point. Perhaps he was intimating that such unfortunates projected the nourishment of the soul onto matter, even as our culture has, and

*Fussell, *The Boys's Crusade,* p. 126.
†Jung, *CW8,* para. 787.

could only be deceived and dissatisfied in the end. (Pardon the pun, but they did not understand real soul food.) The lustful are in pits of flame as they proffer their bodies to burning hungers. Or, as a warning to our material age, the materialists get more matter than they ever wanted as they perpetually push boulders of dead weight about. Clearly, we should beware of what we ask for, for what we achieve may well prove an imprisonment. (Thoreau noted a hundred and sixty years ago that we had grown imprisoned by the abstractions we created. His longest chapter in *Walden* is titled, and decries our growing enslavement to, "Economics.") Dante timelessly imaged the soul's betrayal with his compelling portraits of those who devote their lives to the material and end with dissatisfaction. When we understand the exiled Florentines' analysis of his epoch, and see its parallels to our own, we ruefully confess with Milton:

Me miserable! Which way shall I fly
Infinite wrath, and infinite despair?
Which way I fly is Hell; myself am Hell. [*]

Or with Christopher Marlowe's Faustus: "Why this is hell, nor am I out of it."[†] Contrary to Sartre's bon mot, Hell is not other people; it is ourselves, constrained by the world we have constructed for ourselves, or allowed others to construct for us.

The sense of ennui, restlessness, sometimes even depression that comes from the achievement of one's ambitions, or the failure to achieve them, is the generally unwelcome invitation to disidentify with those goals. (Legend tells us that Alexander wept when he

---

[*]Milton, *Paradise Lost*, II, l. 73–75.
[†]Marlowe, *The Tragical History of Dr. Faustus*, l. 76.

reached the Ganges, for there was no further world to conquer. Apparently it had not occurred to him that there was also a world within of infinite scope and mystery.) Such an invitation requires a revolution in one's thinking, which will require no small amount of courage and sustained effort. "If I am not my roles, then who am I?" the ego will protest. Moreover, one will then be obliged to find a reference other than popular culture, for our culture will be of no help whatsoever.

In the second half of life the ego is periodically summoned to relinquish its identifications with the values of others, the values received and reinforced by the world around it. It will have to face potential loneliness in living the life that comes from within rather than acceding to the noisy clamor of the world, or the insistency of the old complexes. It will have to submit itself to that which is truly larger, sometimes intimidating, and always summoning us to grow up. It will need to live by verifications from within, not through acquiescence to the timidities of its time. And how scary is that, to each of us? No wonder the blandishments of popular culture are so available, so seductive. No wonder so few ever feel connected to the soul. No wonder we are so isolated and afraid of being who we are.

Yet, paradoxically, the very achievement of ego strength is the source of our hope for something better. We need to be strong enough to examine our lives and make risky changes. A person strong enough to face the futilities of most desires, the distractions of most cultural values, who can give up trying to be well adjusted to a neurotic culture, will find growth and greater purpose after all. The ego's highest task is to go beyond itself into service, service to what is really desired by the soul rather than the complex-ridden ego or the values of the culture. During the second half of life, the ego will be asked to accept the absurdities of existence, that death and extinction mock all expectations of aggrandizement, that vanity and self-delusion are the most seductive of comforts, and that the deep, infantile yearnings of childhood will forever go unsatisfied. How counterproductive our popular culture—with its fantasies of prolonged youthful appearance, continuous acquisition of objects with their planned obsolescence, and the incessant, restless search for magic: fads, rapid cures, quick fixes, new diversions from the task of soul.

The relinquishment of ego ambition, as fueled and defined by first-half-of-life complexes, will in the end be experienced as a newfound and hitherto unknown abundance. One will be freed from having to do whatever supposedly reinforced one's shaky identity, and then will be granted the liberty to do things because they are inherently worth doing. One engages in work because it is meaningful, and if it is not, one changes the work. If one has the strength to accept the necessary solitude of the journey, one can appreciate the gifts of friendship and relationship all the more for their precious moments in the face of transience and decay. One can experience the quiet joy of living in relationship to the soul simply because it works better than the alternative. This revisioned life feels better in the end, for such a person experiences his or her life as rich with meaning, and opening to a larger and larger mystery.

Vocation, even in the most humble of circumstances, is a summons to what is divine. Perhaps it is the divinity in us that wishes to be in accord with a larger divinity. Ultimately, our vocation is to become ourselves, in the thousand, thousand variants we are. How easily this invitation is confused with the ego's comforts and the ego's identifications with the charged complexes of our time. As all of the great world religions have long recognized, becoming ourselves actually requires repeated submissions of the ego. A good example of confusion in this area is how the word *personality* has been so debased. We talk of another person as having a good personality when we have no idea from the outside whether they are being true to themselves or not. We think the achievement of personality is validated when we are liked by others, or when we are well adapted to the world around us, but what does the soul have to say about all this? Being well adjusted is a trivial goal when one factors in the soul. The soul has no interest in social adaptation as such. It has as its goal the fulfillment of ends transcendent to the ego. Given that we are each unique, eccentric, when it is not a posture, as so often in adolescence, it is what we are bound to become.

The achievement of personality as a vocation always demands surrender, submission to the larger. The necessary task of the ego is to transcend its own interests, to say "Not my will but Thine," and to cooperate. "Unless you die [that is, the ego agenda dies] you shall not live." Jesus becoming the Christ and Gautama becoming the Buddha are cultural images of individuation, each with its own ethnocentric spin, but each a compelling paradigm. Such paradigms are not to be strictly imitated, for such would be repeating someone else's journey, a journey already brought to fruition. But each serves as a challenge for succeeding generations. The word *Islam* means "submission" to the transcendent. And the Hindu scriptures remind us of the peril of living someone else's life, rather than our own:

It is better to do your own duty
badly, than to perfectly do
another's: you are safe from harm
when you do what you should be doing. *

Familiar words, but we still need to revisit them, not once but over and over.

This service of the ego to the soul is precisely what Jung meant

---

* *Bhagavad-Gita*, III, 35.

by his idea of individuation. It is not ego aggrandizement; it is ego submission to the transcendent. Jung explains that this task is complex, life-long, and demanding:

> *The development of personality means nothing less than the optimum development of the whole individual human being. It is impossible to foresee the endless variety of conditions that have to be fulfilled. A whole lifetime, in all its biological, social, and spiritual aspects, is needed. Personality is the supreme realization of the innate idiosyncrasy of a living being. It is an act of high courage flung in the face of life, the absolute affirmation of all that constitutes the individual, the most successful adaptation to the universal conditions of existence coupled with the greatest possible freedom for self-determination.* *

How easily we are seduced into believing we are serving the soul when we are serving our own needs for ego reinforcement, comfort, security, and the approval of others. How easily we are seduced into rebellion against social norms in the belief that this is individuation, when it is merely self-indulgence masquerading as difference. In both cases, the seduction is so easily achieved because the ego wishes to serve itself and avoid service to the soul. What pulls us out of false rebellion or the easy torpor of the familiar is that the soul's protest has grown too painful to ignore. Then we are called to achieve our particular idiosyncrasies as our gift to the collective. In the end, the meaning of our life will be judged not by our peers or their collective expectations, but by our experience of it, and by whatever transcendent source brought us to it in the first place. As Jung notes,

---

*Jung, *The Development of Personality*, CW 17, para. 289.

True personality is always a vocation and puts its trust in it as in God, despite its being, as the ordinary man would say, only a personal feeling. But vocation acts like a law of God from which there is no escape. The fact that many a man who goes his own way ends in ruin means nothing to one who has a vocation. He must obey his own law. . . . Anyone with a vocation hears the voice of the inner man: he is called. *

Who among us has ever heard such advice from our elders, our culture? We prize something called "success" yet grow the more miserable for having achieved it. If our life ends in ruin, from a collective societal standpoint but has fulfilled the calling intended by the gods, it has been a life well lived. The great religious leaders whom we venerate almost always suffered rejection and persecution, yet faithfully served their *vocatus,* which is why we venerate them. The transient vacuities of our cultural icons—success, peace, happiness, and distraction—pale before the question of whether or not one experiences this life as meaningful. Moreover, the test of meaning is not a cognitive decision, so one should not suddenly quit this present life for any quixotic mission. Meaning is found, over the long haul, through the feeling of rightness within. No one can give that to us, although we may allow others to take it away from us.

Each of us has been enlisted in the fulfillment of our parent's wishes for us, in the proffered security of sanctioned cultural forms, gender roles, and such contemporary values as materialism, self-indulgence, and hedonism. And each of us has suffered, and continues to suffer, for so passively complying. When consciousness is strong enough to undertake the task of submission to and honest

---

*Jung, *The Development of Personality, CW 17,* para. 289, 300.

dialogue with the soul, then one will experience healing, and know the difference between job and calling, between career and vocation. We betray ourselves and our children when we do not make such a distinction. At such moments of surrender to the soul, we are in the presence of the divine, and in harmony with its intent. As R. M. Rilke expressed it through his literary persona nearly a century ago, "I am learning to see. I don't know why it is, but everything penetrates more deeply into me and does not stop at the place where until now it always used to finish. I have an inner self of which I was ignorant. Everything goes thither now. What happens there I do not know."* Such a person has repositioned the ego and is living in the latticework of eternity. Such a person has heard and is responding to the calling to become what the gods intended, the sacred *vocatus*.

Why, after all, are we here? One man who had been driven by his parents' ambitions came late in life to therapy in order "to learn how to be an ordinary person," that is, redeem himself from their complexes before he died. St. Augustine said we were here to love God and enjoy life. Kurt Vonnegut believes we are here to be the eyes and conscience of God. Jung, standing on the silent African veldt at dawn, watching the drifting rivers of animals moving in their timeless way, wrote that we are here to bring consciousness to brute being. Whatever theory speaks to the reader, surely we are called to become more fully what we are, in simple service to the richness of the universe of possibilities.

---

*Rilke, *The Notebooks of Malte Laurids Brigge,* pp. 14–15.

Chapter Eight

The New Myth Emerging from the Psychopathology of Everyday Life

"There was a time when the air was packed with spirits, like flies on an August day. Now I find that the air is empty. There is only man and his concerns."

Hilary Mantel, *Fludd*

AT THE TURN OF THE LAST CENTURY Freud published a book titled *Psychopathology of Everyday Life* wherein he noted that one does not have to visit a mental asylum in order to observe psychopathology; one can observe the machinations of the divided soul in the mechanics of ordinary life. In his book Freud detailed the implicit motives, walled off from consciousness, that interfere with the ego's choices and behaviors—producing slips, forgetfulness, and camouflaging of dangerous feelings through acceptable disguises. Freud, along with Jung and others, helped our age find a new vocabulary, observe meaningful motives in the confounding of consciousness, and, in short, helped us become psychological.

In this new century, we are driven to psychological inquiry, in large part because our social and religious institutions as well as great educational, technological, scientific, artistic, and humanistic accomplishments have failed to prevent the slaughter and madness of the last century. The great Crystal Palace, which in 1851 housed the first international celebration of the newly divine trinity of "Progress," "Machinery," and "Materialism," was by the next century a glass and steel hulk used by the *Luftwaffe* as a navigational point on their bombing runs over London. It seems that not only minor interferences of consciousness, but madness itself lurks beneath the veneer of civilization and the psychopathology of daily life. How else can we look at a world where we are bombarded by sensations, driven by addictions, medicated beyond accountability, agitated into constant motion, and further from our selves than ever, unless we begin to look psychologically, unless we begin to consider that there may be a deeper meaning after all?

Jung added the thought that we also *had* to become psychological, because the spiritually charged images that once linked humanity to nature and to the gods had eroded with the waning powers of tribal mythologies and sanctified institutions. If points of spiritual reference had disappeared for most, the modern sensibility had to look within in order to find the place where those collective images were generated. Perhaps the most important paragraph of the twentieth century was written by Jung when he raised some troubling inquiries:

> *We think we can congratulate ourselves on having already reached such a pinnacle of clarity, imagining that we have left all these phantasmal gods far behind. But what we have left behind are only verbal specters, not the psychic facts that were responsible for the birth of the gods. We are still as much possessed*

today by autonomous psychic contents as if they were Olympians.
Today they are called phobias, obsessions, and so forth; in a word,
neurotic symptoms. The gods have become diseases; Zeus no long
rules Olympus but rather the solar plexus, and produces curious
specimens for the doctor's consulting room, or disorders the brains
of politicians and journalists who unwittingly let loose psychic
epidemics on the world.*

The implications of Jung's observations reverberate throughout our culture and our personal lives. In examining that seeming oxymoron that a *god,* an eternal one, may die, he explains that the name attached to a form may fade, but the energy behind it has only been transformed and reappears elsewhere.

Cultures that sustain cohesive mythological images connect individuals to the four orders of mystery: the transcendent (the gods), the environment (their home in nature), the tribe (the social fabric), and their own psychological grounding (personal identity). History is not kind to such mythic images, however. The luster of the gods fades, and with it, the connecting powers that animated the culture's life and provided a sense of participation in a larger order. Where did the gods go then? Jung presciently asked. The primal energies that gave rise to the ancient *imago Dei* have not gone away; they have gone underground, and because unconscious, have a spectral influence even greater than when they were embodied as gods. The spiritual powers that the gods embodied, the invisible world made visible for a while, fall back into the human psyche and oblige humankind to suffer separation, alienation, and estrangement from them. Suffering this loss is then incarnated

---

*Jung, "Commentary on 'The Secret of the Golden Flower,'" *CW 13*, para. 54.

as personal or social pathology, because it is operating so unconsciously. This is the cultural form of the "psychopathology of everyday life" for our time.

All of the great religious traditions teach that to ignore the gods is the worst of sins. So it stands to reason that to ignore the energies they embodied sets loose autonomous dynamics that will prove dangerous to humankind. As Jung suggests, such depth energies—ignored, projected, turned into physical illness—have become neuroses, or worse. Phobias, obsessions, public moods that erupt in uncontrollable enthusiasms or violence are illustrations of the pernicious powers of these neglected forces.

This recent century, begun with so much hope for progress, for healing, for the solution of the ancient scourges of humankind, became the bloodiest in all history. The neuroses of individual politicians embodied and channeled the unconscious dynamics of the populace and led to more murderous "possession" than that ascribed to Satan during the Middle Ages. The distractions and enticements of popular media—newspapers, magazines, film, and most of all television—delivered much information but in a deadly mix of popular fantasy, collective projections, wishful thinking, obscure motives, and shadowy agendas that only dazzled intelligence.

What fills this existential void, this meaning gap, this time between the gods who have vanished and the gods not yet arrived (as Heidegger put it) is the stuff of our daily life. Where our ancestors had living mythologies, we believe that we have transcended such a need and therefore stand naked and vulnerable before the raw, sometimes destructive powers of our nature. Our hubristic belief that we are in control of ourselves and nature only makes us more unconscious of what is at work within us. Our ancestors could seek the relief of their personal and tribal problems by asking which god had been offended and then offering propitiation to reestablish right relationship with that god. To say that one has offended Aphrodite today would be thought mad. In an earlier era, one would have needed to petition the goddess's grace through acts that expressed a greater mindfulness of her work. Today we use psychiatric terms such as *paraphilias* to designate so-called "pathologies of desire" and believe we have contained and controlled whatever we have named. In fact most modern psychiatry and psychology is limited to nosology (naming), etiology (causality), behavioral modification, and pharmacological alterations. There is little engagement with the purposeful character of symptoms, or a reflective, prolonged, and respectful consideration of what wounded energies need redress. What healing can occur when we know so little about which depth dynamics have been offended or denied within? Cultures that had dynamic metaphors for these energies, and rites of connection—what we dismiss as mere mythology—were far better able to address and heal the soul than the combined forces of modern psychiatry and pharmacology. A culture without living mythological access to the mysteries is a culture in trouble.

On the eve of the world's descent into the maelstrom of World War II, Jung, speaking to the Guild for Pastoral Psychology in London in 1939, noted that humankind poorly tolerates the loss of a mythological connection to the centering energies of the cosmos. We then grow more susceptible to ideologies that promise easy solutions, black-and-white values, and we often require a palpable enemy "out there" to hate since that allows us to avoid self-reflection. In his time, Jung noted, the world had arranged itself into the competing, one-sided ideologies of Marxism and fascism. In such mass movements individual sensibility is easily swallowed, moral nuance forgotten, and responsibility for individual choice avoided. A third group, he noted, internalized this mythological crisis and suffered the conflict as personal neurosis. Only the last group offered hope for civilization, and only then if they could find the meaning of their suffering and finally align their spiritual compass with the purpose of the soul.

Today, Marxism and fascism have been replaced by only slightly subtler but no less spiritually seductive ideologies such as materialism, hedonism, and narcissism. This latter triumvirate mobilizes the spirit of most moderns, but in the end betrays them by failing to connect them to what is healing or innately satisfying. Without a "vertical" sense of participation in divinity, humankind is condemned to a sterile, "horizontal" existence, circling its own absurdity and ending in its own annihilation. (No metaphor more aptly dramatized the horizontal entrapment of modernism than Beckett's *Waiting for Godot,* with his two tramps by the wayside, with nowhere to go, really, and nothing to do, really, and yet afflicted by awareness.) Being connected to the mystery only comes, Jung suggests, "when people feel that they are living the symbolic life, that they are actors in the divine drama. That gives the only meaning to human life; everything else is banal and you can dismiss it. A career, producing of children, all are *maya* [illusion] compared with that one thing, that your life is meaningful."* How can a pill, or a new car, or even a new lover ever provide such meaning as that which restores depth to our lives?

In addition to materialism, hedonism, and narcissism, we must add two other popular ideologies: fundamentalism and the culture of sensation. Since World War II, only the fundamentalist portion of the religious spectrum has grown, precisely because of the general ambiguity into which our age has fallen. What might be embraced as the greatest freedom to choose in human history instead stirs anxiety in many. Fundamentalism, be it religious or political or

---

*Jung, *The Symbolic Life, CW 18,* para. 630.

psychological, is an anxiety management technique that finesses the nuances of doubt and ambiguity through rigid and simplistic belief systems. If I can persuade myself that the world is perpetually founded on the values of another, culturally limited, less conscious age, then I do not have to address the new subtleties of moral choice, the emergent capacities of women, the ambiguities of gender, sexual identity, and preference, and the horrors of nationalism, factionalism, and other tribal mentalities.

Of course people have a right to affirm any set of values that they have sincerely, experientially tested, but fundamentalism is a form of mental illness that seeks to repress anxiety, ambiguity, and ambivalence. The more mature the personality structure, the greater the capacity of the person, and the culture, to tolerate the anxiety, ambiguity, and ambivalence that are a necessary and unavoidable dimension of our lives. A culture that is immature, and believes its values besieged, will fall back into a siege mentality, a sentimental nostalgia for a simpler time, for simplistic black-and-white value judgments, and will project its own shadow by vilifying others. The saddest example of this regressive agenda plays out in our current national drama. America and its civic leaders fumbled the opportunity to open dialogue with the nation and its policies, and generate a good faith exchange with the rest of the world, after the events of 9/11. If one wonders "why do they hate us so," then one should be prepared to ask "them," and listen openly, nondefensively, and intelligently to what they have to say. Such opportunities renew themselves, however, and one may hope for a greater capacity to tolerate differences and ambiguity in the future, lest we become the garrison state we have historically resisted. Such a capacity for genuine conversation with the world will, however, require as much maturation in the nation as it requires for individuals who hope to live in reciprocal relationships.

The culture of sensation is similarly seductive and no doubt has even more adherents than fundamentalism. We are wrapped around by pop culture. News that runs twenty-four hours creates info junkies. Local newscasts find the goriest accident, the most salacious scandal, the most paranoia-stirring threats to public health to serve up for breakfast, for dinner, and to send us toward turbulent slumber at bedtime. Transient nonentities are catapulted to fame, followed by cameras throughout the course of their ordinary days, and described with hyped banalities of the unexamined life. Romances, survival contests, sensationalized disease reports, corporate greed—all feed the ever-increasing lust for sensation. Apparently, where one has no personal life, no depth of character, one must have an artificial life, with someone else's values.

A life, or a culture, based on sensation has no choice but to continually escalate the sensations, for we quickly grow desensitized to their incessant drumbeat and their failed promise. A modern Dantean descent into Hell might be defined as taking a good thing, asking too much of it, exhausting it, and being left with only it.

Stuck as we seem to be with the limits of our sensations, and lacking a relationship to our own reality, we now are left to create the artifice of "reality TV." How much more neurotic can a culture get than to construct a wholly vicarious life? Where we relinquish hope for connection, for depth, for meaning, we find only sensation, and therefore we must do more of it, more often. We have a familiar, ugly name for this phenomenon, and it is *addiction*. The culture of sensation can only produce addiction and broken hopes, just as fundamentalism can only produce rigidity and a very large shadow, as so many clerical scandals illustrate. Few if any of us are free of addictions, if we look closely enough, and none of us are free of broken hopes and anxiety-generating issues. The more we seek to control these aspects of our humanity, the further we drive from consciousness the essential mystery in which we walk. Moreover, neither the fundamentalist culture nor the sensation sensibility will ever bring dignity and depth to suffering, move individuals to larger spiritual engagements, or bring the meaning that arises most from the larger mysteries of life, which will always resist and transcend our desire to control them in service to our own gratification.

When we examine the psychopathology of our daily lives, we find two personal and cultural forms prevailing: *addictions* and *paraphilias*. Addictions are found in our reflexive, frequently unconscious anxiety-management behaviors. It is too simple to label the more overt forms of such management strategies, such as drug abuse, as addiction and let it go at that. All of us have daily rituals, the unconscious motive of which is the warding off of some supposed evil. We have television programs, computers, the internet to plug into, reflexively, to assure ourselves that the world of diversions is out there, predictably, and that we are wired to it. We flee solitude, the only serious treatment for loneliness. We avoid dialogue with ourselves, the only person present in all scenes of our drama. We dismiss dreams, the ongoing commentary offered by the Self as to just how things are going and how they might be better. We ignore our history, with its many clues as to the autonomous agents that are making those self-defeating patterns for us. Our common existential journey begins in an initial traumatic separation that gives us birth and consciousness, yet provides the ground for later addictions, with their potential for anesthetizing consciousness. So we long to be plugged in again.

Accordingly, all addictions have as their motive anxiety reduction through some form of connection with the "other." Given that our human condition is based on separation, from the womb, from the mother, from others, and from our own mortal thread, we can understand how deeply programmed such existential anxiety is for us.

This anxiety is further deepened by the loss of connective mythologies, those charged images that link us to the gods, to nature, to each other, and to ourselves. Cut us off from those images, which has been the grim trend of the last four centuries or so, and the anxiety can only increase. The point is not to judge addictions, but rather to pragmatically figure out over time how ineffective they are for truly connecting. Moreover, they actually misdirect conscious investment in the agenda of the soul. The task for each of us will be found in an increasing capacity to bear our lives without diversion and to suffer the soul's distress until we are led where it wishes to take us.

Without more conscious suffering, we can never find depth or meaning, never really grow, and never really change our lives. But just how attractive is a philosophy and a psychology that embraces suffering rather than offering a ready escape from it? No wonder our culture is so addiction bound, and vast industries have risen to assist us in the management of the anxiety of disconnection. Still, only one who is willing to face the pattern of distraction found in his or her addiction, and suffer our common wound more consciously, to really feel what he or she is already feeling, has any hope of growth. A fundamental truth of psychology, from which our ego repeatedly flees, is that it is most commonly through suffering that we are stretched enough to grow spiritually. The road of continuous ease results in the circular trap of addiction. We remain bound to the repetitive wheel of the same old, same old, without respite, and without hope.

Similarly, paraphilias have us in their grip. From the Greek word for *love*, paraphilias have to do with the many manifestations and modulations of desire, some of which the culture sanctions and some of which it forbids. *Desire* itself derives from a Latin nautical term which means "of the star." To have desire is to have a vector, an intentionality, a direction. To lose desire is to be as adrift as a mariner who has lost the guiding star across otherwise trackless seas. How frequently our culture has confused "desire" with "love." The relentless desire for satiation, desire for escape from struggle, desire for flesh, for success, for any sweet taste in the mouth—all may come at the expense of fealty to the soul. All may imprison the person in the narrowest of cells. This is not to suggest that asceticism equals love of the soul. Sometimes the soul wishes to savor flesh, good food and wine, and the raucous, raunchy, erotic, ecstatic joie de vivre that serves the life force—Eros. The soul desires ever-greater life, and what it desires may have little to do with any of our ego's schemes—for satiation, for peace, for release from struggle and conflict. The program of the soul will seldom be found in flight, but rather in places of spiritual risk and psychic danger—all in service to larger life.

The paraphilias of our time, disturbances of desire, include sexual addiction, pornography, substance disorders, and toxic consumerism, which offer to fill the empty places of the soul. As with addictions, these forms of distorting desire are not to be morally judged; they are to be evaluated as to their effectiveness in feeding the soul what it really wants. The soul's program will vary from person to person, and sometimes from moment to moment, but unheeded consciously, it will be projected onto something outside, not unlike what feeds the gluttonous in Dante's *Inferno* or what is found on the extensive shelves of romance novels in bookstores. Diverted love will be found in the advertisements with which we are deluged, with their hidden promises of release, healing, transformation. It will be found in the legislation that promises Homeland Security without understanding the necessity of an open society remaining open. It will be found in the treacle served up by televangelists, feel-good therapists, and spiritual quacks who promise healing without suffering, release without compensatory cost, and salvation without first visiting Hell. Such brokering of love is unworthy of that force; it has kept humankind clinging to earth for millennia and for sure is a devaluation of the rigors that the soul asks of us.

Add the various eating disorders to the list of cultural neuroses, for they, too, are inadequate responses to, or materializations of, the soul's invitation to drink the cup of life to its dregs. Whether stuffing our spiritual hungers with matter, or seeking to control our ingestion of life through various anorexias, we are driven further and further from the soul through our spiritual projections onto food.

Add as well what a century ago William James called "the bitch goddess: Success." Whatever success is, however defined by the neurosis of the moment, what the ego and the collective culture define as success and what the soul asks of us will seldom have any relationship to each other. We can drive ourselves to be successful and realize later that we are further and further from ourselves, the more so as the goal of success has driven our efforts. If we are such fleeting mortal ephemera, what is fame but a delusion of the ego, an attempt to soothe its existential insecurity? What is success, if we sacrifice others, or the deepest parts of ourselves, to its illusory achievement? What is success if the soul ceases to be our ally?

"Success" has become an unquestioned cultural icon. The difference between an icon and a symbol is that the former contains only its own limited meaning, while the symbol points beyond itself toward a larger realm of mystery. Wouldn't a woman who paid attention to her dreams, and tried to adopt choices based on their direction and value system, be successful, even if she were departing further and further from the approval of her family? Wouldn't a man, being humbled by the power of the encounter with the soul, and seeking to learn what it had to say to him, be successful, even if it meant leaving the value system collectively adopted by his clan? In theological metaphor, would not success be embodied by the person who became what God intended rather than what the ego desired or the culture approved? As T. S. Eliot once observed, in a world of fugitives, the person who is headed in the right direction will appear to be running away.

The erosion of tribal life and of linking mythic systems has more and more melted the glue that held us together. We sit now behind locked doors, in front of glowing cathode tubes, and robotically rehearse our common cultural conditioning. This disconnect has occasioned more and more so-called personality disorders. What were once called "character disorders," moralistically implying a failure of character, then became "personality disorders," as if all failed adjustments are pathological, not the fault of the society that imposed damaging values. Psychodynamic therapists are more inclined today to describe these patterns as "disorders of the Self," suggesting an interruption of the nurturant ego-Self axis.

When a person has experienced overwhelming trauma, and/or has lost connection with the healing energies of the tribe without, or of the ego-Self axis within, then he or she will have a tendency to identify with that wound and make choices out of that limiting, constricted imagination. Additionally, recourse to violence, racism and bigotry, regressive behavior of any type, always derives from a constricted imagination. When we are stuck in history, or the provincial ministry of our complexes, the imagination is always stunted. "The fallacy of overgeneralization," by which our lives circle around the old complexes as splinter mythological systems, is only treated by the enlargement of vision such as comes from compensatory experience, insight, and the risk of the new. So powerful are the archaic images of our personal and cultural history that their autonomy in our lives is assured as long as we do not make them conscious. Added to this power is the reinforcement from our popular culture, which has grown more and more homogenized, more and more narcissistic and infantilizing, and which bombards us with images daily. Inevitably, our creativity is thwarted, and the range of our choices limited. From such deficit, we are condemned to the same dreary cycle of repetitive behaviors, failed "treatment plans," and faux tribalism.

We can be enlarged only when we are exposed to a wider range of images, such as are provided by education, travel, learning, dialogue with others, and the soul's frequent visitors. As the Persian poet Rumi wrote of the guests that our soul sends to visit the house of the ego:

> *This being human is a guest house,*
> *Every morning a new arrival. . . .*
>
> *Be grateful for whoever comes,*
> *because each has been sent*
> *as a guide from beyond.* *

Lest we sentimentalize Rumi, let us remember that some of those "visitors" will be experienced as counter to our culture, defeats to our fantasy of psychological omnipotence, and incursions into our ego's plan for security. Yet from doubt and defeat, much more is to be learned than from compliance with what the ego or tribal culture has already privileged, ratified, and institutionalized.

---

*Rumi, "The Guest House," *The Essential Rumi*, p. 109.

Living Myths

Those myths that served antique societies, linked them to the various orders of mystery, were not created by the conscious mind, nor were they committee reports. They arose out of primal encounters, whether in the collective tribal experience or in the privacy of personal awe. These encounters might occasion joy or terror or wonder, but they always opened a person or a tribe to mystery. The image, whether of deity, material event, or emotional whirlwind, that arises out of such an encounter is a link to the mystery. In time, of course, the ego tends to focus upon the image and not the energy that gave it life. Once the image becomes an artifact of the ego, chances are great that the initial energy has already left it to go elsewhere, as Jung observed of the gods of Olympus. The gods do not die, he said, but the energy leaves their image; yet our clinging to the image, the old belief or dogma, causes the affect-laden experience to lose its power for us. A person who dreams of possessing a new object, or position in life, in order to provide some large measure of happiness, inevitably ends in dissatisfaction. The vitality of the object or position, which unbeknownst to the person is an unconscious aspect of his or her own unaddressed agenda, has been spent, and has autonomously reentered the unconscious, where it awaits a new goal upon which to project.

Our ego tendency to seize upon the image and hold it captive to our agenda for security leads to the oldest of religious sins, the sin of idolatry. The living mystery is hardened into a concept, a belief rather than an experience, and loses the vigor of the mystery. Then one is left only with the artifacts of belief (which need repeatedly to be reinforced, as at religious "revivals" or pep rallies) but not the living experience. We worship strange gods, all of them failing in the end. We transfer the need for the experience of the transcendent onto persons, objects, and causes, and wonder why they disappoint. When one has had an authentic engagement with mystery, it is neither definable nor explicable nor transmittable to others. As Jung explained in a letter:

> *God: an inner experience, not discussable as such but impressive. Psychic experience has two sources: the outer world and the unconscious.* All immediate experience is psychic. *There is physically transmitted (outer world) experience and inner (spiritual) experience. The one is just as valid as the other. God is not a* statistical *truth, hence it is just as stupid to try to prove the existence of God as to deny Him. . . . People speak of* belief *when they have* lost *knowledge. Belief and disbelief in God are mere surrogates. The naive primitive* doesn't believe, he knows, *because the inner experience rightly means as much to him as the outer. He still has no theology and hasn't yet let himself be befuddled by booby trap concepts.* *

The collective fantasies of the modern world are that the old myths can be revivified by acts of will, or that by acts of will new myths will be generated. While we have suffered the loss of the old, tribal myths, by and large, we cannot manufacture new ones—though, for sure, many have tried. Utopian visions appear from time to time and never succeed in the test of real life, for they come from ego-driven "good intentions" only, not the energies that give rise to the gods.

Such images as move our tribe, consumerism for example, betray

---

*Jung, *Letters*, Vol. II, p. 4.

the depth that lies within all of us. Marxism was a rational, well-intended, humanitarian effort to redress the grievous inequities in our economic systems, but it was doomed to failure because it underestimated the irrational factors in humankind and the insurgency of self-interest, and because by materializing values, it underestimated humanity's need for transcendence. In short, seeking to banish superstition, Marxism manufactured surrogate superstitions, creeds, ideologically generated calls to service and sacrifice, and required totalitarian oppression to enforce its ignorance of the human soul. Similarly, modern consumerism is a contrived, self-looping system based largely on artificially generated fantasies of demand. It may bring many comforts to the body but seldom to the soul, and in the end, as everyone knows, it only distracts and disappoints.

Another way of putting this is that when the gods are not experienced inwardly, they will be projected outwardly. The energy we project onto the things of our world—objects, causes, ideologies, relationships—possess a kind of autonomy, for they momentarily carry spirituality for us. As Jung warns, "Our consciousness only imagines that it has lost its gods; in reality they are still there and it only needs a certain general condition in order to bring them back in full force."*

We need only think of the terrifying powers of the mob mentality, the frenzied masses at a political rally or a rock concert, to see how easily this energy is projected onto external figures or images. Whenever the level of conscious attention is lowered, perhaps in times of personal or cultural crisis, the tendency of the ego to project what is not addressed in the inner life increases its fascination

---

*Jung, *Letters*, Vol. II, p. 593.

with the outer. There is an old term for the power that such figures or images then have upon us; it is *bewitchment*. We are bewitched by the almost supernatural character of the psyche's energy whenever we encounter it, whether within or without. So we are susceptible to bewitchment by shiny objects, political and commercial entreaties, slick theologies and New Age spiritualities, precisely because they speak to something deep within us without requiring us to own our own part in them, or pay the price of consciousness and personal responsibility to truly make them ours.

To free ourselves from bewitchment we are obliged to begin to *read the world psychologically.* What this means is that we go the next step, beyond fascination, or psychic possession, and ask: "What is this touching in me?" "Where does this come from in my history?" "Where have I felt this kind of energy before?" "Can I see the pattern beneath the surface?" "What is the hidden idea, or complex, that is creating this pattern?" "Is there something promising magic, Easy Street, seduction, 'solution' here, when, as we know, life will always remain raggedy and incomplete?" And, always; "Am I made larger, or smaller, by this path, this relationship, this decision?" If we work at them, we will always find the answers to these questions. If we work at them, we will find we are living our life more responsibly, and that brings much satisfaction no matter how difficult the choices. However, one further question nags: "Do we really want consciousness, or would we rather enjoy bewitchment?"

One client, whom I recall with great fondness, in repeatedly answering the call of others, found herself frequently exhausted, depressed, and angry at feeling used. Her family of origin had unwittingly demanded that she sacrifice herself to the needs of a wounded parent, as is frequently the case, and this core idea had become the dominating attitude of her life. The unconscious fantasy of the child is that in taking care of the other, perhaps fixing them, the child guarantees that other will be there to take care of them. Of course, this happy outcome never occurs. Only when she realized that saying no to the demands of others would not produce catastrophic abandonment, did my patient begin to venture out into unknown territory, following her own nature and her soul's desire. By "reading" her patterns, and her symptoms, she began to stand up against the compelling dogma derived from childhood experience, which had governed her life, binding her to her history and making her miserable in the present.

The "enemy" we face in situations like this is never the "other"; it is the power of history, which infiltrates the platform of the present upon which consciousness might make other choices. In her dreams my patient was repeatedly visited by a woman whom she knew to be herself, though the appearance was different. This woman would stare plaintively at her and then turn away. The dreamer always felt a pang at this turn, for she knew she was losing something precious. This strange visitation was, of course, her soul's invitation to embrace this "other," this woman who was herself. How can we not embrace, finally, what is most dearly ours? Since we do not consciously make these dreams, how can we not come to trust that agency within, which brings such healing images to us?

This task of becoming psychological in our outlook is very difficult, for it asks a leap of faith, an act of existential trust. It asks nothing less than *to intuit and to value the invisible world that courses beneath the physical*. Since most moderns are bereft of the vital tribal images that served the antique age, we are left only with the seduction and limitations of the tangible world. Yet, for us, as for our ancestors, the individual human psyche is the arena in which both outer world and inner world meet and are experienced. Whatever is real for you is a psychological event, an experience that only you can validate and honor. Yet how easily the timid, fragile, insecure ego is seduced—by fear, by the promise of rescue, by seductive blandishments, by guarantees of instantaneous transformations—away from this immense personal resource. Our culture offers these divertissements to us all the time in our commercial, political, and religious rhetoric. Highly paid people study our psyches in order to persuade us, to manipulate us, even to create values that serve their special interest. And we wish them to seduce us. It is so much easier to be seduced than to assume sole responsibility for our consciousness, for ourselves. This is the deepest psychopathology of daily life—the routine flight from the summons of the soul.

Reading the world psychologically begins with reading our own lives in a more reflective way, discerning the hidden motives, the old agendas, the replicative patterns, the unlived life projected onto others, and so on. None of us can be conscious all the time, or even much of the time. So much of life is on automatic pilot, and we pay for this loss of consciousness over and over in the sabotage of relationships, in our self-stultifying attitudes, and in the shameful power we routinely bequeath to others in managing our values.

Being psychological means that one will need to find the new, the personal myth from within. It will not be found in an external ideology or institution, however benignly intended it may be, for those sources which may have served the past have too often grown self-perpetuating, preserving their own priesthood or corporate leadership, and rigidifying an original primal experience into dogma and formal principles. One will find, sooner or later, that the *pneuma,* or spirit, has long departed those ideas and places. Nor will right thinking or rational principles of conduct and behavior satisfy the soul. We will not be spared our anxieties, moments of deep despair, and appointments with the fellow with the scythe at the door. No amount of ritual prayer, healthful practices, or salutary motives will plumb the soul's depths. Quite likely, the soul will speak to us at least some of the time in ways we do not want to hear. But it is speaking, always, and tells of us of that invisible world, which informs, moves, and shapes the visible world.

The greatest gift of depth psychology is returning to us again the possibility of a deep dialogue with this mystery. To be psychological does not mean that one must enter therapy, although, with the right person, that decision can be transformative. It does mean that one ask, much more radically than ever before, what is going on beneath the surface. We are all susceptible to being bewitched by surfaces, but the energy that moves the whirling constellations, that moved the great myths, and moved our ancestors still moves within you.

Being psychological means being responsible for questioning surfaces until the energic sources beneath are revealed; being modern means being wholly responsible for meaning, choice, conduct. We are here such a short time. Before we depart, it would be nice to think that we reconnected with our journey, that we found *our* myth again, the one truly worth serving. The emergent myth from amid the psychopathology of daily life is already forming in the dream you will dream tonight, in the intuition that comes to you at the hour of the wolf, and in the mystery that is forever renewing itself through the life of each of us.

Chapter Nine

Recovering Mature Spirituality in a Material Age

"Much about good people moves me to disgust, and it is not their evil I mean. How I wish they possessed a madness through which they could perish, like this pale criminal. Truly I wish their madness were called truth or loyalty or justice; but they possess their virtue in order to live long and in a miserable ease."

Friedrich Nietzsche

"Fantastic sea gods stroll at the edge of the world
Crusted with salt and brilliant as fishes."

Sophia de Mello Breyner, "Beach"

RECENTLY I WAS ASKED to speak with a group of brain tumor patients and their family caregivers. In the face of catastrophic illness one inevitably feels victimized, feels a loss of autonomy, and feels depersonalized by being adrift in the vast and complex medical and hospital system. One is not only in medical jeopardy, but one's sense of self is radically assaulted, and usually diminished. So I acknowledged to this group the inevitability of these feelings, along with the unavoidable visitations of anger, grief, fear, and depression. Many nodded their heads, perhaps because someone was validating their experience rather than offering platitudes. I also discussed some of the ways in which they might begin to recover a sense of personal autonomy, and to reconnect with deepened meaning in their journey. I described dream work, the use of the expressive arts, and meditation as means of reconnecting with the voice that is large within each of us. They all seemed grateful for the acknowledgment and the reframing of their circumstances. However, the first comment after my remarks had to do with the need to pray for a medical miracle. This thought is quite natural; yet what I sensed was this person's resistance to the very idea of an inner life and a personal authority. Her orientation was wholly directed toward rescue from without. Of course there are miraculous events in medicine, every day, but we also remain mortal, every day.

As I drove away, I reflected not only on those brave souls, and their difficult struggle ahead, but on how distanced this one woman wished to remain from the possibility that she might be more responsible for her life than she thought. The recovery of a mature spirituality is one of the most difficult tasks of our time. Not only because there are so many banalities and so many distractions, but because we flee from growing up and being wholly responsible for our experience. The sad legacy of having been small and afraid continues to disempower and infantilize.

How different was Jung's puzzling but challenging religious affirmation that especially in the traumatic, the work of the gods may be seen. He wrote, "[God] is the name by which I designate all things which cross my willful path violently and recklessly, all things which upset my subjective views, plans and intentions and change the course of my life for better or worse."* How much more this perspective asks of us—namely, to move from victimhood to participation in the meaning of our journey, and to recognizing that in

---

*Jung, *Letters*, Vol. II, p. 525.

all events, even the traumatic, there is an invitation to greater engagement with depth, with mystery.

In the second half of life there are two major tasks. The first is *the recovery of personal authority.* What does this mean? As we recall, naive and dependent as we all began, we were obliged to try to meet our needs, indeed in some cases even to survive, by adapting to the conditions imposed by our environments—the family of origin, socioeconomic conditions, cultural imperatives, and the like. Each adaptation required the sacrifice of instinctual truths, personal needs and predilections, and the desires of the soul. The daily repetition of necessary adaptations leads to the progressive positing of authority outside ourselves. Yet, over time, the external authorities shift, are internalized as complexes, and begin to govern from within. Even the most overtly powerful among us are subject to these inner tyrants. We believe ourselves conscious agents, when in fact much if not most of the time we are subject to these authority clusters derived from the fortuities of our personal history and the variegated values of our time.

The recovery of personal authority is a daily task imposed upon all of us by the soul. Usually, we will try to avoid such soul demands as long as we can by repressing the agenda of the soul as long as we can, at least until the suffering becomes intolerable to ourselves or those around us and we are obliged to pay attention. As each of us has been conditioned to experience authority as external to us, and has internalized such admonitions and agendas and reflexive responses as our own complexes, so it proves difficult, even intimidating, to take on the task of personal authority. Does the fish know it swims in water? Do we understand that we swim through a medium of reflexive perceptions and responses, all tied to history and not to an outside authority? It is highly unlikely that we will question the field of influence, with its tacit authorities, until the discrepancy between expectation and outcome is no longer deniable.

What constitutes "personal authority"? Stated most simply it means, *to find what is true for oneself and to live it in the world*. If it is not lived, it is not yet real for us, and we abide in what Sartre called "bad faith," the theologian calls "sin," the therapist calls "neurosis," and the existential philosopher calls "inauthentic being." Respectful of the rights and perspectives of others, personal authority is neither narcissistic nor imperialistic. It is a humble acknowledgment of what wishes to come to being *through* us. If the ego does not step out of the way of that energy that wishes to live through us, the energy will trample us in pathological outbreaks, or something vital within us will die, even though our bodies may keep on moving for decades. We all, privately, know this imperative summons every day, though we may flee it: find what is true for you; find the courage to live it in the world; and the world will in time come to respect you (though at first you may confuse others and scare them).

Closely allied with the task of gaining, or better recovering, personal authority is the task of *discovering a personal spirituality*. Too often individuals have had this critical invitation contaminated by their culture or their childhood experiences. They confuse the spirit's longing for largeness with familiar institutions, creeds, dogmas, and practices. Fearing a retreat to the treacle of the past, they abandon the task of sustained reflection on the life of the spirit. And, for sure, many of today's purveyors of spiritual goods are as slippery as soap salesmen. Their coiffed hair, their televangelistic suavity, their oleaginous platitudes infantilize their congregants rather than challenge them to become what they were meant to become. Their messages offer relief from struggle through simple steps, and seduce by surreptitious avoidance of life's summons to depth. Our culture is crowded with such spiritual snake oil. As Jung observed decades ago:

> *Once metaphysical ideas have lost their capacity to recall and evoke the original experience they have not only become useless but prove to be actual impediments on the road to wider development. One clings to possessions that have once meant wealth; and the more ineffective, incomprehensible, and lifeless they become the more obstinately people cling to them. . . . This end result is . . . a false spirit of arrogance, hysteria, wooly-mindedness, criminal amorality, and doctrinaire fanaticism, a purveyor of shoddy spiritual goods, spurious art, philosophical stutterings, and Utopian humbug, fit only to be fed wholesale to the mass man of today.**

It is of paramount importance that our spirituality be validated or confirmed by fidelity to our personal experience. A spiritual tradition that is only received from history or from family makes no real difference in a person's life, for he or she is living by conditioned reflexive response. Only what is experientially true is worthy of a mature spirituality. Experiential spirituality will stretch us, sometimes test us, but will always ask us to be larger than we wish to be. What must Jesus have meant when he invited those around him to take up the cross and follow him? Surely it was not an invitation to a life of ease or collective approval. Similarly, he said that whoever remains with mother and father will not travel with him. We might contemporize that challenge by saying that whoever continues to serve the parental complexes will not be living the individuation task.

A mature spirituality will seldom provide us with answers, and

---

*Jung, *CW 9ii*, para 65, 67.

necessarily so, but will instead ask ever-larger questions of us. Larger questions will lead to a larger life. A mature spirituality is critical for the second half of life because if we do not address these questions directly, chances are we will be living in subjugation to received values which delude, divert, or diminish us.

So often spirituality, like the false self, is fear-driven, which is not to be judged, but a fear-driven spirituality will always diminish rather than enlarge. It has been said that religion is for those afraid to go to Hell, and spirituality is for those who have been there. Any spiritual perspective that seeks to finesse difficult questions of good and evil, that seeks to scapegoat others, or that defers authority to external sources is an infantilizing spirituality. Any spirituality that makes people feel guilty and judged is merely adding to the complexes they already have. Any spirituality that keeps people in bondage to fear, to tradition, to anything other than that which is validated by their personal experience is doing violence to the soul.

By these criteria, many if not most spiritual practices are affronts to the larger life to which we are summoned. Just as our definitions of ourselves are too small, so our definitions of God are too small. And is there not a correlation between these two diminishments we desire, lest we be asked to grow up? Growing up spiritually means that we are asked to sort through the possibilities for ourselves, find what resonates for us, what is confirmed by our experience not the consensus of others, and be willing to stand for what has proved true for us. For this reason, the twin tasks of finding personal authority and finding a mature spirituality are inextricably linked.

As far as we know, the most critical qualitative distinction between our species and others is that we alone suffer the need for meaning. We do not graze in the fields, migrate through the autumnal skies, course in the water's depths on instinct alone, as our fellow creatures do. We are the symbol-making, symbol-using, symbol-needing animal. The capacity to engage life symbolically is what makes our culture possible and our spiritual life necessary. Symbols help bridge us to the mysteries of the cosmos, to natural events, to each other, and to our own mysterious selves. Mysteries are not knowable directly. If they were knowable, they would not be the mysteries—they would have become mere artifacts of our consciousness.

An image rises up from an event—an image of the beloved, an image of nature, an *imago Dei*, and that image allows us to relate to the experience of the mystery in a way that consciousness can grasp. An example of the phenomenological generation of symbols is the story of three eminent scientists and thinkers—Charles Darwin, William James, and Carl Jung—who each found himself in the midst of an earthquake, in different nations and different decades. All three men reported the spontaneous formation of the same symbol of that overwhelming experience; namely, each said he suddenly felt as if he were on the back of a large beast whose intent was to cast him off. Later each man realized that he had experienced an earthquake, but in the initial moment each felt such a primal, archaic character to the event that it could only be apprehended in conscious life as the symbolic image of a beast. This archetypal power of nature was profound, overwhelming all categories of conscious reference, and opened the three men to the profound and wholly Other—the mystery. This animal image was neither the inner experience nor the outer phenomenon, but it bridged the two, which is what the etymologies of both *symbol* and *metaphor* imply. Symbol and metaphor are our greatest gifts, for they make culture and spirituality possible. The animal *lives* the mystery; the human experiences it *as* mystery. Limited as we are, we are nonetheless able to approach the largeness of mystery through the tools of metaphor and symbol. The images of our own dream life are notable examples of such spontaneously generated symbols, which bridge between our finite consciousness and the transcendent.

What most characterizes the modern era, going back four centuries, is that the responsibility for meaning and for the conduct of one's life has progressively shifted from tribal mythology and sacred institutions to the shoulders of the individual. No one, whether pope or potentate, whether from the seat of mace or miter, today has the authority to define what you experience as real for you. The past few centuries have been harsh on external authorities. The claims of divine sanction by various religious and political leaders are still made today, but we know these leaders to be flawed human beings like the rest of us, just as capable of erring judgment and self-interested interpretations. (The motto of England's ruling House of Windsor, to choose one example, is still *Dieu et Mon Droit*, "God and My Right," but we all know that it is a constitutional monarchy and serves at the will of the people.)

In the early nineteenth century, the Sage of Koenigsburg, Immanuel Kant, ended traditional metaphysics and made modern psychology necessary by discerning that we never know reality directly; we only know our internal experience of it. He was not saying that external reality does not exist; rather, that we can only know it subjectively. Our psyche takes the raw chaos of stimuli and organizes it into coherence according to categories of time, number, spatiality, and other elements of our minds. The chair upon which you sit is a swirling assemblage of energy and open spaces that presents as a state we call matter, even as it is also constantly in motion and transformation. It is difficult for the ego to imagine that it is not sitting on something permanent, fixed, but rather a passing energy congruence, as quantum physics has known for a century. (Perhaps paleontologist Teilhard de Chardin came closest to bridging these worlds when he said that matter is spirit moving slowly enough to be seen.) There is a natural tendency of the ego to confuse its subjective state with the objective reality. We stumble into this confusion all the time. We have done it with our religions as well.

Every religion has its origin in some primal encounter with the transcendent, as it presented to an individual or to a tribe. Out of that encounter an image arises, not unlike the bucking beast engendered by the earthquakes, an image that bridges between the mystery and the perceiving consciousness. Over time, the ego tends to privilege its own constructs and confuse them with external reality, or confuse them with the mystery. Our finite sensibility cannot ultimately know that infinite mystery that has been called *God*. We have, however, an experience of transcendence, and call it by the name *God*. But what we call God is not the name, not the image, but the profound energy behind the image, which gave rise to its numinous charge. As Jung has clarified:

> *It is, in fact, impossible to demonstrate God's reality to oneself except by using images which have arisen spontaneously or are sanctified by tradition, and whose psychic nature and effects the naive-minded person has never separated from their unknowable metaphysical background. He instantly equates the effective image with the transcendental* x *to which it points . . . then it must be remembered that the image and the statement are psychic processes which are different from their transcendental object; they do not posit it, they merely point to it.* *

Our images of God, or the profundities of nature, or states of psychic transport, are what is experienced, not the energic source

---

*Jung, *Psychological Reflections*, p. 338.

from which they arise, the source that remains, in the words of theologian Karl Barth, "Wholly Other." (That is what makes it the mystery!) How often have tribes assaulted each other out of their anxious collective egos' need for security through uniformity, compliance, and consensus? The immature person, or culture, proclaims "our God is superior to your God," the way children do. Sadly, throughout the world's savage history, more human beings have been murdered over literalized religious metaphors than any other cause. Can you imagine anyone marching off to slay the infidel chanting, "My metaphor, my symbolic construct, has more potency, more juju, than your metaphor or symbolic construct"? For anyone to recognize that he or she is even using symbol or metaphor is to have gained a mature psychological level of consciousness, much more able to recognize the subjective rather than objective character of such a religious proclamation. He or she is spared the delusion of literalism. If I say that I like a certain flavor of ice cream, and that you will too, you may or may not agree with my taste. But if I insist that my taste is right and yours is wrong, then I have offended your humanity by denying the reality of your experience. We do this kind of violence to each other, as individuals, as cultures, as spouses, as parents, all the time.

The chasm that occurs between fundamentalism and atheism rises sometimes from stupidity, sometimes from inadequate understanding, and frequently from psychopathology. In the former's position, religious values are to be defended as facts, facts that offend common sense and often push the defender into a narrowing isthmus over which he or she is forever doing battle. The latter, seeing that claiming such things as "facts" is untenable, summarily rejects the universal insight toward which religious images may point. He or she concludes that if beliefs are factually shaky, then the whole motif is worthless. Such either/or positions are missing what is most durable: the deep psycho-mythological truth that the image embodies. Moreover, the person who says that such moments of meaning are *only* psychological ignores the fact that soul exists as an experience of autonomous energy wholly transcendent to consciousness, although we are obliged to experience its presence within the subjective arena of our own psychological understandings.

Remember that the word *soul* is our designation of the autonomous energy that courses through the material guises of the world—in you, in me, in nature, in dream images, and so on. As far as we are concerned, it becomes *through* us, by being experienced by us. Thus, for example, another may activate, incarnate love in us, but this is experienced as our subjective state. The truth of religious experience originates outside us, but engages something inside us that is seeking this other. When inner and outer engage, unite, we experience this as meaning. Thus, soul exists outside us, but something central to our nature is of similar nature and desires to connect. This outer movement of soul is what is meant by the word *numinous*, whose etymology means "to nod toward, or beckon" us. Thus, soul solicits us even as we seek it. The German poet Friedrich Hölderlin expressed the paradox this way: "That which thou seekst is near, and already coming to meet thee."

Sadly, the quality of public discussion of these matters has been so poor that great masses of modern humanity have discarded what lies deepest within—their own, inherently religious yearning. This tragic devaluation of the spirit has led many to reject the possibility of the transcendent and to throw themselves into the addictions and diversions of popular culture as antidotes for the pain of this great loss. It has led others to cynicism or depression. Only in recent years did the august American Psychiatric Association deign to admit the possibility of "religious difficulties" as a marginal diagnostic category of interest to therapists. Yet anyone who reflects deeply upon our culture and our common condition will discern that the loss of a spiritual life underlies virtually all of our culture's malaise and our personal psychopathology. Whoever does not feel a participant in a deeper symbolic drama will manifest as a walking collection of symptoms sooner or later. As Jung notes, this issue is central to the governance of a person's entire second half of life:

> *Is he related to something infinite or not? That is the telling question of his life. . . . If we understand and feel that here in this life we already have a link with the infinite, desires and attitudes change. In the final analysis, we count for something only because of the essential we embody, and if we do not embody that, life is wasted.* *

In order to recover, or perhaps to reconstruct, a mature spirituality amid an age of shoddy spiritual goods, we need first to reflect not only on what spirituality means, but also on how it is formed, how it may serve, and what we need to learn from its past.

In the nineteenth century the French thinker August Comte noted how the complex mystery of our world was originally experienced through a psycho-religious perception called *animism*. Animism, from the Latin word *anima*, which means "soul," derives from a naive confusion of outer and inner, objective and subjective realities. Early cultures experienced the world as "en-souled," that is, all things being the embodiment or the carriers of soul energy. The tree had soul (from which we still derive the expression to "knock on wood," as a summoning of the *anima* within the tree to stand by us for good fortune). The earth had soul, whose goodwill and bounteous fruit people needed to arouse through acts of sym-

---

*Jung, *Memories, Dreams, Reflections*, p. 325.

pathetic magic such as sacrifice of animal or human, ritual intercourse in the fields and temples, and so on. Each person carried and embodied soul, and people often recognized it in each other, as in the Hindu greeting with palms together in acknowledgment of the soul in the other, or even projected it onto each other, as in the case of possession.

As we know, the course of human history since that distant era has been to develop a keener differentiation of objective and subjective, lest we be bewitched by projections, or even hallucinations. Yet, as a result, the presence of soul is experienced less and less in the world, and the world is more and more denuded of spiritual depth. Today we consider the animists naive, though we might envy the omnipresent spiritual vitality of the daily world that they had in abundance, in both its terrifying and comforting expressions. We think ourselves superior to them although we all still employ superstitions, as we call them, rituals to ward off evil, and magical thinking in our private, unguarded moments that betray the resurgence of the old subjective-and-objective confusion after all. (Just watch how folks twist their bodies back and forth after having already released a bowling ball.)

With the increasing development of ego consciousness, Comte noted that the stage of animism was replaced by the *theological* stage, whether the gods of the antique world or the formal religious bodies that arose out of the Levant and the Far East. We see the transition from the animistic to the theological occurring when, for example, the immense power of the sea is embodied in a specific deity, Poseidon, whose name appropriately means "earth-shaker." Before setting forth on the wine-dark sea, Homer's mariners respectfully entreated the beneficence of this god, who could so easily annihilate them.

As the great religions become less and less a matter of personal experience and more and more a question of surrender of personal authority to corporate security, they take on a life of their own in institutional and cultural forms. While each person is profoundly affected by these cultural forms, internalized as complexes of affect, value, and response, most are led further and further from the validation of personal revelation into the affirmations of belief in the received forms rather than the immediacy of primal experience. By the mid-nineteenth century many noted thinkers, from Kierkegaard to Nietzsche to Dostoevski, had concluded that "the gods had died." They were making psychological statements even before psychology as we know it, not metaphysical statements. That is, they were witnessing the psychological reality that for most, the cultural forms of the gods, and their attendant value systems, no longer evoked the immediacy of personal experience. The loss of this connection to the soul was felt as alienation, a disorientation, and evoked a nostalgia on the one hand and the nervous rise of secular surrogates such as scientism and materialism on the other.

Comte greeted this change with enthusiasm because he thought it was "progress" toward the age of positivism. By *positivism* he meant that nothing could be considered authoritative if it was not objectively validated. The chief validation was that of the senses, to which the modern sciences lend themselves so readily. Clearly, the modern sciences have brought greater comfort and control to humanity through an increased manipulation of the material conditions of life. However, Comte's nineteenth-century view, the one in which we all were raised, the idea of material and scientific progress as a form of spiritual evolution, has, in the face of recent history, also proved naive and one-sided. Not only did that scientific skill enable the last century to be the bloodiest in the long, lamentable catalog of human butchery, but the failed gods of modernism left the modern adrift in our materialist sea, awash with corporate empires whose books are cooked, governments founded on mendacity, and intellectuals intent on constructing monuments to their neuroses.

We may condescend toward the old animist, but at least his world was spiritually charged in a way in which ours is not. He or she understood that survival, and meaning, depended on the capacity to read the signature of the invisible at work in the visible world. Not only did the animist need to read the signs of nature in order to survive physically, but he or she also had to align his or her choices with subservience to the perceived spirit powers. By limiting our contemporary sense of truth to what can be physically validated, we have limited our deeper access to the world and de-souled it in many ways.

One may especially see this tendency in the limitation of most modern psychotherapy to behavioral modification, cognitive reprogramming, and pharmacology—all useful approaches, but by themselves superficial and unintentionally devaluing of our deepest being. One may see in popular theologies the same heresy as in psychology, namely the confusion of the image with the energy that animates it. Thus people worship forms of belief without struggling with the issues the forms tentatively embody, or emulate behaviors without questioning whether they really serve fuller life. Accordingly, either the image of divinity is to be defended for its presumed historic claim, or it is to be summarily rejected as unworthy of a modern sensibility. In either case the world is de-souled, when what it needs is reanimation; either way, the individual is prey to belief systems that narrow into rigid positions rather than expand to opening dialogue; the mystery is banished and therefore rendered irrelevant to all. Similarly, one may attend a college in order to avoid the radical opening to real education,* go to church to

---

*Education derives from the verb *educe,* which means "to draw forth from within." The original teaching method of Socrates has been largely displaced by

avoid religious experience, and even undertake therapy to avoid the reality of the psyche. All of these practices are in fact common, albeit mostly unconscious, and result only in deeper and deeper alienation from the mystery. And all reduce the measure of life through the disregard of personal experience and deflection of personal authority.

This is the sad state of modernism, no matter where one stands on the religious spectrum. Polls indicate that Americans profess a higher percentage of belief in a deity, attend religious services more, and all the while have a greater reliance upon material comforts than the citizens any other advanced nation. Their religiosity may not be so religious when it is in service to complexes, groupthink, and a persistent avoidance of personal spiritual maturation and humbling service to the mystery.

Truly, one should be wary of religious experience, for it may ask something of us that we would prefer to avoid. Most people intuit this threat, this likely summons to largeness, and for this reason, many cultural manifestations of religiosity are surreptitious efforts to avoid actual religious experience. No wonder, then, we seem so disaffected, so adrift, so easily suckered by pop ideologies and fleeting fashions of attire, behavior, and thought. No wonder, then, that a culture that has lost its soul drifts into unconscious pacts with whoever offers to lead it, whoever proclaims clarity of values, or, more often, whoever promises to distract the citizenry. Daily obeisance to the television set threatens to become the chief soporific of our time, supplanting religious inquiry, intellectual growth, discernment, discrimination of values, as well as enabling avoidance of whatever personal demons we may have.

---

professorial deference to received scholarly authority. By and large, our students are taught how to take exams but not to think, write, or find their own path.

All of this distracted flight may fairly be called a *Seelekrankheit,* a sickness of the soul. Still, others have sought to live stoically and with integrity in the presence of absence. As poet Stephen Dunn recounts:

Tell them that in the end I had no need
for God, who'd become just a story
I once loved, one of many
with concealments and late night rescues,
high sentence and pomp. The truth is
I'd learned to live without hope
as well as I could, almost happily,
in the despoiled and radiant now. *

The despoiled now may not be as richly endowed as the spirit-appareled world of our animistic ancestors, but it remains radiant.

Such radiance in the present moment still moves all humanity, and from that experience metaphoric images rise to bridge them to the mystery. After these spontaneously appearing images lose their luster, we seek to re-create the experience through the cultural forms of dogma, ritual, and cultlike practices. Dogma serves as a reassuring program of answers to questions that arise: to explain, to communicate, and in time to defend the past for the person who did not experience it directly. The dogma itself does not carry the mystery, though it may sincerely seek to sustain its impact. Rituals have the intent to re-create the encounter with the mystery, to summon up the spirits, and hopefully reanimate the original en-counter. Through reiteration, however, rituals tend to lose their connection to the primal energy and increasingly become hollow

---

*Dunn, "A Postmortem Guide," *Different Hours,* pp. 120–121.

forms. In time, they tend to become rigid, inflexible entrapments of soul rather than summoners to largeness. Similarly, the cultural forms of dress, behavior, ethics that distinguish one group from another can grow arbitrary, disconnected, and cultlike and become the source of alienation from other groups with other forms of the same experience.

Lastly, institutions grow up around these cultural forms, at first in homage to the primal events, and then as guardians of their history, and ultimately as encapsulated entities that are most invested in preserving themselves, long after the spark of primal experience has left them. The chief project of *modernism*, that movement of literature, art, music, psychology, philosophy, and troubled sensibility over the last two hundred years, was to witness the eroded authority of such institutions and to dismantle their claims to govern the modern soul. Fundamentalism spends its anxious time trying to defend the secondary minutiae of historic claims, seeking arks on Mt. Sinai or defending parthenogenesis as a biological event rather than a spiritual metaphor, all the while employing bad science and bad theology in futile arguments. Institutions that claim power over our nature will have to pay nature's denied due, and will end by abusing their flock. Some people leave all cultural religious forms in disgust, despair, or desolation, and walk into the sterile kingdoms of atheism and materialism, in which no transcendent expression will be found.

The question remains, then, how we are to reconstruct a viable spirituality in a time of sterile materialism, failed institutions, and hawkers of shoddy spiritual merchandise in New Age bookstores. Any project to revivify by going back is doomed to failure. New wine does not come from old wine bottles. Nonetheless, there are some paths through the past that are well worth our exploration. Each of us is the inheritor of a profoundly rich symbolic tapestry. In each of our traditions there are images that can still speak to us if we can differentiate from the perspective of another time and place the universal issue that each of them embodies.

It is useful to consider the following four questions when we examine any mythic image or cultural form that solicits our attention. They are:

1. What is the universal, timeless question that this form, image, narrative seeks to address?
2. What is the response this person, or this tradition, offers to that question?
3. How does my contemporary culture address that same issue?
4. How much of that is confirmed by my own experience?

Beneath the unfamiliar cultural form of each image resonates timeless issues: "How are we to understand death?" "By what values, or discernment processes, do we make difficult choices?" "How does one sort one's way through the contemporary brambles to find one's path?" And so on. Our culture has very inadequate answers to these kinds of questions, if any at all. Since these questions never go away, they go underground, into the unconscious. Or they are projected into cultural masques through our movies and songs. Or, denied altogether, they leave us very much alone in the universe, where rather than suffer those questions honestly and openly, we are left prey to triviality and banality.

So as we sort through the rubble of historically charged images, by what standard do we gather them to our heart? It cannot be their institutional authority alone. It cannot be because our family or ethnic tradition embraced them. It can only be if they move us, that is *set off a resonance within us*. If such resonance occurs, the activation of like to like in some hidden harmony, then we know that

that image has some meaning for us. We feel it. No amount of willpower or faith can, as such, arouse such resonance for us. When the spirit has departed, we cannot will it back. Though we may not understand why, when the spirit is present, we will be moved.

Upon reflection, three essential points became clear. First, that the eternal questions will arise in quite different guises in all times, and persist in determining the value of our lives whether we are conscious of them or not. Second, that those who went before us experienced profundities in forms that may, or may not, still stir us as well. We owe it to them, and to ourselves, to inquire seriously. And third, that our culture is failing miserably to bring us to these questions, which deepen our humanity and bring worth and weight to our journeys. This last fact constitutes a betrayal of the largeness of the soul, and therefore a deception of the individual person by the collective.

This test of *resonance* is critical to our capacity to gather a spirituality that brings deepened connection and meaning into our lives. As we have seen, many if not most of our values are imposed upon us by the Zeitgeist, by gender roles, by economic constructs, by the psychodynamics of our family of origin. Sometimes these values may in fact be in agreement with the design of our soul, but many times they are not. Yet, as we recall, the child is outvoted, needy, and dependent, and therefore obliged to subordinate the truth of his or her inner life to the demands and models of the outer life. Whatever inner protest one may feel at this age often goes unexamined, until in time even we forget what we once knew, or felt. Only when it begins to hurt too much to deny any longer, or we are privileged to find other examples, other permissions in the world, and only when we have gained the capacity to take care of ourselves, can we begin to reclaim our lives from our history. Remember that the chief characteristic of the modern era is that the responsibility for choosing values has shifted from the tribe and the institution to the individual. Such a privilege is also a responsibility.

When the principle of resonance, that is, inner confirmation as opposed to external authority, is accepted as the surest guide to the conduct of a life responsive to the soul, then we are forced to become psychological. We experience *metanoia,* a transformation of consciousness—the recognition that we are in fact spiritual beings who are cast into a material form in a material age. We moderns think we got rid of the old energies, or brought them under our control, but they re-form in the unconscious as virtual deities. As Jung explains, "All ages before us have believed in gods in some form or another. Only an unparalleled impoverishment of symbolism could enable us to rediscover the gods as psychic factors, that is archetypes of the unconscious. . . . All this would be quite superfluous in an age or culture that possessed symbols."*

Despite the polls that suggest there is a surge of religiosity in America, the operative value, that is what actually most mobilizes and directs energy, is not traditional religion but its overvalued surrogates: economics, power, affluence, hedonism, and popular divertissements. Whether conscious or not, we all are *Homo religiosus.* As theologian Paul Tillich observed, our religion will be found where our ultimate concerns are expressed. To that we might add a corollary that our de facto religion is found where our deepest energies are most invested. For many it will be found in the domination of their souls by economic obsessions. For others it will show up in a neurosis, perhaps in seeking to win the favor of others at any cost. Again, Jung is to the point when he says:

---

*Jung, *The Archetypes of the Collective Unconscious, CW 9i*, para. 50.

The question is not religion or not, but which kind of religion, whether it is one furthering man's development, the unfolding of his specifically human powers, or one paralyzing them. . . . We can interpret neurosis as a private form of religion, more specifically, as a regression to primitive forms of religion conflicting with officially recognized patterns of religious thought. *

Even those who profess a conscious set of religious beliefs and practices may not in fact be living in good faith with themselves if in the unconscious those values are simply those imposed upon them, or those which make their participation in the collective more comfortable, or those which serve as anxiety management, or those which result from spiritual laziness. We can be such strangers to ourselves that most of what we profess may be an unexamined surrogate or an imposed value. The fact that so many of us suffer crippling guilts induced by our traditions is a sadly recurrent example of a religious construct that only breeds neurosis. In fact, so often the conscious values we adopt, and cherish, are apotropaic defenses against evil, rationalizations of our wounds, flights from the terror of being alone, or unwitting confessions of intimidation at the prospect of conducting our lives on our own authority.

To thoughtfully examine our culturally induced religious life is in no way to denigrate the great world religious traditions. Remember, we are to search them all with serious intent to find what pieces speak to us. Those great images still have enormous linking and healing power; however, each of us has to make that discovery on our own. In a poem titled "A Coat," W.B. Yeats described how he had woven the patchwork of many mythic traditions into a coat

---

*Jung, *Psychology and Religion, CW 11,* para. 167.

to wear in the frost of the modern age. William Blake said that he could see eternity in a grain of sand, and I believe he could. If you or I cannot, then we need to find our own ways in which to read the surface world and glimpse the movement of deeper currents within it. This process is not psychologizing, that is reducing everything to subjective experience alone, but it is acknowledging that without that subjective confirmation, nothing finally will have a reality for us, no matter how much ego, or nervous consensual flattery, may will it to be true.

As Jung further challenges:

I strip things of their metaphysical wrapping in order to make them objects of psychology. In that way I can . . . discover psychological facts and processes that were veiled in symbols beyond my comprehension. In doing so I may perhaps be following in the steps of the faithful, and may possibly have similar experiences; and if in the end there should be something ineffably metaphysical behind it all, it would have the best opportunity of showing itself.*

What Jung is suggesting is that the "truth" within the image can only be true for us if it becomes a psychological fact, that is inwardly apprehended and experienced by us. This has always been the case; Jung is simply making more conscious to us the process by which images become holy or the opposite, lose their energy. Wealth, power, even good health may be seen as cultural artifacts that embody an unconscious religiosity because they activate a psychological response for so many. "Following in the steps of the faithful," as Jung calls it, is a process by which the primal images of

---

*Jung, *The Secret of the Golden Flower, CW 13*, para. 50.

religious tradition may flame anew in the soul of the modern. On the other hand, you may find that any received image is in fact dead to you, perhaps to be grieved, but this is preferable to living in a habitual loyalty to the past that contributes nothing to your present integrity. Serving a past image unconsciously may very well prove to be that oldest of religious heresies—*idolatry!* Idolatry is often a comforting artifact of the ego, but it is an impediment to the renewing agenda of the soul.

Whatever moves us deeply, occasions awe and wonder is religious, no matter through what venue it may come to us. For this reason, many of our popular forms of entertainment carry charged imagoes that have a religious function for us, whether we know it or not. Our culture's preoccupation with sexuality and violence, for example, illustrates the way in which these primal energies course through our days at all times, even though we may deliberately wall them off from our conscious lives and practices. Another culture might have proclaimed, "These powerful experiences are the *gods;* we call them Ares and Aphrodite, and you must respect them, pay conscious homage to them, or they will bring great harm to you and your family." We are still learning, to our profound dismay, that when we reject or repress those gods, they invade our conscious lives as neuroses, compelling fantasies, projections onto others, or manifold social disorders.

The images that carry energy for us derive from the *mundus imaginalis,* the spirit world that animates the material world, and provides the linkage between the world we can see and the world we cannot. This autonomous activity of the soul whereby the deeper realm reaches toward conscious embodiment was called by Jung "the transcendent function," namely that mutual activity of self and universe that seeks to transcend the barriers between the conscious and the unconscious realms.

A familiar example of the "transcendent function" will be found in the daily act of dreaming. We do not summon dreams up. If you think so, try to order up a certain category of dream and see if the psyche pays any attention to you. But on an average of six times per night, we are visited by this other world, which is nonetheless our world. Such tremendous expenditure of energy is neither random nor lacking in purpose. Nature does not waste energy. Attending this meeting point of inner and outer worlds is the chief office of depth psychology, the mystical tradition of the world religions, and the daily task of each of us. From this meeting point, creative energies arise, revelation appears, and each of us is initiated into a larger, developmental spirituality. The images that arrive each night are not the deity, as such, though the visiting gods have suffused those images with their energy. Thus it is through such images that we bridge to the gods again. Dream images are an incredible gift from the soul. Who then, are we, to reject them, treat them casually, rather than pay careful attention to what the soul is seeking to say to us? Of many a patient I have asked, "From where did your dream come? Did you invent it?" "No, of course not," they reply. "Then we must learn to track and respect that place within you which seems to know so much about you, and has your interests at heart." This is how we begin to find our inner authority, and recover a personal psychological integrity.

Finding a mature spirituality will only occur when we internalize the fact that our egos are only a small part of a larger mystery. It is a mystery at work outside of us, in the cosmos, in nature, in other people, and in ourselves as well. We are called to ask serious, more courageous questions of ourselves, for without these probing questions, we will simply fall back into the old patterns, which work neither for us nor for our culture. We realize we are going to have to become psychological by scrutinizing the world around, and the world within, with greater depth and focused awareness. We have to see the religiosity that is present in virtually all things in our world, and then ask ourselves if we find such forms worthy of the soul or not. We are going to have to risk attending to this liberating principle of resonance. If something resonates within, it is somehow about us, and for us, and if it does not, it will only betray the soul in the long run, no matter how much ego wills or tradition venerates. A mature spirituality requires a mature individual. A mature spirituality already lies within each of us, in our potential to take on the mystery as it comes to us, to query it, to risk change and growth, and to continue the revisioning of our journey for so long as we live. It remains to be seen how ready we are to take the step toward this responsibility for personal authority. That is an appointment that each of us is called to keep.

The new myth will not come from above. Only totalitarian ideologies, or ego-crafted appeals to our complexes, will appear in such fashion. The new myth will come as it always has, rising from the depths, greeting the tribe, summoning the individual to serve that which enlarges rather than diminishes. The new myth, a deep, resonant energy field, is already birthing in the depths of you, the reader. Your summons is to respect what comes to you, and to honor anew the ever-changing forms of those deep mysterious energies humankind historically personified and honored as "the gods." In Rilke's words:

Gods—we project them first in audacious images
which constricting fate destroys for us again.
But they are the Immortals
Who in the end will hear us. *

---

*Rilke, *Sonnets to Orpheus*, II, 24, author's translation.

Chapter Ten

Swampland Visitations

"In the midst of my days I shall go to the gates of Hell."

Isaiah 38:10

"O Lord, give each person his own personal death.
A dying that moves out of the same life he lived,
In which he had love, and intelligence, and trouble."

R. M. Rilke

THERE IS A POWERFUL FANTASY of progress that lurks beneath the surface of contemporary culture, a fantasy to which we have all subscribed in some form or another. While scientific and technical advances over the last two centuries have greatly improved the comfort and length of our lives, they have facilitated no comparable moral progress. The bloody catalog of the last century was in large measure achieved because of that technical prowess. We learned to kill more efficiently and cover the earth with our bloody prints. Nonetheless, the fantasy of progress still runs deeply within our culture, for how many of us have not at one time or another confused material progress with spiritual advance? Nowhere is this fantasy more identifiable than in our preoccupation with health, with youthful image, and with resistance to aging and mortality. These apprehensions are hardly new. In the seventeenth century Thomas Nashe wrote "A Litany in Time of Plague":

Beauty is but a flower
Which wrinkles will devour;
Brightness falls from the air;
Queens have died young and fair;
Dust hath closed Helen's eye.
I am sick, I must die.
    *Lord, have mercy on us!**

Nashe understands the brevity of life, the transience of beauty, and how time and tide come to each in turn. He and the preponderance of his contemporaries could frequently appeal to a secure belief in the God in heaven and the promise of an afterlife. While such a belief is still available to many, for most moderns, those distant gardens of the skies have faded.

Instead, for most of us today, the search for relief from our common condition has shifted to the fantasy that through vitamins, health practices, cosmetic surgeries, right thinking, and right conduct, we can prolong life, avoid aging, and some coming day, perhaps through cloning, defeat death itself. While none of us, myself included, wishes to deny the great contributions that have been made by improved nutrition and medical intervention, entanglement in such fantasies has the long-term effect of furthering our alienation from the ministries of natural process and, worst of all,

---

*Nashe, "A Litany in Time of Plague," *The Norton Anthology of Poetry*, p. 202.

deflecting us from lucid, luminous moments of consciousness during this brief transit.

It might strike the reader as peculiar to reflect that something like good health might prove a "fantasy," a fantasy which, heavily invested with psychological energy, can actually distract one from the depth and dignity of this journey. I am hardly against good health or long life; I oppose the way in which these obsessions lead us further from our natural lives, which is hardly in our best interest. In calling such investments a fantasy, I'm not suggesting they are unreal, but rather that they solicit a value investment that in the end will betray us. A fantasy is an invested image, which, for however long it lasts, carries or distracts consciousness. It matters, then, to pay attention to what images are carrying our soul's investment, lest we find them, over the long run, pragmatically ineffective. The avoidance of our mortal, transient condition is pathological. To be mindful of our fragile fate each day, in a non-morbid acknowledgment, helps us remember what is important in our life and what is not, what matters, really, and what does not. It has been my experience that those who handle aging and mortality least well are those who fear that they have not been in *this* life, that they have not been *here*, that they have not lived the life they were called to live. Those most preoccupied with appearance are typically those most resistant to the task of inner authority, for they continue to seek validation from the world out there.

Added to this fantasy of transcending our natural reality is the understandable desire to avoid what I call "the swamplands of the soul," those dark places where fate, fortune, and our own psyches frequently take us. No amount of right thinking or right conduct will spare us swampland visitations. Much so-called New Age thinking has seeped into general public consciousness, and this populist philosophy offers seductive, ungrounded spiritual practices that seek to finesse the question of suffering. They intimate transcendence of swamplands, provide gurus who will do the simplistic thinking for us and remove us from the suffering that forges larger and larger consciousness. They foster narcissism, naiveté, self-absorption, and indifference to others, promise magic versus the daily work of constructing our lives, and reward us with only superficial engagements with the wonder and terror of being here.

We need always to distinguish *pain* from *suffering*. Pain is physiological and should always be alleviated when possible, for pain can erode the spirit's vitality. Suffering is spiritual, for it inevitably raises questions of meaning. If we are free of suffering, we are less likely to engage with those questions that ultimately define who we are. The rigor and depth of questions raised by suffering jar us out of complacency, out of the casual reiterations of untroubled life, and bring us to the daily dilemma of enlargement or diminishment. An old medieval adage has it that "suffering is the fastest horse to completion."

Would the world's great religions have become part of our heritage without the suffering of the Christ, the Buddha, Moses, Abraham, Mohammed, and others? As the Koran asks, do we expect that the pathway to the Garden of Bliss will be less troubled for us than for those who have preceded us? Just how often did Greek tragedy praise early death, lest long life bring one to more and more swamplands? And yet we lust for longer life. To what end? In service to what values—mere animal existence? There is a West African metaphor that someone's "feet are in agreement." That is a metaphoric euphemism for death. Only the dead have their feet symmetrically lined up. In life, our feet, like our lives, are forever living contradictions and paradoxes.

If we live long enough, we face necessary appointments with

death, with loss, with betrayal, with anxiety and depression, and a host of other dismal denizens of the deep. Fate, fortune, and the autonomy of the unconscious will frequently take us to places we do not wish to visit. When we arrive in swampland zones, we are always faced with a task. That task demands of us something larger than we customarily wish to provide. We are implicitly asked: "How am I to enlarge consciousness in this place; how embrace life here amid peril; how find the meaning for me in this suffering?" Identifying and accepting this task contributes to the enlargement of soul; flight from this task perpetuates our sense of victimization and keeps us on the run from the gods and from our own larger life.

Remembering that our ego's central project is maintaining itself and privileging its own narrow position, we can see that without some challenge to that agenda, we would never grow larger than the messages of childhood and the limits of the familial and cultural environment into which fate placed us. The ego's agenda of reinforcement, comfort, order, control, security is not to be judged but rather to be recognized as potentially limiting our humanity. We all have a fantasy of arriving at a conflict-free plateau or a sunlit glen without struggle, without the demand for increasing consciousness, without being pulled deeper and further than we wish to travel. Interestingly, there is such a place—it is called Death. Without journey, risk, conflict, we are already spiritually dead and are simply waiting for the body to drop away as well. Then we will have missed the meaning of our being here in the first place.

Let us visit some of the most common swamplands, which are the inevitable and necessary counterpoints to our fantasies of untroubled lives. In these zones of discord and suffering, we will be brought to great conflict of opposites. Yet, as Jung has made clear,

fidelity to "the Self is manifest in the opposites and in the conflict between them. . . . Hence the way to the Self begins with conflict."*

Guilt

One of those conflicts that frequently torment the sensitive soul, especially those in the second half of life who are willing to look at
their history and its effects, is guilt. No one who is alive is free of it,
although there are those whose souls are so damaged that they've
repressed the capacity to feel responsibility for suffering they've
brought to themselves and others. Their sometimes sociopathic,
sometimes psychotic lives seem free of guilt, but they are obliged to
live in an emotionally sterile wasteland instead. For most of us, guilt
is a ubiquitous companion, frequently interfering in our lives, and
even making choices for us whether we know it or not.

We need first to establish that when we use the word *guilt,* we
know how we are using that word and in what context. The initial
understanding of guilt is as a necessary companion to a life of value,
a life in which responsibility is assumed, in which moral vision matters. When we have brought harm to ourselves or others, it is a
measure of maturity to assume responsibility for it. One of the wise
precepts of the proliferating twelve-step recovery programs summons individuals to acknowledge the wrongs they have committed,
to redress them wherever possible, or to at least make the attempt
to symbolic compensation and restoration. If this restorative task is
not undertaken, pernicious guilt falls into the unconscious and produces even more self-defeating behaviors and areas of pain, which
reintensifies the addictive cycle.

---

*Jung, *CW 12,* para. 259.

Collectively, nations also carry guilt for the harm they have brought others. (Only very wise and strong leaders, such as Bishop Tutu and Nelson Mandela in South Africa, will bring their nation to the bar of justice and ask forgiveness.) Only the strongest of us can face the damage we have brought others, whether intended or not. Nonetheless, such acknowledgment of responsibility for harm is far less likely than unacknowledged guilt to be an unconscious anchor that weighs upon the soul and siphons off its energy. Guilt denied will find some other way through which the piper will be paid. The capacity to accept responsibility for this harm, for choices made, for choices not made marks the maturity level of the ego and adds depth and gravity to the soul. None of us has clean hands in this world; only the unconscious think so, and they are most guilty of projecting their shadow onto others.

There is a second form of guilt which is inescapable for anyone who would pretend a modicum of consciousness. This form of guilt we might call *collective*, or *existential* guilt, for it is an unavoidable by-product of the interconnected circumstances of our lives. Those of us who live in the so-called First World live on the backs of the less fortunate. Within our own societies we live in exploitative circumstances, whether we so intend or not. We slay our fellow creatures for food. We desecrate nature to make malls in service to contrived consumerism. We are passive in the presence of evil. We contribute our fair share of bigotry and prejudice to the weight of the world's woe. We fall far short of even our own professed values and standards, and find ready rationalizations to justify our behaviors. And we all look the other way, lest we see something summoning us to moral responsibility and action. It is not sentimentality to acknowledge these shortcomings, these sins of commission and omission; it is moral sensitivity and psychological maturity to acknowledge our role in them. This existential guilt is inescapable, even by the most ethically nuanced person, and acknowledging such guilt is only being honest.

Most of the time, however, when we reflect on guilt, we think of that queasy feeling, the vague paralysis that creeps over the body and makes us feel miserable. Having acknowledged the two forms of legitimate guilt, for which honest confession is appropriate, let us also acknowledge that much of this third form of guilt is not about what we have done, but about who we are. *Much of this guilt is disguised anxiety.*

As children we learn that our safe passage through this world depends on meeting the conditions set for us by our respective environments. Deeply programmed into us by adulthood is the fear of the loss of the love, approval, and cooperation of the "other" in our lives, be it parent, partner, or institution. When our own instinctual guidance, or the protective interference of the complexes, leads us to truly personal expression, we activate an old, archaic warning system. Guilt then acts as an internal governor, shutting down our natural selves and recalling the agenda of adaptation rather than authenticity. What is called guilt in this instance is most often a management of anxiety, whether we know it or not at the time.

How many lives are stunted by this guilt, this fear that being ourselves will not be acceptable? How many talents unexpressed, how many ventures stillborn in the bed of guilt—all in the name of sweet reasonableness? This form of guilt, because it is tied to our archaic systems, because it addresses our most common reflexive system—the management of anxiety—is the too familiar enemy that aborts promise, sabotages capacity, and keeps one from joyful immersion in the journey of life. The only antidote to this form of paralyzing guilt is resolve, the determination to risk being who we are meant to be by stepping into choices that enlarge rather than bind us to the past. Such paralyzing guilt always binds one to the past, and therefore there can be no future without a movement toward more honest action in its face.

Grief and Loss

This past week I talked with a ninety-year-old who is still vital and engaged in her life, but about to bury her second daughter. If we live long enough, subscribe to that fantasy of immortality in which so much of our culture is vested, we will inevitably be brought to the loss of all for whom we care, or they will have suffered our loss. Loss seems to be the price of abundance, the counterpoise to the richness of life, and remains always, even in moments of attainment, its silent, necessary companion. Grief, which etymologically is related to the word *gravity,* from the Latin *gravis* ("to bear or carry") is in due proportion to our commitment to life. The more we would soar, the more we are bound to the limits of this earth, the flux, flow, and rhythm of attachment and loss. The only way to avoid loss is to avoid attachment, but to live without commitment is to live in an arid place, as we know.

Our life begins and ends with loss. We lose the safest, least demanding place we will ever inhabit, with all needs met, and fall into a world of peril and contingency. And we end the journey with the loss of our mortal state. Natural as it is to seek to hang on, the inevitability of loss rather asks that we treasure what we have, appreciate it for its precious, momentary presence in our lives, and know that its gift to us is found precisely in its impermanence. What would be ours in perpetuity is less treasured. What is fleetingly here is most dear. The Greek myth of immortal Tithonus relates how he found his life meaningless because every choice this hour could be reversed in another. So he petitioned the gods to grant him mortality, so that his life, through his now risky choices, could be experienced as meaningful. They so blessed Tithonus.

Grief is honest acknowledgment of loss, which is based on honest acknowledgment of value. Without value, there is no substantive loss. In grieving we honestly celebrate the gifts we have been given. Lamenting the loss of one whom we love, for example, is most painful indeed, and yet the very grieving is a celebration of the richness that life has brought us. We cannot have the richness without the possibility of loss, and without loss we cannot fully treasure the gifts we have been given.

Again, it is the natural tendency of our ego to seek to control, and its greatest horror is loss and decline. Therefore it always lives in a near steady state of terror, whether acknowledged or not, for it always hovers over the abyss of loss. The famous prayer of the twelve-step programs seeks an awareness of the distinction between the powers of which we are capable and those of which we are not. This daily discernment provides the only way in which any serenity can be achieved. The German word for "serenity" is *Gelassenheit*, which could be translated more literally as "the condition of having let go." The serene countenance of the Buddha is based on his recognition of the folly of seeking control, dominance, and containment. Having triumphed over both fear of loss and desire of sovereignty, he is free, and therefore serene. How far such serenity is from the frenzies of our market-fueled fantasies of acquisition, control, and ownership, and therefore how constant is our terror of loss and our flight from the honesty of grief. Again, only through relinquishment, which is a deliberate act of letting go of the false hope of permanent purchase on life's treasures, can one experience serenity, and at the same time savor the plenitude that has so richly come to each of us.

Betrayal

Who has not betrayed another, and who has not been betrayed? We are such fragile vessels that we fall far short of the ideals we would affirm. We betray our children by being less than we can be for them, even if we spend a good part of the time in conscientious sacrifice to them. We betray our friends and partners whenever our own agenda intrudes, as it always will, and yet who is strong enough or conscious enough to keep that hidden agenda at bay? Which of us has not felt an existential betrayal; who has not assumed he or she had a Job-like contract with life, and then had life treat him or her in a shabby fashion, which felt like a betrayal?

That we might not have such a contractual arrangement with the universe still does not protect us from a sense of betrayal, and those who most assume such a deal will feel the greatest betrayal. As one beginning patient hopefully questioned, "If I do my therapy, I will not suffer cancer?" There is no quid pro quo, and the "betrayal" is the betrayal of our expectations for such contracts. As Ecclesiastes recognized millennia ago, the rain falleth on the just and the unjust alike. So much for "deals."

Yet life demands that we set forth in an atmosphere of trust with each other. We trust that each of us will stop at the intersection and wait our turn. Accidents occur, but the necessity of trust remains. Those who are incapable of trust live in a conspiratorial, fear-flushed world and suffer the overgeneralizing, paranoid fantasy of betrayal. Often this sensibility is derived from actual slights, injustices, and abuses in the past. But what is so horrible is that such a wounded soul is bound to the stunted message of the past, and is governed by its fears and its limited range of human engagements. Such a person, so defended against betrayal, will never experience the richness and depth of relationship. In protecting our vulnerability we blunt all our possibilities.

Nonetheless, in each of these swampland visitations, we face a task. Even betrayal can sting us into enlargement, just as it may lead us to diminishment. In the bitter bite of betrayal, one may constructively ask, "Was I overly invested in some projection onto the other person?" Most relationships, especially those most intimate, have an aura of disappointment about them, for we silently feel the other has betrayed us by not meeting our agenda for that relationship. As we have already seen, such expectations are projections onto the other of our own mislaid responsibilities for ourselves. We are always letting the other down, as they let us down, even when we both try not to. An awareness of this agenda, and its inevitable betrayal, can lighten relationship by bringing us to a more realistic appraisal of possibility, and a more responsible assumption of the task of our own journey.

Betrayal may unmask our hidden dependencies. What were we really asking of the other? What were we counting on them to cover for us? Where were we not grown up in expecting the other to protect us from life's demands? Jack Spratt and his wife certainly had a rational division of labor, but the rest of us have to clean the platter by ourselves in the end. Holding the tension of opposites in any relationship—legitimate expectations of reciprocity on the one hand, and the assumption of responsibility on the other—leads us to a more evolved consciousness and a more evolved relationship. The subtext of most relationship is dependency, rather than mutual support of the independence of each party.

Just as the experience of the Self is frequently felt as an affront to the ego, so each of these swamplands overthrows the ego's autonomy. The challenge in this "defeat" is for the ego to grow, and thereby achieve some greater autonomy in the world.

Doubt and Loneliness

Doubt is a profound and effective spiritual motivator. Without doubt, no truism is transcended, no new knowledge found, no expansion of the imagination possible. Doubt is unsettling to the ego, and those who are drawn to ideologies that promise the dispelling of doubt by proffering certainties will never grow. In seeking certainty they are courting the death of the soul, whose nature is forever churning possibility, forever seeking the larger, forever riding the melting edge of certainty's glacier.

The suppression of doubt is the secret seed of fanaticism in all its forms, and therefore the secret drive engine in bigotry, sexism, homophobia, fundamentalism, and all other forms of contrived certainties. As Jung reminds us, "People who merely believe and don't think, forget that they continually expose themselves to their own worst enemy: doubt. Wherever belief reigns, doubt lurks in the background. But thinking people welcome doubt: it serves them as a valuable stepping-stone to better knowledge."*

The suppression of doubt is typically the defense of a neurosis, a defense against the paradoxes of life from which we invariably grow. In fact, most of the time we do not wish to grow. Those who say that they know what kind of art they like, or what kind of god, or what kind of moral structure are saying that they like what kind of art, god, structure they know, that is that which makes them feel more comfortable. Being pried free of spiritual constraint is the gift doubt brings. The suppression of doubt ensures that we are left with a partial truth, a one-sided value, a prejudicial narrowing of the richness that life has to bring.

As a young person I had great guilt in doubting some of the beliefs and practices of my elders. I now see that the "guilt" I experienced was actually the anxiety of being on my own spiritual journey. I feared losing their approval, the comfort of their certifications, and their companionship. But something deeper pushed even harder and I came to see that doubt led me to an ever-larger world in which contraries may in fact finally embrace. Further, doubt is necessary for democracy to really work. Totalitarianism is terrified of any doubt of its powers, its certainties, or its precepts; democracy flourishes when we express our doubts over a policy, over the motives of our leaders. Compare this with those who flee troubling ambiguity by wrapping themselves and their vehicles in flags, drown honest debate with chauvinistic clamor, and encourage a pseudo-patriotism that ill serves its nation by silencing serious dialogue that might lead to more refined judgment.

The paradox is that the hysterical certainties propagated by political and religious institutions are in fact an unconscious confession of their own insecurity. Wherever certainty is brandished so vehemently, it is generally in compensation for unconscious doubt, and therefore is dishonest. Our anxieties lead us to grasp at certainties. Certainties lead to dogma; dogma leads to rigidity; rigidity leads to idolatry; idolatry always banishes the mystery and thus leads to spiritual narrowing. To bear the anxiety of doubt is to be led to openness; openness leads to revelation; revelation leads to discovery; discovery leads to enlargement.

Doubt is also the necessary requisite to a radical openness to the

---

*Jung, *Psychological Reflections,* p. 354.

mystery. How easy it is for us to condescend to the ideas so fervently embraced as truisms by our ancestors, yet we perpetuate similar unexamined truisms today. What humankind has learned over and over is that the more we seem to know, the larger the mystery grows. The physics, chemistry, and genetics we learned decades ago is inadequate for the growing evidence and new questions of today. The mechanisms of the body, the interactions between body and mind, and the presence of a force that transcends mere observation—our awareness of all three grows more and more elusive. How can we not doubt *everything* when the world is so rich, and our conscious capacities so limited? Our doubt, then, is a form of radical trust, a trust that the world is richer than we know, so abundant that we can hardly bear it, and our growth requires a willingness to embrace the paradox that doubt is the key to its further riches.

But doubting also threatens us by bringing us to our essential loneliness, the place without external validation, the place where we most risk being who we really are, and feeling what we really feel. Loneliness is not one of the greatest disorders of the soul, but the fear of loneliness is. We are all lonely, even when amid crowds and in committed relationships. When we are alone, we are still with someone; we are with ourselves. The question is, *how* are we with ourselves? Those who manage to find respect for themselves, who learn to dialogue with themselves, who find that their dreams and other such phenomena are communicating with them from some deeper place within them are not really alone. We spoke earlier of the paralyzing power of guilt, the recognition of how far short we all fall in meeting the expectations of others and of ourselves. How necessary the task, then, of self-acceptance, self-forgiveness, self-love, and the embrace of our aloneness.

We have all heard of the necessity of self-love, but most of us have little clue as to how this is possible, or what it might even mean. We know that narcissism is not self-love but rather the confession that one cannot love the self. How necessary it is to rehear the words of that itinerant rabbi who said that one is to love one's neighbor as oneself. Most of us heard that commandment and failed to be told, or failed to grasp, that such love is only possible to the degree that one can love oneself. The failure to accept ourselves makes it very difficult, if not impossible, to accept others, despite our desire to do so. As Jung has so eloquently written of this biblical admonition:

> *Acceptance of oneself is the essence of the moral problem and the acid test of one's whole outlook on life. That I feed the beggar, that I forgive an insult, that I love my enemy in the name of Christ—all these are undoubtedly great virtues. What I do unto the least of my brethren, that I do unto Christ. But what if I should discover that the least amongst them all, the poorest of all beggars, the most impudent of all offenders, yea the very fiend himself—that these are within me, and that I myself stand in need of the alms of my own kindness, that I myself am the enemy who must be loved—what then?**

How much lonelier it is to live our soul's journey in a state of isolation from ourselves, no matter how many others are clustered around us. The flight from our loneliness proves to be a flight from ourselves, then. How much have we burdened our relationships as a treatment for loneliness, when all the while we have neglected our relationship to the only one who's been with us from the very be-

---

*Jung, *Psychological Reflections*, p. 239.

ginning? As Jung has observed this paradox, "Loneliness is not in-imical to companionship . . . for companionship thrives only when each individual remembers his individuality."† If we cannot bear being with ourselves, how is it that we ask another to do that for us? In fact, the capacity to be with ourselves, as we really are, finite, imperfect, and deeply flawed, will prove not only to be the "cure" for loneliness but our secret gift to others as well.

Depression

A colleague was visiting a small mountain village outside of Asheville, North Carolina, years ago, when Prozac first appeared on the scene. He dropped by a local pharmacy, the only one in town, where the pharmacist proudly announced that the majority of the adults in his village were on Prozac. "Progress," he boasted, was no stranger to this mountain redoubt. Indeed, the success of psychopharmacology has been so great that we have been called "the Prozac Nation." Psychiatry today is less a psychotherapeutic enterprise than a pharmacological crapshoot, and we have become a people who believe we will find happiness in a pill of some sort.

Let us revisit the subject of depression begun in the third chapter. Recall that in order to approach the subject of depression we have to recognize that the same word is being used in reference to what are startlingly different causes, states of being, and levels of meaning. Perhaps as many as a quarter of us suffer from a chemical imbalance that, like diabetes, is best treated by attempting to right the imbalance with medication. Yet because of the training of our physicians, and the mind-set of our culture, too many suffering the

---

†Jung, *Memories, Dreams, Reflections,* p. 356.

symptoms of depression are just given a prescription and it all ends there. Never mind what issues of meaning have been raised, what side effects may be encountered, be assured that your physician, your insurance company, and your pharmaceutical sales rep will be pleased you are on the pill, rather than engaging in much more ambiguous questions.

Another kind of depression is reactive in character and occurs most typically when we have suffered a loss of some kind—the loss of a loved one, a reversal in the outer world, or the loss of a value we once cherished. Not to react to this loss would be pathological, and would indicate that we had placed no value in the first place on what's been lost. A reactive depression is only pathological when it lasts too long or interferes too much in the conduct of our lives. But who is to say what is too long or too much? A reactive depression is a subjective state that can only be evaluated by subjective criteria, namely how you suffer it, what it does to you, and what it might keep you from doing. Medicating this state is likely to confuse if not obscure this useful questioning.

The third kind of depression, from which we all suffer from time to time, may be called intrapsychic depression and occurs as an autonomous reaction of the psyche to the impact of our culture, or the choices we have made in living our lives, upon our souls. No matter how successful we have been in the outer world, judged by standards external to us, if we are not living in accord with the intent of our soul, depression is likely to follow. The more I try to do what "I" wish to do, and the less it is what the soul intends, the more depressed I will become. In such moments of intrapsychic conflict, the potential value of the depression emerges, if we can ask a larger question than how to rid ourselves of the bad feeling— "What, then, is the summons of my soul?" If I am able to humbly submit myself to this question, I may face large changes in my outer life, the replacement of old values upon which I have grown too dependent, or be called to an agenda of growth that intimidates me. But I will become less depressed.

How critical it is for us to differentiate these quite different states of being that all fall under the generic word *depression*. If we fail to understand their origin, confuse their common symptoms with differing causes, then we will likely fail to work our way through the depression to its meaning. I once counseled a young man who had suffered testicular cancer from which he was, understandably, reactively depressed, who struggled to separate from a family of origin that had oppressed and depressed him greatly, and moreover was in the grip of a biologically based depression—all at the same time. What he needed was a combination of medication and psychotherapy, and as a result of both, he got on the track of his real life much faster and much more consciously than if we had left any piece of the puzzle out. But how often do our psychiatrists, or our physicians, or our therapists for that matter, neglect to explain and educate us about the different kinds of depression, wind up treating them all alike, and as a result leave so much unaddressed?

The majority of us suffer, if not an enervating depression, then at least pockets of depression, for who among us has managed to live a life wholly in accord with the soul when we're all trying to serve the cultural agenda at the same time? If we look at this existential condition, we find that we all have a set of questions to address: What is depression but life wishing to express itself but being "pressed down"? What wishes to live within us? Find that, and give it energy, value, and enactment in the world, and the depression will lift. So we need to ask: "Where am I stuck, blocked by archaic fears, and therefore repeating, reinforcing the conditions that have produced my disabling depression?" "What new life is seeking to live through me, and what must I do to bring it into being?" After all, intrapsychic depression is the psychodynamic reaction of our own nature; to respect nature's intent is to begin the healing project.

So often in midlife and the second half of life, one encounters depression, as the soul escalates its protest over the life which we have chosen, or had chosen for us. The ego attitudes, no matter how sincere and culturally reinforced they may be, are exhausted, yet we redouble our efforts. Why would we not grow more depressed?

As Jung metaphorically expressed it, "A neurosis is an offended god."* What he meant is that an energy in us has been repressed, oppressed, split off, projected onto others, and thereby has been wounded or "offended." Just as the ancient world might describe the origin of spiritual suffering as a slighted god, so our healing solicits a deepened conversation with the psyche. The respect owed a "deity" is the respect we owe those motive-driven energies that course within us and seek fuller expression. To deny them is to pathologize what is divine in us and to deepen self-estrangement.

An intrapsychic depression is thus an invitation to the recovery of a deeper dimension, a reorienting of the surface of life to its depths. In coming to acknowledge the agenda that the depression solicits may occasion greater anxiety, but the agitation of growth, change, the movement into a larger life is far preferable to the misery of diminishing, life-thwarting depression. An approach that emphasizes distraction, as popular cultures does, or medication, as many psychotherapists do, as palliatives to the authentic sufferings of the soul, betrays our larger interests, no matter how well in-

---

*Jung, *CW 7*, para. 392.

tended the treatment is. The therapeutic secret of a depression is not found by suppressing it with biochemical agents, but by asking its meaning. This investigative approach is enlarging, and the soul will not fail to offer direction if we are willing to be open. Some, myself included, have even come in the end to bless their depression, for it obliges them to become more conscious and to change their lives.

Addictions

As we have seen, we live in a culture that breeds addictions, for our psychic roots are severed from a deep mythic ground. This mythological dislocation increases the steady hum of anxiety, always just beneath the surface of even our most mindless forms of escape. No one is free of addictions, for addictions are anxiety-management techniques the purpose of which is to lower the level of psychic distress we feel at any given moment, whether we are conscious of the distress or not. In no person's life are these anxiety-reduction patterns absent. For one person stress is relieved by a cigarette, for another food, for another a phone call to a friend, for another work, for another some simple repetitive activity such as cleaning the house, for another compulsive prayer.

What all these disparate acts have in common is that they are treating existential anxiety, whether consciously or not, that they have a compulsive character, which means that they have a life outside our conscious control or awareness, and that at best they offer only partial soothing of the stress. If we did not find some relief as a result of the behavior, we would move to one where we did. But such relief is at best momentary; then the anxiety rises again, and the palliative behavior must be enacted again—and therein lies the addictive hook. The less the life we have built, or the life we have received, or the life that is foisted upon us, serves our soul's desires, the more we will suffer the anxiety that leads to addictions. So in our compulsively alienating society, addictions find ready breeding grounds, leaving only the question of how costly the side effects of the addictive behaviors prove.

Well-intended efforts to "cure" addictions, or suppress the drug trade, or create new social programs are doomed to failure, for the core issue, the floating anxiety that is endemic to a culture that lives by artifice rather than natural values, is never addressed consciously. Similarly the efforts of the religious right to suppress overt addictive behavior merely drives the anxiety into the underworld, where it has no choice but to find its outlet in child or spousal abuse, health problems, barely controlled angers, or the thousand other leakages through which any repressed emotion inevitably finds expression. The fatuous admonition of a former First Lady to "just say no" sounds seductive at first, but ultimately proves ineffectual in the face of the encroachments of anxiety that drive to find defenses of some kind. Perhaps the subtlest, and most pervasive, of addictive management techniques is habit itself, for habit is one of the means by which we hold off ambiguity and anxiety. Simply reflect on how irritated, that is how anxious, you feel, when your habits, your daily routines, your conventional expectations are interrupted.

While the origin of addictive behaviors is understandable, and forgivable, their effect on our lives, and those around us, can be devastating. Not only do we remove ourselves from more authentic, more developmental engagements with life, but we are also caught in a circular response to life that can only replicate itself, and the pain that lies at its core. Moreover, in this repetitive cycle addictions bind us both to the past and to an anticipatory anxious fantasy of what the unknown future might bring. Even worse, addictions narrow our lives by obliging us to obsess on the "treat-ment plan." Through focus on the repetitive behavior, the person "treats" the anxiety through distraction and displacement. The smoker worries about the next smoke, the drinker about the capac-ity to achieve an alteration of mood, the shopper and gambler worry about the mounting fiscal cost, while the eater computes the number of calories, the compulsive perfectionist worries about the next sin or shortfall, the worker labors under the impossible burden of getting it all done, and so on.

Can it be that the treatment is worse than that which it is treat-ing? To ever break the stranglehold of addiction, one is going to have to face what the compulsive behavior is a defense against. To go down into that anxiety state, to really feel what we already feel, and to learn that we are not really destroyed by it, is to "go through" the addiction to its other side. It is to break the tyranny of anxiety without ceasing to feel anxious.

Usually one is only willing to face these disturbing feelings when one is forced to, in desperation, because the cost has become too much. The cost in money, the decline of health, the burden on re-lationships, the narrowed life—all cost us more than the core anxi-ety warrants. To consciously acknowledge the anxiety will certainly require resolve, but it may be done if one understands the cost of the addictive cycle. As great as our anxieties may be, it may also be that we fear even more being robbed of life by those "treatment plans" we evolved. Originally servants, they become our masters, and we may conclude that this is not acceptable. After all, as Hei-degger observed once, "the terrible" has already happened. Ac-knowledging this means one may find the resolve to feel what one feels, and suffer what one has already suffered, and find the recov-ery of one's journey possible once more.

Anxieties

At bottom, all of our problems can be traced back to the omnipresence of anxiety. As we saw earlier, we all share the common condition of existential anxiety occasioned by overwhelmment or abandonment. The specific role anxiety plays in our stories derives from the variegated conditions life has brought us, the reactions of our own nature and character, and the great variety of possible outcomes.

It is first useful for us to differentiate angst from anxiety from fear. *Angst* is the German word for anticipatory anxiety or dread that accompanies the human condition because the threat of annihilation is palpable and present from our first to our last breath. Our fragile estate floats over a great abyss, and no matter how diverting our strategies may be, there is no day in which we do not know this simple fact. An acceptance of this angst as normal is healthy; its denial is pathological, and will sooner or later result in some life-estranging behavior, or worse, the trivialization of the journey. The task brought to us is to live our lives fully, in the presence of the threat of annihilation. The failure to do so is the abrogation of life, and we its failed authors. So if life is nasty, brutish, and short, as philosopher Thomas Hobbes once opined, then live it nonetheless. So often I run into folks who judge themselves as inadequate somehow or flawed because they are anxious. Only the psychotic or unconscious are free of anxiety, and what a price they have paid.

Anxiety is free-floating, unattached, not unlike the fog that obscures the road we drive. Fear, however, is specific and if we can convert our anxiety into specific fears we will have taken a powerful step. The reader no doubt thinks trading anxiety for fear is hardly a victory. But anxiety is ambiguous and paralyzing; the specifics of fear, however, are something that consciousness can address. Our fears are typically derived from our powerless past, but from a conscious, much more empowered present, fears may be confronted. In most cases these anticipatory fears may fail to materialize; if they do, we can generally handle them, or survive them. What was overwhelming to the child is often merely problematic to the psychologically larger adult. However, when one learns that beneath the current anxiety there is a buried filament that reaches back to a childhood fear, then one learns the secret of the disabling power of the anxious present. To see in the cloud of anxiety the specificity of a fear, to confront the fear as an adult, is to break the tyranny of anxiety. But to be free entirely of anxiety is unrealistic and delusory, no matter how energetic one's mental gymnastics or addictive "treatment plans." At least one should not add the corrosive power of shame to our common condition of anxiety.

If we look hard enough, we will find anxiety, or its management, at the roots of so much we do. It is disconcerting to realize this fact, but in recognizing the ubiquity of anxiety in our lives and in those around us, we may feel greater compassion for ourselves and for each other. Philo of Alexandria is reported to have said, "Be kind. Everyone you meet is carrying a big problem." If we can accept that about ourselves and each other, accept the normality of anxiety, seek the roots of identifiable fears in that anxiety, then simply do the best that we can and forgive the rest, we may at last become less anxious.

How Do We Avoid Swamplands?

The common fantasy of our culture is that we can avoid, or solve, such swampland visitations as we have described. We would like the second half of life to be clutter free. Guess again. Fate, the movement of the deep forces of nature, the autonomous powers of our history, and our own choices will take us to swamplands from time to time, and no amount of right thinking, right behavior, right theology, or even right psychology will spare us from such descents. Those who promise otherwise are charlatans.

Under the stress of the swamplands, we are most likely to regress further by continuing to employ those understandings, those strategies, those attitudes that brought us there in the first place. If one is in a deep hole and has only a shovel in one's hand, surely the temptation is to use the same shovel to dig even deeper. Don't we need instead to see that the swamplands are an inevitable and necessary counterpart to our conscious fantasies of power? Is it an accident that the more we have conquered in the outer world, the more the disquiet of our inner world? The ongoing curriculum of life does not demand that we avoid suffering; it asks instead that we live more meaningfully in the face of it.

Despite the blandishments of popular culture, *the goal of life is not happiness but meaning*. Those who seek happiness by trying to avoid or finesse suffering will find life more and more superficial. As we have seen, in every swampland there is a task, the addressing of which will enlarge one's life not diminish it. Life is not a problem to be solved, finally, but a series of engagements with the cosmos in which we are asked to live as fully as we can manage. In so doing we serve the transcendent meaning that is meant to be brought into being through us. In fleeing this fullness of life, we violate our very purpose.

In the second half of life there are many experiences of defeat and disappointment. We lose friends, our children, our energies, and finally our lives. Who could manage in the face of such seeming defeat? And yet the task of life asks that we embrace this agenda of apparent loss as much as the agenda of acquisition that the first half of life served.

As Jung notes:

> *In the secret hour of life's midday the parabola is reversed, death is born. The second half of life does not signify ascent, unfolding, increase, exuberance, but death, since the end is its goal. The negation of life's fulfillment is synonymous with the refusal to accept its ending. Both mean not wanting to live, and not wanting to live is identical with not wanting to die. Waxing and waning make one curve.* *

The flight from the swamplands of the soul, however unpleasant they may be to consciousness, is the flight from the wholeness of life, a wholeness that may only be expressed in paradox, and any psychology or worldview that excludes paradox is excluding half of life itself.

The central paradox of our current feel-good culture is that we grow progressively more and more uncertain and less and less persuaded that our lives really mean something. Feeling good is a poor measure of a life, but living meaningfully is a good one, for then we are living a developmental rather than regressive agenda. We never get it all worked out anyway. Life is ragged, and truth is still more raggedy. The ego will do whatever it can to make itself more comfortable; but the soul is about wholeness, and this fact makes the ego even more uncomfortable. Wholeness is not about comfort, or goodness, or consensus—it means drinking this brief, unique, deeply rooted vintage to its dregs.

As we have so often seen, the task of ego consciousness in the

---

*Jung, *Psychological Reflections,* p. 323.

second half of life is to step out of the way and embrace a larger spiritual agenda. Contrary to the fantasy of the youthful ego, this larger life will quite often be found in the savannahs of suffering—not on the lofty peaks of New Age transcendence, or in fundamentalism's fearful flight from complexity, but down in what Yeats called "the fury and mire of human veins." Only in this way do we grow, and do we find, amid suffering and defeat, the possibility of meaning so rich we can scarcely bear it. For this embrace of suffering, this acceptance of paradox, we deserve to be valued. As Jung put it so aptly, "This apparently unendurable conflict is proof of the rightness of your life. A life without inner contradiction is only half a life, or else a life in the Beyond which is destined only for angels. But God loves human beings more than the angels."*

Though we may not understand it at the moment, each swampland visitation is an enrichment, for it is an opening to a deepened consciousness, which can only be purchased through the experience of the opposites. This engagement of opposites leads to enlargement, not diminishment. If truth be told, we wish we didn't have to grow, but life is asking more of us than that. Our daily obligation to destiny must become like that of the soldier described by Nikos Kazantzakis, whose prayer is "the report to a general: This is what I did today, this is how I fought to save the entire battle in my own sector, these are the obstacles I found, this is how I plan to fight tomorrow."†

---

*Jung, *Letters*, Vol. I, p. 375.*
† Kazantzakis, *The Saviors of God*, p. 107.

Chapter Eleven

The Healing of the Soul

"Though inland far we be,
Our Souls have sight of that immortal sea
Which brought us hither."

William Wordsworth, "Ode: Intimations of Immortality from
Recollections of Early Childhood"

"If you don't break your ropes while you're alive
do you
think ghosts will do it after?"

Kabir

DURING THE COURSE of his long and distin-
guished career, the Irish poet W. B. Yeats often changed
his themes, style, and personal philosophy, sometimes
leaving behind the audience he had cultivated. When he was up-
braided for this confusing constancy of change, he replied:

The friends have it I do wrong
Whenever I remake my song
Should know what issue is at stake.
It is myself that I remake. *

---

*Cited by Richard Ellmann, *Yeats: The Man and the Masks*, p. 186.

His devotion to change grew both from his fidelity to his talent and from the urgings of his soul. Bringing both together was his vocation.

How, then, are we to weather the sea changes of our voyage, how sustain the journey and heal the soul at the same time? Sometimes the healing of the soul occurs naturally, instinctually, when we, or our environment, do not interfere with the processes. That we even have to take up the question of spiritual healing is a measure of where we stand in the history of civilization. If the images of our popular culture effectively supported the desires of the soul, then we would have no need of reflection, or therapy, or books to stir us to an enlarged consciousness. For centuries now, the technologically advanced cultures have made immense strides in engineering the material world, health care, transportation, and communication, and have constructed ever-new virtual realities, yet we grow concomitantly more and more separated from nature, and from an instinctual relationship to our own life. So much has this divergence come to be the central source of our suffering that even the word *soul* is suspect, coopted as it is by New Age finesse artists on the one hand, and avoided as it is by the educational and scientific communities on the other. (Recall that even psychology has banished *psyche*, or soul, from its serious consideration, in favor of the lesser forms of behavior and cognition and biochemistry.) We suffer progressive failures of nerve before the mystery, which grows ever larger the more we make advances elsewhere. This failure of nerve leads us to smaller questions, and smaller lives.

For all the changes that have occurred over the last four centuries, perhaps our greatest loss is the diminution of dialogue about that mystery toward which the word *soul* is meant to point. We might call Hamlet our first modern comrade. He has clear marching orders, like us, but his resolutions are "sicklied over with the pale cast of thought and lose the name of action," like ours. In other words, he is neurotic like us; his conscious intentions are undermined by inner, unknown agencies, like ours. He confesses that he could be bounded in a walnut shell, and count himself a king of infinite space, were he not, like us, troubled by bad dreams. He is a stranger to his world, and a stranger to himself, and yet he seems very, very familiar to each of us.

Or we could find our modern brother in Goethe's Faust, who wishes to know all, at any cost, yet blanches when the bill arrives. We see how the noble Faust becomes "faustian" when he can no longer connect his search for knowledge to an ethical grounding. We learn through Kafka's "A Country Doctor" that the world once summoned the priest in his black gown and then, when he could not save, transferred their demands to the physician in his white gown, and now he has proved unable to save them either. Have we not learned the limits of our institutions, and the shadowy agendas haunting even our noblest ideas?

From such prophetic artists, from the million voices in the rehab clinics, from the anguished cries of those who are lost, alone, and despairing, from those who are dumbed out in television land, or wandering like lost herds through the malls, or aimlessly preening for acceptance at social galas, we learn how far the luminous soul of each has been driven underground. If we want to begin to address the healing of the soul, we have to be willing to both look within ourselves for clues, and radically look, with spiritually attuned eyes, at the world in which we live. For, as Jung has described so eloquently:

Anyone who wants to know the human psyche will learn next to nothing from experimental psychology. He would be better advised to put away his scholar's gown, bid farewell to his study, and wander with human heart through the world. There, in

*the horrors of prisons, lunatic asylums and hospitals, in drab
suburban pubs, in brothels and gambling-hells, in the salons of
the elegant, the Stock Exchanges, Socialist meetings, churches, re-
vivalist gatherings and ecstatic sects, through love and hate,
through the experience of passion in every form in his own body,
he would reap richer stores of knowledge than textbooks a foot
thick could give him, and he will know how to doctor the sick
with real knowledge of the human soul.**

So if we are to approach the more conscious unfolding of our
own lives, we are obliged to return to the questions that began this
journey. Living the questions that serve the ego, or the culture's insecurity, will only infantilize. Rather, we need questions that ask
that we grow up.

What has brought you to this place in your journey, this moment in your life?

We are a storm-tossed skiff adrift on many streams, with contend-
ing currents, driven by a source far to our rear, and toward a port
with no certain name. Seldom did we ever believe we were acting
against our own interests, nor did we believe that we were in the
grip of the unconscious, precisely because it was unconscious. But
here we are, and it is unlikely that any of us would have predicted
where we have arrived today—with whom we are partnered, what
careers we have launched and abandoned, our many appointments
with defeat and disappointment.

Yet two forces have been at work at all times. The one is a mys-

---

*Jung, *Psychological Reflections*, p. 81.

terious current that carries us forward, toward whatever the gods intended, and the other some thousand counter-currents that come from the world around us, the world we were obliged to internalize. To borrow the metaphor of Beowulf, we have been on this "whale-road" for some time, in part driven by fate, in part driven by external pressures, in part correcting our course through increased consciousness, and in part compelled by the ineluctable unfolding of destiny. (*Destiny* is a word that originally meant following a course, as a river within its banks, subject to modification, risking drying up, flooding at times, being replenished, but always coursing toward an outlet in the large, tenebrous sea of the soul.)

If we do not pause from time to time to slow the rush, to ponder this question of what brought us to this place in the journey, this moment in life, then we may be sure that we have abdicated any responsibility for the journey, forsworn any capacity for choice and concomitant meaning, and relinquished the future as well. We are told that what we do not know will not hurt us; it does, and others as well. If one does not reflect on these various forces, one may be sure that these same forces will continue to work their way toward unconscious replication. Anyone who avoids this question may be intelligent, but not conscious. Consciousness is a task that renews its challenge every morning.

What gods, what forces, what family, what social environment have framed your reality, perhaps supported, perhaps constricted it?

As we saw, the classical Greek imagination personified the powers at work in the world, powers to which even the gods were subject, with such names as *moira* (fate: the givens that determine our makeup, such as our genetics, our family, our Zeitgeist), *nemesis* (the consequences of our choices, which track us, punish us through undesired repetitions), *sophrosyne* (the balancing of cause and effect over time, or what goes around comes around). Further, they identified aspects of our character such as *hubris*, the tendency to self-deception and the inflationary overconfidence that we are always capable of making conscious decisions. They further imagined that when we are ignorant of these powers at work in the world, and in our own souls, we "offend the gods," who are their archetypal embodiment. Thus, we can be possessed by mad Ares in our rages, overthrown by Aphrodite when we subvert the ministries of love, or pulled to ground in our inflationary flights of ego exuberance by the leveling powers of any offended deity.

The classical imagination dramatized an archetypal stage on which we are always at play, whether we know it or not, always in the presence of the demanding scrutiny of the gods, whether we acknowledge them or not. We are not summoned to perfection; that is the realm of the gods; we are rather called to mindfulness, to approach such fields of divine reference with sensitivity, respect, and humility.

Central to the biasing of our personal vision is the fate-driven childhood matrix in which our first lessons about self, about other, and about the transactions between are programmed. The implicit and the explicit messages of the family of origin are, next to the archetypal field, the deeply compelling powers of our own nature, the most powerful determinants in our lives, for they constitute the primal messages internalized and are deeply ingrained by daily repetition in the years when we are most impressionable, most dependent, least capable of rational reflection.

In ever-widening circles we have to include our neighborhoods, our tribes, our nations, our cultures, our Zeitgeist as further influences on such vital matters as self and world, and the many expectations that come with social contracts. For some persons the family and the culture are supportive of their nature, and for others, most others, their nature finds itself opposed by the powerful collective forces around it. As a result, a deep split evolves between fate and destiny, between the forces of determinism and the possibilities inherent in all of us. This inevitable split is our common condition—the only differences among us are how deep the split, how pathologizing to us, and how divergent from the agenda of the soul.

When we begin to reflect on the patterns that our history reveals—knowing that we never intended to repeat our wounded history over and over, never expected the symptoms that impose themselves on consciousness, and never intended the conflicts that have arisen between our good intentions and our true effect upon others—then we know that there are other forces at work outside the frame of consciousness and we are led to wonder: "Whose life have I been living?"

If it is not ours, so to speak, whose life then? Yet we are the only character who is present in each scene, so we must be held accountable in the end. In many cases we are living the unlived life of our parents. Wherever they were blocked, so we may be blocked, or suffer the drive to overcome their limitation, or distance ourselves from that particular dilemma in the course of our own journey. When we are carrying the unconscious life of the family, we are programmed most commonly to repeat the pattern, or seek to compensate for it, or to find some "treatment plan" for it, such as addictions, overwork, or mindless avoidance of the soul task that life brings.

The recovery of one's own life from the multitudinous forces at work within it becomes an imperative, and it begins with accountability. If you do not like your life, change it, but stop blaming others, for even if they did hurt you, you are the one who has been making the choices of adulthood. Even if you have chosen out of those hurts, you are nonetheless accountable for those choices. You are always accountable for living your life, and not someone else's.

Consider these questions in the light of the following dream in three scenes dreamed recently by a man in his late forties who has been in sales most of his adult life. He found his relationships with women turbulent and transient, his commercial success lacking in abiding satisfaction, and his only refuge in music, for which he has no little talent and much passion:

I am in a large living room of an old house. (Victorian atmosphere.) There is some kind of counseling session going on. I think it is supposed to be individual, but there are others there and I am irritated. We have been tested. My notebooks have gotten good grades.

There is a tall, intelligent, aloof woman. I am attracted to her. I find that she is a prostitute part of the time. I am upset by this but also encourage her to do this. I am afraid to let her know how much I disapprove of this.

I am looking at a display for some new, avant-garde music. It has an illustrated dust jacket. Suddenly the illustrations grow animated and come to life.

After decades of analytic practice, I remain impressed, indeed astonished, at the power of some psychic center in each of us to produce such compelling images and present them to consciousness. Who would ever make these things up consciously? And yet we all are living these dramas every night, and by light of day enacting them, as such intrapsychic images govern our moods and our choices. We are, in the end, mythological creatures. Our mythic movements are in response to the value-laden force fields that hum just beneath the visible surface of things. So let us look more closely at the dream.

Remember the man's dilemma. He has been very successful in his business life, if money is a sign of success, but his relational life has been unsteady, and his general mood state has evidenced a malaise that borders on depression. Look now at the images.

Part one of the dream places him in an old house, with Victorian dimensions. We all live in such old houses, for a house is a common symbol of a residential ego structure whose values and scenarios, even after the passage of generations, still govern the choices of the living. In the context of this charged history, an effort toward understanding is transpiring; the dreamer has undertaken a deliberate therapeutic relationship. While his therapy sessions are of course focused on the present, they naturally swarm with the historical presences that we all carry all the time. As his conscious life has been interfered with by such presences, so he expresses irritation. At the same time, he, that is his ego consciousness, feels that he has played the cards handed him by life well, that he has achieved good grades from whatever evaluations befell him. (From the standpoint of materialistic culture, he is right; from the standpoint of psychic life, he suffers.)

In part two, his relationship to the inner world (what Jung called the *anima,* Latin for "soul" that which is compensatory to his outer masculine identity and role) is troubled. He is attracted to this part of his psychic life but also learns that it has engaged in prostitution. His inner split is so clear when he both disapproves of selling his inner life and encourages prostituting it at the same time. In fact, he is fearful to bring the issue up for discussion, for, after all, a guy's gotta make a buck, play the game, get ahead.

In part three we find a transformative element. When music appears, new and at the edge of creative expression, the dust of history is animated, and the soul springs to life. Consciously, the dreamer knows the inherent value of music to him, and all that music embodies for him, and yet consciously, as most of us do most of the time, he daily trudges off to a life that takes him further and further from what he loves. Why would he not have some depression, as the psyche weighs in with its vote? Why would he not have unstable, inconsistent relationships with women when this is the relationship he has managed to his inner feminine? The psyche, for all its mystery, is very clear, and very logical, once we have begun to open the ego's resistance to an honest dialogue. It is encouraging to report that at this writing, he has listened to his dreams, is taking Flamenco lessons on his guitar, and the work continues.

We dream this way every night. And every day the world is full of clues as to the will of the soul, if we are willing or desperate enough to begin to pay attention. If and when we do begin to take this inner life seriously, our locus of sensibility, our psychic gravity, begins to change. From this internal change, profound changes of the outer world become possibilities.

Why, even when things are going well, do things not feel quite right?

While the world is full of clues to us, most of the time we do not see them. As Jesus reportedly protested in the Gnostic Gospel of Thomas, the kingdom of God is spread all over the world and we do not see it. Such clues are found not only in our dreams, but in our patterns, in how others relate to us, how our body reacts, how our feelings rise as autonomous critiques and expressions of value, how energy is available for some things and not for others—clues everywhere. Clues everywhere!* But these clues are so often

---

*T. S. Eliot's "The Journey of the Magi" depicts the three wise guys from the East who visit the manger in Bethlehem. Looking for power, for magic, for shazam, they miss clues scattered all around them. The reader, viewing the scene from the promontory of history, understands the clues and wonders how the three wisenheimers can be so opaque. So are we all, when clues stare us in the face, so are we all.

drowned by the cacophony of messages from the world around us, as well as the committee of complexes within. Their voices say, "please Mom and Dad," "make money," "be successful," "get married," "raise children," "make them dutiful so that they will take care of you," "choose security over truth," "choose what your peers choose," "seek authority in the consensus," and so on.

These interfering voices are quite familiar to us, for we have lived with them for a long time. They once came from parents' mouths, or from one's tribe, and offered a path to acceptance by others. Who could resist such siren calls? So why is it, then, that so many people, having obeyed these imperatives to the best of their ability, are so unhappy with their lives and with themselves? Why is it that "success" in achieving these goals so often feels empty? Why, having followed the plan, served the marching orders, does one not feel an inner assent, a rightness which confirms?

Why does so much seem a disappointment, a betrayal, a bankruptcy of expectations?

The simplest answer to these questions is found in the fact that so much we do serves the values of collectivity and violates the essential nature of our individual selves. Even when we accomplish what we set out to accomplish, the achievement seldom feels right because it is seldom about us at all. As Joseph Campbell said on television once, we can spend decades climbing the ladder, only to realize too late that we have placed it against the wrong wall. That wall may be someone else's wall, but not yours. So much feels a betrayal of expectations because, as we saw in the chapter on relationships, we are imposing the very large agenda of the soul upon finite, fragile things, fragile people, and fragile roles. No person, no role in life, however rewarding, can ever carry the complete aspirations of the soul—only our move toward wholeness can. Wholeness is not found in perfection, which is neither achievable nor desirable—the former because we are too flawed and never live long enough to get it all right, and the latter because it would exclude its opposite and thereby undermine wholeness.

As we have seen, the youth needs projections to pull him or her into life. Who would have left home at all if they could not believe that their career would offer emotional satisfaction sufficient to appease the hunger within? Who would have entered a relationship without the fantasy of homecoming, of nurturance and security in large measure? Who would have brought children into the world if they knew the children would become new objects of worry and emotional vulnerability rather than carriers of their parents unlived life?

The first half of life feeds on these projections, but so often during the second half of life, these projections lose their powers in the face of the abrasions of daily life, and one suffers ennui, disappointment, or even a sense that the presumed contract has been betrayed. The projected values were intended to win approval, gain love, success, security, and an abiding sense of community. So why, then, the ennui, the hum of malaise beneath the surface, the sleepless nights, the reliance on substances for comfort or anesthesia, the lure of an illicit relationship?

Could these so-called symptoms prove precisely the clue for which we seek? Are they not the rejected gods of the underworld, speaking in their symbolic ways? Is what we seek to be found not "out there," but beneath our noses? If such projections are necessary for the first half of life, then their erosion, their bankruptcy may be necessary for the second half of life. For then we are obliged to inquire into them, find what values of the soul they have been carrying, and begin to own those values more directly as *our* task, not that of our career, partner, or children. What, indeed, does it profit one to gain the world that the projections have offered, and find that the price is loss of relationship to one's soul? It is in the swamplands of disappointment, then, that the task of personal ownership of the soul may be reclaimed. It may be hard to thank the soul for plunging us into swamplands, but there, in those dismal depths of defeat, disappointment, and depression, we may recover the high journey of soul work each of us is meant to undertake.

As long as we continue to cruise along, buoyed by the successes of projections, we will be seduced into unconscious identification with trivial values. Once when I drove up to work in a newly leased vehicle, someone observed that I "must be so happy." I was dumbfounded because I could not understand what this person was referring to. She reported that her friend was so happy because she had a new car, so I must be so happy, too! I was speechless. I said something about a car being a piece of metal which moves me from one place to another, but chose not to add that I might be happier if we had a more equitable society where people on the streets we drive had a home and food to eat tonight. Thank goodness, then, for the "betrayal," the swamplands, so that we may be rescued from such trivia and become more mindful of what may really matter in the long journey of the soul.

The bad news for the ego's fantasy of sovereignty is that we suffer; the good news for the soul is that we suffer. Such suffering can bring us to a radical reconsideration of the meaning and direction of our lives. So often I have seen patients who knew perfectly well what they were called to do, and what decisions they should make, but were understandably afraid of the rejection of others, loneliness, and most of all having to grow up and be wholly responsible for themselves. In many cases, they ran from this impending appointment with the soul, and in some cases, they chose to suffer the rebirth of a relationship to the soul. The projections, if examined carefully, diminish life through their narrow frame; growing up enlarges life, makes it more interesting, and we might even become thereby somewhat less of a problem to those around us.

Why do you believe that you have to hide so much, from others, from yourself?

Who among us did not learn to conceal, having first learned that to reveal is to be at risk? The less supportive the environment, the more troubled or preoccupied the family, the more costly the child's disclosures of his or her natural narcissistic needs will prove. Accordingly, most children learn to protect themselves, to seek the satisfaction of their needs surreptitiously, or not at all. In fact, sometimes children lose touch with their needs altogether and spend a life of chameleon-like adaptation to the demands of those around them. Thus, so many of us live as strangers to ourselves. The message of one's essential powerlessness is overlearned and one feels little permission to express oneself forthrightly. Here again, permission will not be given; the adult must seize it. What once passed for amiability, for a cooperative spirit, for "niceness," becomes, in the second half of life, an unacceptable liability. This accommodating reflex, so necessary an adaptation for the child, requires the daily sacrifice of integrity as an adult—then it is not so "nice." When we come to recognize that we *are* a truth, a truth meant to be lived, a truth the denial of which harms not only ourselves, but others as well, then we are much more inclined to speak directly and candidly. The abrogation of this truth is a violation of the soul, and the soul will always respond to this bad faith somewhere down the line, and sooner rather than later.

One patient's mother was so extremely fragile emotionally that he learned that to shout, or even speak loudly, or to bring his needs to the table in any way resulted in her hysterical outbursts or withdrawal from him. Accordingly, he learned to manage his mother at an early age. He devoted himself to her needs and stifled his own. Is it any wonder that years later he entered the nursing profession, work that consciously appealed to his sense of service, but that unconsciously linked him to a familiar relational pattern? He came into therapy under a mandate from his hospital for his outbursts of anger in the presence of patients. Is is any wonder that beneath all that accommodation of others lay the enraged child who had never experienced true reciprocity from others?

Notice how this patient had unconsciously set himself up by his choice of profession. He was always going to have to assume more than half the responsibility for the relationship with patients who were legitimately debilitated and needful. When he began to consider the roots of his rage, he was nonplussed even to learn that he'd been wounded by life. Learning that he was angry, which his outbursts revealed with their leakage through his repression, he began for the first time since childhood to pay attention to his feeling life. It would be nice to report that his life improved suddenly. In fact it got worse, in a sense, as he grew aware of the large life that not only had been denied him, but with which he had colluded in denying himself. Such recognition, such paying of forgotten dues, is the requisite for reforming one's life.

Learning to be honest and to cease hiding oneself requires enormous courage, especially given the fact that the adaptive reflex—that is, the complex—is wired to an archaic place where great danger lurks. Realizing that that danger is linked to the powerless past of childhood, and not to the competent, coping adult one has become, is necessary to firm up the resolve to live with more candor. So often a person will, in defense of the old complex, convert honest speaking or presentation into its opposite, fearing selfishness, rather than see it as the authentic expression of the self.

Just as there is a progressive energy at work within us, so there is a very conservative power that seeks to limit growth by limiting vulnerability. As all growth requires facing what we fear, we naturally learn patterns that protect against the fear. If we cannot speak the truth, our truth, to ourselves, we will be unable to speak it to the world either. Speaking it to the world requires that one learn to speak it to oneself first, and then to realize that our truth is who we are. To deny the complex truth we embody is more than a personal wound—it is a wound to the world by our refusal to participate in it, a reluctance to add our unique aspect to the whole. Seen in that light, it may fuel each of us to risk greater disclosure of who we are, for we are brought here to add our small portion of the truth to the world, our uniquely colored chip in the larger mosaic of being.

Why does life seem a script written elsewhere, and you barely consulted, if at all?

Do you recall sitting in second or third grade and watching as a visitor came to your classroom, that larger, older person whom you believed wise, authoritative, and powerful? Do you recall believing that the big folks in the world knew what was really going on and were, by and large, in charge of it all? That classroom visitor could now be you, stepping into the room and receiving the projections of all the little folks therein. You know better, that you are only who you are, and that you are barely removed from their world; nonetheless, they look upon you with awe. You've become a big person just by living long enough, at least in their eyes. In your eyes, if you are honest, you have not even become a big person yet, although you may be playing large roles. What then does it take for us to become a "big person," with a childhood history consciously reflected upon, versus a "big person" who is still being run by that child?

It is not unrealistic for the child to think that there is a script waiting for him or her out there, hopefully wise, productive, and supportive, and that learning that script will best take the child to the place he or she needs to go. I surmised as a child that "they" took you aside upon entering high school and told you the script and what it was about. I chose high school because, not knowing about puberty, I observed that high school kids had bigger bodies, looked as if they knew what was going on, and clearly were on the adult side of that chasm that separated them from me in my tiny state. How dismayed I was to later learn that "they" do not exist, that there is no wise script, and that while there are many scripts given us, no one quite knows how they came to be, who wrote them, or what they are really about, although at the same time no one seems particularly willing to throw these scripts away.

As we have seen, the most important messages of life come from the primary relationships with mother, father, and siblings, and then, in ever-widening circles, the culture as a whole. These messages are internalized and we accede to them, seek to evade them, or unconsciously solicit treatment for them. These messages, or complexes, are splinter mythologies, embodied in daily life as fractal personalities, and together they enact the ego's daily dance. Most of the time the ego is in service to these scripts even when it thinks otherwise. Even in adolescence, when we may begin to question these scripts, we lack the powers of successful revolt, and continue to fantasize that pursuing them will in the end lead us where we are supposed to go. Thus, we marry, go to college, join the army, produce children and careers, and only from time to time question why or to what end.

But the question *why* continues to be asked in the unconscious. The psyche will continue to make corrections, express its protest, seek a fuller embrace of one's archetypal nature. The psyche is autonomous and will express another, deeper script than that which we received from our fated family of origin, culture, and peculiar histories. The task then is relinquishing the dependence on the fractal scripts for the larger project, which propels us in the direction of wholeness. When we can make this shift—and it takes the whole of the second half of life to swing our vessel around, so powerful are the old currents—then we can feel embraced and supported by a larger energy once again. This larger energy is the will of the psyche toward *individuation*, Jung's metaphor for the innate drive toward wholeness. Paradoxically, surrender to this will does not bring inflation, grandiosity, or a free pass from suffering, but it does bring about a sense of purposefulness once again. This sense of rightness comes about through the alignment of the ego with the will of the soul.

We all had that sense of who we were for a short time in childhood, and then it got lost. It is possible to get it back and to live a larger life if we are humble enough to confess that what we have been doing with our lives has not proved sufficient. The loss of alignment with the soul is both the origin of suffering and the invitation to its redemption.

Why have you come to this book, or why has it to come to you, now?

Upon reflection, this book is simply telling you what you already know, and have always known. But you may have forgotten what you knew, or been intimidated by the largeness of what your life asks of you. To use Wordsworth's metaphor from the beginning of this chapter, we all retain an intuitive tie to that great, immortal sea from whence we came. If this book speaks to you in any way it is because it is about you, hence the re-cognition, the re-membrance. Additionally, there are moments in one's life when things are meant to happen, when outer and inner are aligned. We have mastered the language of the outer world through physics and chemistry, but the principle of *synchronicity* acknowledges that there is an inner world of causality as well. When the moment is ripe for us to hear, then the word is spoken.* Perhaps, the word is always being spoken, but it takes our readiness to hear.

Why does the idea of the *soul* both trouble you *and* feel familiar, like a long-lost companion?

The soul (*anima, alma, ame, Seele, psyche*) is simply the word for our intuited sense of a presence that is other than the ego, larger than the ego, and sometimes in conflict with the ego. The soul is the archetype of meaning and the agent of organic wholeness. Such an idea may be intimidating to the ego consciousness, for here is something further beyond its control. As Jung reminds, "It is not I who create myself, rather I happen to myself."[†]

The idea of the soul is further intimidating because it asks something of us; that is it summons ego consciousness to an accounting. The soul asks us to a larger frame of reference, to an eternal perspective amid our time-bound egos and their reductive, fear-driven agendas. Such a presence reminds us that we are never alone when alone, that there is another that provides continuity to our fractured

---

*There is an ancient Chinese proverb that avers that when the right word is spoken, it will be heard a thousand miles away.

†Jung, *Psychological Reflections*, p. 322.

days, organic unity to our broken selves, and transcendence to our fallen condition. The soul is intuited in childhood, pushed aside by the adaptive choices of consciousness, and recovered in adulthood only when we are willing to open to it. I was in my fourth year of analysis in Zurich, obviously committed to the process, before it really hit home to me that there was an active place of wisdom, deeper than my conscious knowing, that had been speaking to me all the while. What an obvious recognition, yet how recalcitrant my consciousness had been. That trek from head to heart took four years.

When we ask the meaning of a mood, reflect upon our history, inquire into the dynamics of a physical symptom, ponder a dream, we are in a dialogue with soul. When we are wrung by life, flung into dismal depths, then lifted higher than we thought possible, transformed from what we were to what we become, we are in the presence of soul. But we are always in the presence of soul, whether consciousness reflects upon it or not.

Many years ago, when I was in graduate school, a colleague who was in the theology school asked me to walk on a blustery day from the campus to the village, where there was a stationer's shop. He wanted to buy a copy of *Time* magazine, which featured the Swiss theologian Karl Barth on the cover. We went to the only two stores in town that carried magazines and they had no copies. On our way back to the campus, my friend spied a small Ma and Pa store about three windswept blocks away, a frigid detour for our mission. We went into that store, which seemingly sold only bread, eggs, and milk, and, wondrously, it had one copy of *Time* waiting for my colleague. As we continued the walk, I jokingly asked him if he thought some divinity had sent him down that street to the one copy of *Time* left in that small town. He thought a moment and then somberly replied, "I hope not." I knew instantly that he had taken my question seriously and that, earnest theology student that he was, it was easier for him to wrestle with the idea of chance than the notion that he was in the hands of a divinity. His remark was thoughtful, and religiously respectful of the largeness of the question. In this small event, something large had risen. So, too, the idea of the soul may intimidate, or it may support, each of us.

In a poem titled "Autumn," R. M. Rilke describes how not only the leaves are falling, but all things, this heavy earth, all falling through space, and we with it. Yet, he concludes:

> *And still there is one who in his hands gently*
> *Holds this falling endlessly.* *

Notice that the poet does not name the one whose hands hold the cosmos, but he does intuit that all that fall are sustained nonetheless by something even larger. So the idea of the soul, the felt presence of the soul, intimidates while it sustains, and the summons to the ego is to relinquish its fantasy of sovereignty and be held in that fall.

Is the life you are living too small for your soul's desire?

Consider these questions. Answer them honestly to yourself or they will prove of no value. If they hurt a bit, or intimidate a lot, then they are hitting home for you. Answer them honestly, and you are on the way to the insight that leads to wisdom, the wisdom that leads to change, the change that leads to a larger life, and the larger

---

*Rilke, "Autumn," in Flores, ed., *An Anthology of German Poetry from Hölderlin to Rilke*, p. 390.

life that ultimately provides healing because it is the life the gods intended for you.

1. Where has life, in its unfairness, stuck you, fixated you, caused you to circle back and back upon this wounding as a provisional definition and limitation of your possibilities? Why do you continue to cooperate with the wound, rather than serve something larger, which serves you in return?

2. Where has life blessed you, given you a gift? And what have you done with that gift? How have you accepted the responsibility that goes with it?

3. Where are you blocked by fear, stuck, rigid, resistant to change?

4. What is the fear beneath the fear? The fear that intimidates you only gains its power from the wiring beneath it, the wiring of history, which leads to a deeper fear, a fear from your past. This circuitry activates the old message that this fear, this issue, is larger than you, and so you ignore the conscious, empowered adult you have become since then.

5. Where was your father stuck, and where has that stuck place shown up in your life? Where was your mother stuck, and where has that stuck place shown up in your life? Are you repeating their lives, their patterns, or trying to overcome them by compensation, or treating the problem in a way that brings harm and further self-alienation? Is this the legacy you will pass on to your children?

6. Where do you avoid conflict, the necessary conflict of values, and therefore avoid living in fidelity with who you are?

7. What ideas, habits, behavioral patterns are holding you back from the large journey of the soul? What secondary gains do you receive by staying mired in the old—security, predictability, validation from others? Are you now tired enough, hurting enough to begin to take the soul's journey on?

8. Where are you still looking for permission to live your life? Do you think that someone else is going to give it to you? What are you waiting for, someone else to write the script of your life for you?

9. Where do you need to grow up? When will this happen? Do you think someone else will do it for you?

10. What have you always felt called toward, but feared to do? Does this possibility still summon you, symbolically if not literally? What new life wishes to come into being through you?

Why is now the time, if ever it is to happen, for you to answer the summons of the soul, to live the second, larger life?

There is much in our age that is evil, and much that is good, but, worse, there is much, much more that is trivial, distracting, and delusory. Consciousness has brought great gifts, and great horrors, upon us, but consciousness is only part of the story. As Jung reminds, "Consciousness is always only a part of the psyche and therefore never capable of psychic wholeness: for that the indefinite extension of the unconscious is needed. But the unconscious can neither be caught with clever formulas nor exorcised by means of scientific dogmas, for something of destiny clings to it—indeed, it is sometimes destiny itself."*

We live amid politicians and theologians who infantilize us by fear-mongering, and scientists and psychologists who trivialize life by addressing only what can be empirically verified. We are so much larger than that. Just as much theology has forgotten the psyche, so much psychology has retreated from the soul—in both cases they

*Jung, *Psychological Reflections*, p. 334.

are intimidated by the truly large. You may expect little help from your contemporary culture, from your peers, and from your family in this task of reconnecting with the soul. Yet you are not alone, for there are many others persons out there who feel as you do, who yearn as you do for a second, deeper life. In fact, there is a hidden community of individuals who are on their own path. At times they will feel quite alone, estranged from all that once gave comfort, but their very solitude is the surest sign that they have been launched upon the journey that, amid suffering and joy, brings the richness of life.

In our time, our sense of homelessness leads us to our common home; our separate journeys provide our community. As Hermann Hesse once wrote, "We have to stumble through so much dirt and humbug before we reach home. And we have no one to guide us. Our only guide is our homesickness."* This spiritual homesickness gives us the journey; the journey gives us our life, once again.

Our progressive realization of the calling of the individual soul constitutes our greatest gift to the world. What we deny of the soul's imperative will sooner or later impose itself upon us from the outer world. These spiritual chickens, it would seem, always come home to roost somewhere. The powers of the cosmos, which nod, beckon, solicit our conscious attendance, and intimate the soul's intent, shine from every crevice in our lives. As the poet Paul Eluard observed, there is another world, and it is this one!

Everywhere we look we see intimations of the soul. Learning to read the texture of the surface and see the mythic forms coursing

---

*Hesse, *Steppenwolf,* p. 153.

beneath is the task, not only for the depth psychologist, but for anyone who wishes to inhabit modernism with a scintilla of consciousness. What we are then to do with the repeated summons is up to us.

So, here you are, in this mysterious now. With your history receding like the sound of a hunter's horn along the wind, with your future rushing toward you like the next season, now is the moment, the only moment that exists, in which becoming can be and in which consciousness can make a difference. Perhaps the highest achievement of consciousness is not the self-serving reiteration of its own glories, its agenda of regressive reinforcement in the face of the large, intimidating cosmos that is our home, but rather its capacity to acknowledge that it has been called to witness, and to serve, to serve something much larger. There *is* in you room for a second, timeless, and larger life. For, as the poet Walt Whitman wrote in "A Clear Midnight":

> *This is the hour O Soul, thy free flight into the wordless*
> *Away from books, away from art, the day erased, the lesson done,*
> *Thee fully forth emerging, silent, gazing, pondering the themes*
> *   thou lovest best,*
> *Night, sleep, death and the stars.* *

Even when surrounded by many others, your journey is solitary, for the life you are to choose is your life, not someone else's. Alone, we nonetheless move amid a community of other solitudes; alone, our world is peopled with many companions, both within and without. Thus, this paradox stands before each of us, and challenges: We

---

*Whitman, "A Clear Midnight," *Leaves of Grass,* p. 387.

"must be alone if [we] are to find out what it is that supports [us] when we can no longer support [ourselves]. Only this experience can give [us] an indestructible foundation."* Finding what supports you from within will link you to transcendence, reframe the perspectives received from your history, and provide the agenda of growth, purpose, and meaning that we all are meant to carry into the world and to share with others. The soul asks each of us that we live a larger life. Each day this summons is renewed

and leaves you, unspeakably, to sort out
your life, with its fearsome immensities,
so that, now boundaried, now limitless,
it transforms itself as stone in you and star.†

---

*Jung, *Psychology and Alchemy, CW 12,* para. 32.
†Rilke, "Evening," II. 9–12, (author's translation).

Bibliography

Alison, Alexander, *et al.*, eds. *The Norton Anthology of Poetry*. New York: W.W. Norton and Co., 1983.

Bhagavad-Gita. Trans. Stephen Mitchell. New York: Three Rivers Press, 2000.

Bly, Robert, *et al. The Rag and Bone Shop of the Heart*. New York: Harper-Collins, 1992.

———. *The Soul Is Here for Its Own Joy: Sacred Poems from Many Cultures*. Hopewell, NJ: Ecco Press, 1995.

Dunn, Stephen. *Different Hours*. New York: W.W. Norton and Co., 2000.

———. *Loosestrife*. New York: W.W. Norton and Co., 1996.

———. *New and Selected Poems 1974–1994*. New York: W. W. Norton and Co., 1994.

Ellmann, Richard. *Yeats: The Man and the Masks*. New York: Dutton, 1948.

Flores, Angel, ed. *An Anthology of German Poetry from Holderlin to Rilke*. New York: Anchor Books, 1960.

Freud, Sigmund. *Psychopathology of Everyday Life*. Trans. A. A. Brill. New York: New American Library, 1960.

Fussell, Paul. *The Boys' Crusade: The American Infantry in Northwestern Europe 1944–1945*. New York: The Modern Library, 2003.

Hesse, Hermann. *Steppenwolf.* New York: Henry Holt and Company, 1963.

Hollis, James. *The Archetypal Imagination*. College Station: Texas A and M University Press, 2000.

———. *Creating a Life: Finding Your Individual Path*. Toronto: Inner City Books, 2001.

———. *The Eden Project: In Search of the Magical Other*. Toronto: Inner City Books, 1998.

———. *The Middle Passage: From Misery to Meaning in Mid-Life*. Toronto: Inner City Books, 1993.

————. *Mythologems: Incarnations of the Invisible World*. Toronto: Inner City Books, 2004.

————. *On This Journey We Call Our Life*. Toronto: Inner City Books, 2003.

————. *Swamplands of the Soul: New Life in Dismal Places*. Toronto: Inner City Books, 1996.

————. *Tracking the Gods: The Place of Myth in Modern Life*. Toronto: Inner City Books, 1995.

————. *Under Saturn's Shadow: The Wounding and Healing of Men*. Toronto: Inner City Books, 1994.

Hopkins, Gerard Manley. *A Hopkins Reader*. Ed. John Pick. New York: Doubleday, 1966.

Johnson, Robert. *WE: Understanding the Psychology of Romantic Love*. New York: HarperCollins, 1983.

Jung, Carl. *The Collected Works*. 20 vols. Trans. R. F. C. Hull. Princeton: Princeton University Press, 1973. [*The Collected Works* are abbreviated *CW*.]

————. *Letters*. 2 vols. Princeton: Princeton University Press, 1973.

————. *Memories, Dreams, Reflections*. Trans. Richard and Clara Winston. New York: Vintage Books, 1963.

————. *Psychological Reflections: A New Anthology of His Writings 1905–1961*. Eds. Jolande Jacoby and R. F. C Hull. Princeton: Princeton University Press, 1978.

Kazantzakis, Nikos. *The Saviors of God*. Trans. Kimon Friar. New York: Simon and Schuster, 1960.

Malraux, Andre. *The Walnut Trees of Altenburg*. Chicago: University of Chicago Press, 1992.

Marlowe, Christopher. *Dr. Faustus and Other Plays*. Oxford: Oxford University Press, 1998.

Maugham, Somerset. *Complete Short Stories*. New York: Doubleday, 1952.

Milton, John, *Paradise Lost*. New York: Penguin, 2003.

Mood, John. *Rilke on Love and Other Difficulties*. New York: W. W. Norton and Co., 1975.

Oliver, Mary. *New and Selected Poems, Volume One,* Boston: Beacon Press, 1992.

O'Neill, Eugene. *Complete Plays.* New York: Viking. 1988.

Pagels, Elaine. *The Gnostic Gospels.* New York: Vintage Books, 1981.

Rilke, R. M. *The Notebooks of Malte Laurids Brigge.* Trans. M. D. Herter Norton. New York: W. W. Norton and Co., 1949.

——. *The Selected Poetry of Rainer Maria Rilke.* Trans. Stephen Mitchell. New York: Vintage, 1989.

Rumi, Jeladaden. *The Essential Rumi.* Trans. Coleman Barks. New York: HarperCollins, 1995.

——. *Fiha-Ma-Fiha Table Talk of Maulana Rumi.* Ed. Bankey Behari. India: B. R. Publishing Corporation, 1998.

Wagenbach, Klaus. *Kafka.* Trans. Ewald Osers. Cambridge: Harvard University Press, 2003.

Whitman, Walt. *Leves of Grass.* New York: Bantam, 1983.

Yeats, W. B. *Selected Poems and Two Plays of William Butler Yeats.* Ed. M. L. Rosenthal. New York: Collier Books, 1962.

Index